Fly Fishing for
Western Smallmouth

Art —
This will help you
get into some
bronzbacks!
David Paul

Fly Fishing for Western Smallmouth

DAVID PAUL WILLIAMS

HeadWater Books

STACKPOLE BOOKS

To Q, who makes all things possible, including this book

Published by
STACKPOLE BOOKS
5067 Ritter Road
Mechanicsburg, PA 17055
www.stackpolebooks.com

Printed in the United States

First edition

10 9 8 7 6 5 4 3 2 1

Cover photo by Steve Bohnemeyer
Cover design by Wendy A. Reynolds
Photos by the author except where noted

Library of Congress Cataloging-in-Publication Data

Williams, David Paul.
    Fly fishing for western smallmouth / David Paul Williams.
        pages   cm
    Includes index.
        ISBN 978-0-8117-1239-2 (paperback)
        1. Smallmouth bass fishing.   2. Fly fishing.   I. Title.
SH681.W52   2014
799.17'7388—dc23
                                                                                            2014009598

CONTENTS

CHAPTER ONE: The Lure of Smallmouth   1

CHAPTER TWO: The Best Western Destinations   9

CHAPTER THREE: Understanding Smallmouth   43

CHAPTER FOUR: Habitat   59

CHAPTER FIVE: What Smallmouth Eat   81

CHAPTER SIX: Thirteen Top Tips and Techniques   91

CHAPTER SEVEN: Thoughts on Western Flies   105

CHAPTER EIGHT: Seasonal Smallmouth   141

CHAPTER NINE: Gear: The Basics and More   151

CHAPTER TEN: Boating for Bass   161

CHAPTER ELEVEN: Stewardship and Conservation   183

Float Trip Appendix   193

Acknowledgments   197

Index   199

CHAPTER ONE

The Lure of Smallmouth

Barely a few oar strokes from the launch, my brother's fly rod snapped to the water as a smallmouth intercepted his rubber-legged bug, and it was game on. Not huge or even big by Yakima River standards, that fish and the next three showed a willingness to fight that belied their size. Barely a hundred yards of river had passed when a big dog whacked his bug, his 6-weight rod severely tested. Giving as good as it got, the fight ended when the hook pulled out on the last powerful surge, leaving my brother with his mouth agape, a smile on his face.

That is the lure of smallmouth. The fight is why anglers pursue them, often foregoing all other freshwater fish.

Over a century ago, Dr. James A. Henshall wrote:

> The black bass is eminently an American fish; he has the faculty of asserting himself and making himself completely at home wherever placed. He is plucky, game, brave and unyielding to the last when hooked. He has the arrowy rush of the trout, the untiring strength and bold leap of the salmon, while he has a system of fighting tactics peculiarly his own.
>
> *Book of the Black Bass* (1881)

Since that time, anglers across the country have discovered that smallmouth—not salmon, not steelhead, not trout—are the toughest bruisers on the freshwater block. Some years back I was reviewing a Kelly Galloup video shot on a famous Michigan river, hoping to glean trout-fishing tips from such an eminent fly fisher. Kelly caught a few respectable-sized trout, then hooked a fish that really put a bend in his rod and excitement in his voice. While fighting the fish, he said on camera that it was a much bigger trout than his previous fish and likely was several pounds in size. When he finally landed the fish, it turned out to be a foot-long smallmouth bass that fought with the ferocity, strength, and doggedness of a trout many times its

After fishing around the world for many species, this angler was impressed by the unyielding fight of his first smallmouth bass. And they can be found in all western states.

The author's brother, Michael T. Williams, raised on trout, now guides for smallmouth as well.

weight. Kelly's comments about the fight in smallmouth are the perfect answer to the question, why smallmouth.

I've been catching smallmouth and learning about them for 40 years, and the one element that never ceases to amaze me is how much fun they are to catch. Sometimes they take the fly with such subtlety the strike is easily missed. Other times they smack it with what seems like joyful exuberance. Once hooked, they skyrocket out of the water like a submarine-launched cruise missile, shaking and shimmying in an effort to disengage the faux food. If that tactic doesn't work, they put their heads down and use their bulk to bull their way toward the bottom, using their robust body to take every advantage of current or underwater structure, never giving up, never surrendering. That's how the little guys battle. The big smallmouth are even tougher to land.

Henshall's words about fishing tactics ring true. If trout are pugilists and salmon are wrestlers, smallmouth are mixed martial artists where rules are few and unbridled aggression wins. Smallies use every iota of skill and energy in their attempt to get loose. I don't win all fights even with a strong rod, stout leader, and sharp hooks on my side. These guys are that tough. But there is more to the smallmouth fishery. Much is made in the

Smallmouth lurk in the broken-rock shadows. You can draw them out by bouncing a weighted fly along the rocks.

There's something about the color yellow that triggers smallmouth to bite. Yellow works best in clear water. Switch to dark brown or black in off-color water.

angling community about fishing only for wild fish. Almost without exception, any smallmouth caught in the West will be a wild fish, bearing no sign of a blunt nose or shredded pectoral fins, not scarred or frayed by the concrete sides of a hatchery pen. Raised in the wild, generation after generation, smallmouth must be strong to survive.

Smallies are the tigers of the sunfish family, which includes largemouth bass, bluegill, and crappie. They aggressively feed, eating anything—crayfish, leeches, aquatic invertebrates, minnows, even their own kind—smaller than them. Eager to feed and to defend their territory, they willingly strike flies, a trait that makes them the perfect fly-rod fish.

Smallmouth have been swimming in North American waters since the late Pleistocene glaciation. Originally found in the Hudson Bay basin, the Saint Lawrence–Great Lakes region, and the middle Mississippi River basin, they were long limited to those waters by natural geographical barriers like the Appalachian mountain range. Thanks to New York Governor DeWitt Clinton, who envisioned then built the Erie Canal, smallmouth made their way northeast into New York. From

there they expanded throughout New England and the Mid-Atlantic states.

Like other northeastern fish such as American shad, the spread of smallmouth mirrors that of the railroads crossing the West. Railroad men, seeking to take their sportfish with them as track was laid across every western state, carried smallmouth in specially outfitted rail cars, and planted the fish in ponds, lakes, and streams throughout the West. Hardy stock, the adult fish and their eggs traveled well in 5-gallon milk jugs, making them easy to transport from site to site. Smallmouth taken from Lake Ontario via New York arrived in California not long after the 1849 Gold Rush.

Spurred by Hensall's *Book of the Black Bass*, the first book touting the sporting attributes of bass, anglers began to embrace them. Sportsmen seeking to share the wealth of this transplant sent them north from California into Oregon and Washington, where they quickly established themselves throughout the Columbia River drainage. Smallmouth rapidly settled into their new waters; three years after being first introduced into Washington's Yakima River, a local angler landed a monster

Smallmouth are efficient predators. They swim in soft water, waiting for the moving water to bring food to them.

that took second place in a national fishing contest. Utah, Wyoming, Montana, and other Wild West places that trigger images of cowboys, cattle drives, and gunfights are smallmouth bass strongholds.

Call them smallmouth, green trout, smallies, bronzebacks, browny, brown bass, or any other alias, they now live everywhere. Today's traveling anglers or hidebound homebodies can find smallmouth in 47 of the 50 states—Florida, Alaska, and Louisiana are the three holdouts. The Canadian Shield lakes are part of the original habitat. Canadian fishery managers, matching their United States counterparts, have expanded smallmouth from their original habitat in the midcentral provinces to other provinces, including the westernmost British Columbia. These fine fish can be found in several Mexican states and in other places around the world.

Yellow perch are a frequent bycatch in smallmouth waters. Perch young of the year are an important smallmouth forage food as well.

Smallmouth satisfy anglers seeking the solitude of a step-across mountain stream, the pleasures of boating a sun-filled desert reservoir, or a few hours on close-to-the-front-door urban waters. Smallmouth add months to the fishing calendar. When lowland lakes warm, leaving trout gasping for breath, smallmouth fishing rocks. When trout rivers are blown out by snowmelt, the hot weather that melted all that snow has warmed smallmouth stillwaters and stirred the fish from the depths.

The reigning world record smallmouth—a record standing since 1955—was just shy of 12 pounds, taken by David L. Hayes from Dale Hollow Reservoir on the Kentucky-Tennessee border. But not all big fish come from warm southern waters. Fish weighing just a few ounces shy of that record have been caught in cold, relatively infertile Canadian waters. Idaho has fish that come close. One rule of thumb that holds true across cold and warm climes is that the biggest fish live in lakes and reservoirs. Of course, for that rule to be true, sections of the Columbia River must be characterized as a reservoir. Anecdotal evidence points to an 11-plus-pound smallmouth taken from a fish trap on a Columbia River tributary.

In most western states, a 4-pound smallmouth earns the angler bragging rights. A 5-pound smallie is as big a bass as most anglers ever see. A 6-pounder really gets the heart pumping. Every year some western waters produce a prespawn female bronzeback of 7 pounds or more. Many biologists think a new world record will come from the Golden Triangle of western smallmouth fishing—Oregon, Washington, and Idaho.

Largemouth bass, certainly the Florida strain, grow more than twice the size of their smallmouth cousins and garner all the television hoopla and million dollar purses associated with professional bass tournaments. Largemouth have drawn the attention of fiction (Carl Hiaasen's *Double Whammy*) and non-fiction (Monte Burke's *Sow Belly: The Obsessive Quest for the World-Record Largemouth Bass*). Manufacturers have built a multimillion-dollar economy of specialty boats, high-powered motors, rods for every application, reels, lines, lures, and corporate sponsorship around largemouth bass fishing. Little boys and girls grow up dreaming about being on television, arms aloft, a wriggling largemouth bass in each hand, smiling at the adoring crowds while being crowned winner of the Bassmaster Classic. If you seek fame, then largemouth certainly offer a path. But even the most ardent largemouth angler acknowledges that smallmouth are *way* more fun to catch.

When those bass tournaments are held in the West, frequently the winning angler pictured is holding a bronze tiger-striped smallie, rather than a green largemouth. Smallmouth show up in tourney catches because they outcompete largemouth, and with the exception of certain California lakes and reservoirs, western largemouth don't get much bigger than smallmouth.

Gear chuckers not in the know disparage the fly rod as a bass-catching tool. Not many know that the man who founded Bass Anglers Sportsman Society, *Bassmaster* magazine, and the Bassmaster Classic outlawed fly rods in tournaments because he felt they were too efficient and gave an unfair advantage.

Let's take a look at some of the smallies' warmwater game-fish companions. Many species populate the West, though likely not more than one in fifty fly fishers have ever intentionally caught these other species.

Carp, also known as Mississippi steelhead, are rapidly gaining in popularity, so much so that some Montana trout guides have added carp trips. Anyone who has caught a carp on a fly rod understands why they are so much fun. Their special sensory organs make them devilishly difficult to hook, and their big, robust bodies make them a challenge to land in moving water. I frequently target them when also fishing for smallmouth. Columbia River carp can easily broach the 20-pound mark.

Those who think chicken livers and stinkbait are the only way to catch channel catfish are out of touch with fly-rod reality. Cats are highly piscivorous, occupy many of the same rivers and lakes as smallmouth, and willingly eat flies. Every cat I've caught was taken as a by-catch while fishing for smallies. Cats fight like, well, cats. Plus they get big. Oregon and Washington record cats top 35 pounds, more than enough to get the blood racing.

Carp swim in the same waters as smallmouth and crunch plenty of crayfish. It makes sense to use gear that can handle these big minnows. SUE MORRISON

This carp was hooked in the same Yakima River run where other anglers were landing smallmouth.

Walleye have spread far beyond their native habitat, so much so that they have their own professional tournament trail sponsored by corporate giants like Walmart and Cabela's. Scores of die-hard weekend fishers spend their leisure hours searching for their personal best fish. The Columbia River system has tons of walleye, ranging to over 20 pounds.

Walleye fishers talk about the difficulty of catching quality-sized fish, but no walleye angler ever regaled his buddies about the battle royale that tested both tackle and angler before "ol bugeyes" was finally subdued. That's because all within earshot would know it was a big fib. The phrase "feisty walleye" is an oxymoron of the first rank. Only partly tongue in cheek, I believe walleye should be declassified as a gamefish and moved into the food fish category. It's not the fight, it's the taste. The mere mention of a walleye fish taco turns even the most well-fed walleye angler into a salivating monster.

Yellow perch are another popular warmwater gamefish. They share three traits with walleye: they are found most everywhere, they don't fight worth a lick, and the fillets sure taste good dipped in a beer batter then deep fried.

Black and white crappie are fun to catch on a fly rod, as they will smack small forage fish patterns subsurface and traditional dry flies on top. Crappie reach multipound size in some western states, though the further north you travel, the smaller the fish.

Bluegill are the bantamweight brawlers of the sunfish family. If bluegill reached half the size of steelhead, steelhead would soon be a forgotten fish. Bluegill top out at about three pounds and are usually found in the same waters as largemouth.

It has been doubted by some that the Black Bass will rise to the fly, or at best they are uncertain in their modes and times of doing so, as compared with the Brook Trout. These doubts are mostly raised by those who angle for the Black Bass in precisely the same way as for the Brook Trout, upon the supposition that the two

Catfish are another species typically encountered when fishing for smallmouth. This one ate a D-Dub's Rabbit Bugger.

The combination of excellent forage base, long growing season, and lack of fishing pressure makes for exciting fishing. JAY NICHOLS

fish are identical in habits and instincts. But while their habits of feeding are very similar . . . they differ greatly in other habitual features and idiosyncrasies.

Henshall, *Book of the Black Bass*

The coldwater salmonid mystique gets in the way of fly fishers accepting smallmouth as worthy gamefish. Steelhead, salmon, and trout have long been held in the highest esteem by anglers, particularly among the fly-fishing community. American sport-fishing tradition emigrated from the British Isles where coldwater fish were the primary quarry. British sportsmen and women, perhaps mirroring British class-ruled society, fished mostly private water and developed rigorous rules as to the "proper" way to fish. According to those rules, all trout fly fishing must be done with dry flies and all dry flies must be cast upstream. The one dissenter, G. E. M. Skues, broke the rules, fished nymphs, and was excoriated by the rigid-rule crowd.

American anglers in general, and fly fishers in particular, emulated their British cousins and developed a trout-centric view of the angling world. Early American trout-fishing literature is replete with authors demanding adherence to the code of the dry fly. Atlantic salmon could be fished with a subsurface fly, but that fishery had its own rigid dogma as well. Over

time, the dry fly or nymph debate has mostly faded into the background; however, the coldwater fish (trout-centric) view of what constitutes fly fishing endures today.

> If the earthly creature we know as smallmouth bass did not exist, we would have to invent them as counterpoint to the rarified air of trout.
>
> Henshall, *Book of the Black Bass*

Coldwater fishers have been led by coldwater writers to believe that coldwater fish swim at the apex of the freshwater fish world. Trout (and by association, those who pursue them) have been characterized as more refined, more intelligent, and clearly more sophisticated than any other freshwater fish species. If trout writers are to be believed, all trout live in the purest of waters, sip the tiniest insects off the surface—the trout version of taking afternoon tea complete with crustless cucumber sandwiches—then retire until the evening repast. When trout writers and their readers deign to discuss bass, they cast aspersions in a wide tailing loop. Rarely do they distinguish between black bass species, perhaps by choice, perhaps by selective ignorance. They opine that bass are nothing more than coarse, stupid, brutish creatures that eat their children and live in swamps too distasteful to visit.

Black and white crappie compete for the same forage fish as smallmouth. They are usually found around brush piles and downed wood.

Both descriptions, the sublime and the ridiculous, nail trout *and* smallmouth on the head. Both species live in pristine water with 30-foot visibility and in water nearly opaque. Smallmouth live and feed in what is characterized as trout water, like tailouts and riffles. Smallmouth take tiny mayflies, barely dimpling the slick water. Smallmouth exuberantly launch themselves at hovering dragonflies and damselflies, and lo, pity the poor terrestrial that finds itself floating in a stream about to become a smallmouth snack.

At times trout and smallmouth seem gullible beyond all belief, though more often bouts of smallmouth gluttony are triggered by their raging metabolism. Trout, their metabolism more under control due to the cold water, don't have that same excuse. It is true that big and not-so-big smallmouth eat little smallmouth. Conveniently overlooked by the trout mud-slingers, many popular streamer fly patterns intended to catch trout imitate young-of-the-year trout. Samuel Slaymaker designed his Little Brook Trout, Little Rainbow Trout, and Little Brown Trout bucktail streamers to catch trout—fish that also eat their children.

America's trout streams sprouted thousands of new fly fishers when Norman Maclean's *A River Runs Through It* hit the silver screen. Despite Henshall's *Book of the Black Bass*, the writings by Ted Trueblood, Joe Brooks, and Ray Bergman, and the recent book by Bob Clouser, smallmouth have remained under the hype radar. Smallies don't need Brad Pitt's startling blue eyes or Tom Skerritt's strong jaw to gain converts. No artificially created hyperbole or overblown praise needed. Conversion, or at least acceptance, into the growing smallmouth angling fraternity merely takes hooking a smallmouth and experiencing what it's like to be tethered to a bronze bulldog.

CHAPTER TWO

The Best Western Destinations

The West is incredibly diverse, both as a geographical expanse and within any given state. It has huge impoundments like Lake Powell, which cross state lines; it has the Columbia River, which crosses international borders; and it has remote mountain streams, which rarely see an angler, much less a fly fisher.

What follows is a sampling of the West—a taste of the best stillwaters and rivers in the 11 western states—intended to entice. Some destinations will be close and well known to readers of this book. Some will be distant, enjoyed perhaps but once in a lifetime. Each destination has been selected because it offers some of the best smallmouth bass fishing there is.

Trout and salmon anglers have a tradition of traveling long distances to experience a fishing destination, many of which have been written about so much they've taken on a life of their own. Waters like Henry's Fork in Idaho or the Firehole in Yellowstone National Park draw fly fishers from around the world and, in doing so, focus attention on the resource. Preservation of the resource follows. As more fly fishers gain an appreciation of smallmouth, there's no reason why smallmouth waters can't attain that same cachet and inspire that same desire to protect the fishery.

ARIZONA

Arizona is more than desert, saguaro cactus, and the Grand Canyon. Arizona offers an extraordinary diversity of smallmouth bass habitat, ranging from high mountain streams to nearly sea-level reservoirs. All share the common element of bright sunshine.

Black River

The 2011 Wallow Fire trashed the upper Black River watershed as it burned through 500,000 acres of the Apache National Forest. With the vegetation seared to a crisp, there was nothing to hold back rain-driven ash, mud, and debris, which turned a number of the small tributaries into a thick, fish-smothering stew. The river will recover because that is the nature of rivers. The question is, what of the smallmouth? Arizona Fish and Game and the White Mountain Apache Tribe agree the smallmouth are doing just fine in the main river and might expand further upstream to fill a void left by the decimated trout.

The Black River combines spectacular scenery, solitude, and smallmouth. Q. LINDSEY BARRETT

The Black River is small enough to fish without wading, though in the summer heat, wet wading is a good choice for keeping cool.
Q. LINDSEY BARRETT

The smallmouth bass portion of the Black runs through remote and scenic country to form the boundary between the San Carlos Apache Reservation and the Fort Apache Reservation—each with their own access and fishing permits. The shortest route to the river from a paved road enters on the Fort Apache side. Note that past the midpoint of the river, tribal jurisdiction changes and another pass is needed. Before venturing forth, it makes sense to get a current road condition report from www.wmatoutdoors.org. Keep an eye on the weather. Rain triggers flash floods and turns the roads to impassable goo.

May and June are the best months to find smallies up to 4 pounds. A good place to start is Black River Crossing. Hike upstream or downstream as far as your legs are willing to take you, as the fishing gets better the further you hike from the crossing. Crayfish are the primary forage. If you opt to camp on the river, Matt Rustin of the White Mountain Apache Tribe warns to be wary of black bears and store your food securely. The Black River has Arizona's highest concentration of bears, so be bear-smart.

Verde River

The Wild and Scenic portion of the Verde River offers smallmouth in the solitude of the Tonto National Forest. The river can be accessed at several points by car or floated in rafts, canoes, kayaks, or pontoons. In the lower section, the marathon-length Verde River Trail snakes along the river. If you have the

time, there are several multiday floats. Most of the river can be run by a novice, the exception being the reach between Beasley Flats and Childs where Class III and IV rapids are found. The Verde offers 70 miles of smallmouth and a few largemouth between Camp Verde and Horseshoe Dam and more river downstream to Bartlett Reservoir. At present, permits are not required for groups of less than 75 people (yes, that's the right number). User-provided portable toilets and fire pans are required.

The river is fishable in all but the coldest months. In the dead of winter, the stream becomes a put-and-take trout stream. The trout that survive anglers move into the coldwater tributaries when the main river heats up. Smallmouth fishing comes on toward the end of April and continues through late fall. The fish aren't huge—most will run around a foot long—but the river holds some larger fish. All the usual suspects—crayfish, baitfish, and spun deer hair topwater bugs—work here.

Roosevelt Lake

The current Arizona state smallmouth record, a smidge over 7 pounds, was taken from Roosevelt Lake, and that's reason enough to include it here. The lake, formed by the nutrient-rich Salt River flowing out of the White Mountains and Tonto Creek dropping off the Mogollon Rim, has a slot limit requiring the release of all smallmouth between 13 and 16 inches, with the result that the average bass approaches the upper limit of that slot. Threadfin shad and crayfish set the table for the smallmouth in this 21,000-acre impoundment. If you're into racing from spot to spot, a boat allows that. Most fly tossers use float tubes or pontoons to explore the many coves, bays, and points. Late summer and fall draw anglers who look for shad boils—schools of shad pinned to the surface by bass—and throw topwater flies into the melee.

After the dam was raised 77 feet in 1996, central Arizona was hit by a drought that lasted almost 10 years. In 2005, the lake started filling, flooding thousands of acres of desert. In 2010 the lake filled and spilled water over the dam for the first time. The lake is experiencing the "new lake syndrome," resulting in tremendous food production, and the fishery benefits.

The north shore of the Salt River Arm is rocky and has steep drops. There are plenty of rocky coves at the Tonto Creek Arm. The hourglass-shaped lake has bulbous ends and a narrow waist, and it features reefs, islands, and rocky coves that harbor plenty of smallmouth. Cholla Campground off Highway 188 makes a good base camp for exploring the southwest side of the lake. The inlet end (toward Bermuda Flat) has flooded brush that attracts smallmouth looking for schools of shad. A float tube or pontoon boat will put you in with the fish.

When western high lakes have chilled or smallmouth waters in the northern-tier states are suffering blizzard conditions, imagine yourself catching Roosevelt smallmouth in winter T-shirt weather. Better yet, do it.

Lake Havasu

Lake Havasu is a testament to how a focused fishery enhancement project can turn fishing fortunes around. After years of decline, the lake is back. Years of placing spawning, rearing, and habitat structures and ongoing enhancement efforts have improved the fishing.

Smallmouth have really come on in Lake Havasu and the Colorado River as it runs into the lake. There is some thought that they, and the redear sunfish, benefit from the infestation of quagga mussels. Smallmouth, many in the over-two-pound category, range throughout the lake from the Blue Water Casino all the way north into Topock Gorge. Miles of bays, coves, rubble piles, and cliff faces provide the best smallmouth bass fishing in Arizona's Southwest Region. This is mostly clear water, so fluorocarbon tippets are best for subsurface flies.

A boat is a big help finding the fish, but several state and county parks offer shoreline access as well. If you fish from a boat, make sure to obtain the additional Colorado River stamp to augment your regular fishing license. Threadfin shad, small sunfish, and crayfish are the main smallmouth foods, with some gizzard shad beginning to show up in the lake.

Some anglers believe that when water skiers and jet skiers churn up the water, the smallmouth bite turns off. The further you get from heavy boat traffic near Lake Havasu City, the better the catching and fishing experience will be. A wind-protected

Shad move into the submerged brush in a desperate attempt to avoid getting eaten. Topwater flies like Gene Trump's SMP work in these situations. Q. LINDSEY BARRETT

When the wind is up on Lake Havasu, head for the channels on the Bill Williams River.

bay near the Bill Williams National Wildlife Refuge has plenty of nooks and crannies to be explored by both boat and bank anglers.

CALIFORNIA

Smallmouth habitat in California, ranging from a subalpine lake, to a wine-country river, to warm and dry Santa Barbara County, is remarkably diverse.

Russian River

Most of the people who travel along the Russian River head toward the wineries and overlook the fine smallmouth bass fishing. The fish can be found from Asti all the way south to Duncan Mills, with prime fishing being around Healdsburg. Further downriver, the 5-mile from Guerneville to Monte Rio is a popular canoe, kayak, or pontoon float. Canoes and kayaks can be rented at Johnson's Beach in Guerneville. The river runs through deciduous forest and vineyards, passing through several small towns. On hot summer weekends, plan for plenty of company from the "inner tube hatch." Fish run upward of 3 pounds with plenty smaller than that. Target the rock piles and fish crayfish patterns along with small baitfish patterns that look like Sacramento suckers or pikeminnows.

Kings River

The river rises in the Sierra Nevada then flows into Pine Flat Lake about 30 miles from Fresno. Most people think of the river above the lake as a trout fishery. Not many know that smallmouth migrate out of the lake into the river after spring runoff ends. Depending on winter snowpack and spring sunshine, that can be late May. Going in June to fish the lower 5 miles of river is a safe bet. A hiking trail provides access to the lower river. The usual smallmouth patterns that imitate crayfish, suckers, and pikeminnow hold sway here.

Ice House Reservoir

This 680-acre flatwater with a name unlikely to evoke a warmwater fishery is a California sleeper spot. Situated at an elevation of 5,450 feet in the Eldorado National Forest, the relatively few anglers who fish the lake target rainbow and brown trout. They overlook the smallmouth that hang out along the rocky shore to eat crayfish, nongame minnows, and juvenile trout. In the heat of summer, the lake can experience an anabatic wind where heat from the Sacramento Valley builds thermals that sweep upslope, sucking carpenter ants from midelevation forests, and drop the ants over the lake where the air cools. If you fish this lake in the summer, make sure to have a few carpenter ant patterns at hand because the fish—trout and smallmouth—gorge on the ants.

In early fall, most anglers have put away their rods. Too bad, as they miss some of the best fishing of the year. STEVE BOHNEMEYER

Bass pond off the Russian River in California. Get on the water early to fish the morning shadow line as the sun strikes the water.

Float tubes allow a stealthy approach when fishing ponds. They are invaluable when vegetation growing to the water's edge chokes off bank access.

Four campgrounds are located in the area, and a good road runs along the north side from the dam up to Strawberry Point. A not-so-good road continues on from there.

Cachuma Lake

Cachuma is an anomaly in the land of largemouth bass. It's a Southern California lake with smallmouth that are overlooked by tunnel-visioned largemouth bass anglers. Located in Santa Barbara County, the lake warms early, so smallmouth may start their spawn as early as March. Fishing remains good in the shallows until summer heat drives the smallmouth deeper during the day. In summer, try to be on the water early morning or late evening. Suckers, sculpins, other forage fish, and crayfish feed the smallmouth all year round. The fish reach 7 pounds or more.

Santa Barbara County operates the Cachuma Lake Recreation Area. It has camping and boat launching facilities.

COLORADO

Some of the best urban smallmouth fishing in the West is within minutes of downtown Denver. Or head to the more remote northwest corner to float-fish a stream.

Aurora Reservoir

The city of Aurora claims "the best water grows the baddest fish." In 2011, Aurora Reservoir gave up a new Colorado state record smallmouth of nearly 7 pounds. In 2012, a Denver newsletter named the reservoir "The Best Park for Fishing." At 820 acres, the variety of shoreline to explore includes Senac, Lonetree, and Marina Coves. The best months are May, once the water warms from the winter ice, and September and October, as the water cools again and smallmouth return to the shallows.

If you bring your own boat, you'll need to purchase an annual watercraft pass, or you can rent a boat with or without an electric motor at the lake. No gas motors are allowed on the water, so anglers need not worry about dodging personal watercraft or water skiers. Clouser Minnows in size 6 and 8 are the ticket here.

Quincy Reservoir

This is another Aurora city reservoir that has the added bonus of being smaller than the Aurora Reservoir—only 160 acres—and is limited to artificial flies and lures. It also has a shorter fishing season that begins March 1 and ends October 31.

Yampa River

The general consensus has the Yampa as Colorado's best (and perhaps only) smallmouth stream with plenty of fish running to the 5-pound mark. The river turns into a smallmouth fishery below where the Elk River joins, and gets better below Hayden all the way to the confluence with the Green River. Yampa smallmouth are known for their girth, which is caused by their gluttonous crayfish consumption. Fishing is best after runoff ends in July. In low-water years, flows get skinny by September, making floating challenging. The river is accessible at Double Bridges, Yampa River State Wildlife Area, South Beach, Juniper Canyon, and Maybell Bridge. Juniper Canyon

The traditional Clouser Minnow is constructed with bucktail. Color variations abound but like baitfish, they all follow the dark-over-light scheme.

and Cross Mountain Gorge below Maybell are drifts for experienced boaters only. Fishing from a boat is best, as much of the land below Hayden is in private hands. The river is day use water, as the private land restricts multiday camping floats.

The Yampa River is in the Upper Colorado River Endangered Fish Recovery Program. Started in 1988 and extended through September 2013, the program has targeted smallmouth for removal from the Yampa. At first the bass were captured and dropped into Elkhead Reservoir; in 2011, the program started killing the bass it captured. If you fish the Yampa, consider retaining your catch.

Elkhead Reservoir

Not far from the Yampa River is Elkhead Reservoir, a 900-acre impoundment sitting at an elevation of 6,365 feet. This high desert flatwater sits in sagebrush and grass-covered hills overlooked by Bears Ears Mountain. Originally built in 1974 when damming Elkhead Creek, a major Yampa River tributary, the earthen dam was raised another 25 feet in 1996, almost doubling its size. The lake fishes well into October with crayfish setting the table for smallmouth wherever a rocky substrate is found. Elkhead State Park and the new Bear's Ears Campground provide boating, camping, and fishing access.

IDAHO

Idaho is a beneficiary of three rivers—the Snake, Owyhee, and Bruneau—flowing north out of Nevada. These three rivers and the Clearwater form the basis of Idaho smallmouth fishing.

C. J. Strike Reservoir

Really three reservoirs with one name, C. J. Strike, filled by the Snake and Bruneau Rivers, offers March to September smallmouth bass for boaters and bankers alike. As with most smallmouth waters, the fishing heats up as the water warms in May and June. In the main reservoir, target the dam face and nearby coves in spring and early summer. The Snake River Arm is mostly a boat show where success can be found by probing along the coves and other sheltered areas. The Bruneau Arm has good boat and bank access from Jack's Creek and Cottonwood Campground. C. J.'s water level fluctuates little throughout the year, making fish-holding spots and fishing predictable. Summers are hot in the desert, so the fish move deeper as the water gets toasty. September and October can be fine fishing when the water and air temperature drop.

You won't catch huge numbers of fish here, but you'll have a good shot at a fish that pushes the scale past the 5-pound mark.

In bright sunlight, the bass retreat out of the shallows. Cast where the water starts to deepen.

The broken rock structure on Idaho's Clearwater River attracts food, which then attracts fish. The sandy beach across the river will only support small fish.

Dworshak Reservoir

Dworshak Reservoir has produced every new Idaho state smallmouth record bass since 1995 when an elk hunter on his way home from a day in the field stopped to make a few casts. His 8-plus-pound record has been eclipsed several times, most recently in October 2012 by a fish only a few ounces shy of 10 pounds.

Dworshak is big water, 57 miles long and 17,000 acres at full pool. It also is crayfish country. Fish the shallows and catch lots of smaller bass. Dredge the depths, 20 feet or more down, with a Type VI full sinking line or T-14 head to find the big fish. It takes patience, but on Dworshak, the patient nab the big ones.

Clearwater River

The North Fork of the Clearwater River fills Dworshak Reservoir, and it is a fine smallmouth fishery in its own right. Idaho Fish & Game snorkel surveys have found smallmouth as far upriver as Bungalow Ranger Station. Better fishing is found from the upper end of the reservoir to where Idaho Highway 11 connects with the North Fork. Try the campground about a mile below Canyon Ranger Station.

The main Clearwater has few fish in the stretch below Dworshak Dam to the mouth near Lewiston. The cold water released from the dam is simply not conducive to smallmouth, as the river below the dam may be as much as 20 degrees colder than that above the dam. There is a much better population from Orofino, upstream to Kooskia. Idaho Highway 12 runs along the river to provide easy access. The other side between Orofino and Kamiah can be accessed by crossing the river at Greer and walking the abandoned railroad tracks.

Snake River

The Snake River was rated by a national bass fishing magazine as one of the top five smallmouth rivers in the country. It's hard to pick a section of the Snake that doesn't have smallmouth bass, and most sections are underfished. The Hells Canyon impoundments, Oxbow and Brownlee, hold big fish up to 8 pounds.

Prime fishing for trophy bass is March and April before the river turns cold and dark with snowmelt. By June, the water typically settles out and fishing picks up again, holding through September. Early in the year the shallow waters around Lewiston are a good bet to find prespawn females. Focus on those areas with the most sun and protection from the wind. After the spawn, look for broken bedrock and cobble-bottomed stretches, because that's where the smallmouth will be grubbing for

Many of the western rivers flow through remote country. Boaters need to be self-sufficient and prepared to respond to emergencies.

crayfish. The easiest way to fish the Snake is by boat, as there is little bank access until the confluence with the Grande Ronde—and that side of the river is in Washington. The river from the Heller Bar launch on the Washington side all the way down to Lewiston's Hell's Gate State Park is filled with fish. If you have the time and river savvy, the 46.3-mile run from Pittsburgh Landing to Heller Bar has great beach camping, spectacular scenery, and plenty of fish.

Upstream from Heller Bar the river changes character. River levels that fluctuate with melting snowpack and upriver dam releases that alternately expose or cover rocks create powerful boat-sucking hydraulics and the dynamics of numerous whitewater rapids. The river is also subject to periodic stiff upriver winds that make rowing a wind-buffeted raft wonderful exercise. The Snake is not a river for beginners, but the fishing and the scenery are worth the effort. Starting eight miles above the Grande Ronde, the river is managed as part of the Hells Canyon National Recreation Area. During prime time, entry permits are required, as are user-supplied fire pans and portable toilets.

MONTANA

In 2012, Montana experienced a state-wide drought after struggling through record high water in 2011. Still, it produces plenty of trophy-sized smallmouth in a state better known for trout.

Noxon Reservoir

Noxon Rapids Dam impounds the Clark Fork River as it flows north toward the Idaho Panhandle. Surrounded by snow-capped Cabinet Mountains and bounded by pine forest, at first glance Noxon doesn't appear to be bass water. Looks deceive as there are any number of western Montana, northern Idaho, and eastern Washington bass anglers who believe this 30-mile stretch of river offers some of Montana's best bass fishing. Some say it rivals that of Fort Peck Reservoir. Noxon is the site of numerous bass tournaments held each spring and early summer. The best fishing is toward the Thompson Falls end of the reservoir.

A pontoon is a great way to explore the small bays, rocky points, and cliff faces for smallmouth. Don't be surprised if you find a largemouth smacking your bug, as the state record bucketmouth was caught here. The reservoir also has northern pike, four species of trout, mountain whitefish, and yellow perch. Best bass fishing months are May and June before the milfoil blooms and September and October as the weeds begin to die off. The usual cast of forage fish, crayfish, and leeches feed the bass, but don't be afraid to fish topwater sliders, gurglers, and poppers.

Look for a small campground and nice boat launch at Marten Creek. If you camp there, understand that you are in bear country and take appropriate precautions. Use the bear-proof containers provided at each campsite. Other public launches are sprinkled around the reservoir.

Flathead River

The smallmouth in the Flathead River are the result of a mistake. The US Fish & Wildlife Service intended to plant largemouth bass in Crow Reservoir in the mid-1980s. Instead it planted smallmouth, and the fish quickly scooted down the outlet to establish themselves in the Flathead River. For those who wonder how the mistake could have been made, largemouth and smallmouth fry are hard to distinguish.

Most locals target the area around Perma at river mile 11. The Kookoosint Fishing Access, 4 miles upstream from the confluence of the Flathead and Clark Fork, offers a nice concrete launch and accommodates trailered boats even at low water. The site makes a good entry point for a 9-mile run downstream to Pair-O-Dice Fishing Access on the Clark Fork. Flows typically peak in June then drop quickly and maintain flows through the summer months.

Kookoosint is perfect kayak or canoe water for exploring upriver, with bank access upstream until you reach the Flathead Indian Reservation border. To continue upstream, you need a tribal fishing permit. Montana Highway 200 follows the river upstream until the river bends north at Dixon. No permits are required at present on the lower river once it leaves the reservation.

The lower Flathead is a wide river dotted with islands, back sloughs, weed lines, and other in-river structures. All that structure attracts fish food and the smallmouth bass that dine on it. The fishing ranges from days when fish are tough to locate as they move throughout the river, to 30- or 40-fish days. The best fishing is after the river settles down postrunoff. Crayfish patterns get plenty of attention early in the year. Later on, juvenile whitefish patterns get whacked. There is some thought that

Montana's Thompson River forms Noxon Reservoir. Flow-through reservoirs act like a lake, but one with current that can be accenuated when water is drawn for power generation.

Anyone who thinks Montana is just trout country needs to fish the Flathead River. BROOKS SANFORD

Flathead smallmouth are exceptionally robust, bearing more weight per inch than smallmouth found elsewhere.

Don't be surprised if a juvenile whitefish pattern attracts a toothy northern pike as well. The average northern runs about 7 pounds, with fish up to 20 pounds available.

Tongue River Reservoir

Southeastern Montana boasts Tongue River Reservoir where the smallmouth exceed 5 or maybe 6 pounds, with the trend running toward even bigger fish. There is a report of a fish over 7 pounds tipping the scale at Paxiao's Tongue River Marina. If true, it would have broken the old state record by half a pound.

At 3,500 feet elevation, smallmouth fishing starts early and runs well into June when the water temperature may reach 70 degrees F. The south end of the lake runs a few degrees warmer than the north end, at least in the early part of the season. In May, the 12-mile long reservoir is inundated with hordes of

Leave your 5-weight rod home when fishing Montana's Flathead River. In addition to smallmouth, it holds some tackle-busting northern pike.

The Yellowstone River is famous for its trout. Not many know it is an outstanding smallmouth river as well. BROOKS SANFORD

crappie and crappie fishers. August and September are two great smallmouth months. By October, the weather becomes change-able with cold fronts putting down the fish for a few days. Tongue River Reservoir State Park on the northwest corner provides a good base of operations.

The primary forage is spottail shiners, pumpkinseed sunfish, and crappie, along with crayfish. The shiners are a deep-bodied minnow with a dark lateral line easily imitated by Clouser-type flies. The water has a variety of structure, including drowned timber, islands, flats, and rocky points—all of which attract fish at various times.

Yellowstone River

The Yellowstone is the longest free-flowing river in the Lower 48. In the upper reaches, Yellowstone cutthroat reign. From Billings to where the Powder River joins northeast of Miles City, the Yellowstone is a southeastern Montana smallmouth river. Within that reach, the highest fish concentrations are between Billings and Forsyth; 3-pound fish are common. Montana fish biologist population surveys reveal that bigger fish—those ranging up to six pounds—are plentiful as well. So plentiful that the department encourages harvest of smallmouth in the Yellowstone in order to maintain balance in the fish populations. The river suffers water clarity issues during runoff and early summer thunderstorms. August, when the small-mouth in the reservoirs have gone deep, is the best month to hit the river as the water is the warmest and clearest. No permits are presently required.

Crayfish are a rarity in the Yellowstone, so smallmouth munch emerald shiners, western silvery minnows, and flathead chubs. The shiners and minnows, slender and silver in color, get about four inches long. Once the chubs grow past the 6-inch mark, they escape predation.

Before putting a boat on the Yellowstone, take a look at the Montana Water Access Site (http://fwp.mt.gov/fishing/search Fas.html) then click on the Eastern Fishing District Field Guide to download a PDF that describes the Yellowstone access sites. Also get a copy of *Paddling Montana* by Hank and Carol Fischer, as it has information about river hazards, including diversion dams.

NEVADA

The best Nevada smallmouth bass fishing can be found in the northern part of the state in what is technically part of the Great Basin Desert. This is sagebrush country rising to juniper- and pine-covered mountains.

Rye Patch Reservoir

The Humboldt River was dammed to provide an irrigation source for the Lovelock Valley in north-central Nevada. Rye Patch, as with most other western irrigation reservoirs, suffers from severe water fluctuation, which can limit fishing success. When the reservoir is full, it stretches 22 miles through hills that used to be filled with gold. Now the water is filled with

You can cover all the water on Nevada's South Fork Reservoir in a boat. Or you can walk the shoreline before the sun moves overhead and cast to cruising fish.

smallmouth that range up to 3 pounds. In 2013, the reservoir was barely at minimum pool, so put this on your go-to list when it fills again.

South Fork Reservoir

Only 16 miles south of Elko, South Fork Reservoir is accessed through the South Fork State Recreation Area. Set against a backdrop of the 100-mile-long Ruby Mountains, the reservoir covers 1,650 acres at full pool with an average depth of 67 feet. The inlet end, fed by the South Fork Humboldt River, has shallow flats where tubes, pontoons, and small boats can be launched. A gravel road nearly circumnavigates the lake, save for the dam at the northwest end. A doublewide concrete boat ramp and campground are along the east shore. South Fork is open all year with no night closure. Bass are catch-and-release only from March 1 through June 30.

South Fork Reservoir long held the state smallmouth record until it was wrested away by Sheep Creek Reservoir. Plenty of smallmouth still run up to 4 pounds.

Pay attention to the rocky points and bluffs, as they attract smallmouth forage. Early season efforts should focus on water that is 3 to 10 feet deep. As the weather and water warms

through July and August, the fish move toward the face of the dam and into the westside transition zones. You should also fish the points northeast of the boat ramp. Kick boats and power boats provide easy access to all hot spots.

Humboldt River

Smallmouth rivers are rare in Nevada, despite bass being introduced into the state in 1889, one of the earliest introductions in the West. The south fork of the Humboldt runs north out of South Fork Reservoir until it joins the main Humboldt west of Elko. At 330 miles long, the Humboldt, named for German naturalist Alexander Von Humboldt, is the longest river in the continental United States that begins and ends in the same state. The river flows east to west but never reaches the Pacific Ocean, as it disappears into the Humboldt Sinks.

Historically, the river was a cutthroat and brook trout stream, as revealed by diary entries from early explorers and settlers heading toward Oregon and California. Deteriorating water quality from past mining and ranching practices substantially reduced the native fish population. In addition to smallmouth, the river has double-digit channel catfish, rainbow and brown trout reaching 8 pounds, and hybrid rainbow/cutthroat over

5 pounds. Smallmouth enter the system whenever South Fork Reservoir spills water. The bass have populated the South Fork and main Humboldt down toward Palisades with the best fishing above Barth Pit. Pay attention to deep holes around railroad trestles and bridges where the current has scoured the bottom. A big river fish will run 3 pounds.

The river is not a navigable water because in Nevada the abutting landowners own the river bottom. Much of the river runs through private land, and anglers need permission to access the water. The best time to float the river is from Memorial Day through the end of June, with flows running between 175 and 250 cfs measured at the USGS Humboldt River gauge at Carlin.

Sheep Creek Reservoir

A few miles south of the Idaho border, Sheep Creek Reservoir lies on the Duck Valley Indian Reservation. For years the Nevada state record bounced back and forth between Wild Horse and South Fork reservoirs. In 2009, Sheep Creek Reservoir broke into the record books with a smallmouth weighing a smidge under 6 pounds. A year later, another Sheep Creek fish trashed the old state record by almost 3 pounds, tipping the scale at a shade under 9 pounds.

The reservoir covers 788 acres at full pool and is open from April 1 through October 31 with night closures in effect. The water is usually murky with visibility maxed out at about four feet. When the water first warms, wade fishing the shallows is a good tactic. Once the aquatic weeds grow, a floating device makes more sense. Brown and black leech patterns take bass and will surely get whacked by some big rainbows as well. Don't expect to catch huge numbers of bass, as Sheep Creek is managed by the Shoshone-Paiute Tribes as a rainbow trout fishery. Do expect a few big fish.

NEW MEXICO

New Mexico irrigation reservoirs suffered through low water in 2012, harming water clarity. Focus on the rivers and reservoirs with little irrigation draw for best success.

Rio Grande River

The fifth longest river in the United States, much abused along its 1,885 miles, offers some fine smallmouth bass fishing from a few miles above Pilar down through the Rio Grande River

In shallow water below South Fork Dam, the bass move through the vegetation looking for aquatic insects. When the sun leaves the water, they scrounge for crayfish in the broken rock.

Western irrigation reservoirs have suffered extensive water losses, harming the fish populations. When the rains return, the forage food will explode and bass populations will rebound.

Gorge. Don't bother stopping by the BLM Rio Grande Gorge Visitor Center to ask about where to find smallmouth bass in the river. They don't seem to know fish are in the river flowing barely feet from the center.

Instead, turn onto Road 570 from State Road 68 at Pilar. Follow the paved road upstream until you see a likely pullout. Access along the river is limited due to private property, but once on the water you are free to wade or float and fish. River permits, mostly of the self-issued variety, are required for much of the upper river. Some areas require daily parking permits as well.

The primary forage is crayfish, numerous small baitfish—including Rio Grande chubs, redside shiners, and fathead minnows—along with aquatic invertebrates such as dragonfly nymphs. The fish top out around 15 inches. Mid-June, when the runoff begins to abate, marks the beginning of the best fishing and runs through early July. Fishing picks up again as the water cools in late September and extends into October.

Water clarity is important for success. Locals say 2 to 3 feet visibility is prime. If it's less than that, go elsewhere.

Navajo Lake

The reservoir, created by Navajo Dam on the San Juan River, heads in southwest Colorado and runs 20 miles into northeast New Mexico. It's big water—New Mexico's answer to Lake

Powell—and it produces big fish. The former state record, only 2 ounces shy of 7 pounds, was caught here. When the New Mexico Department of Game & Fish does its spring population surveys, fish that equal or exceed that record always show up. Unlike a number of New Mexico reservoirs, Navajo has little irrigation drawdown. The benefits are that it stays relatively full and the water stays clear. At an elevation of 6,100 feet, the water also stays cooler throughout the summer than many of the lower-elevation reservoirs, so the best fishing starts somewhat later and runs into July, then picks up again in the fall when the water temperature drops. Navajo Lake State Park is located at the southern end of the lake near the dam.

Navajo smallmouth feed on rusty crayfish, other warmwater fish, and the conveniently stocked rainbow trout fingerlings.

Ute Reservoir

Located near the west Texas border on the north edge of the Llano Estacado lies Ute Reservoir. Fed by the Canadian River and Ute Creek, it has no irrigation withdrawals, so it stays full and the water clear while the irrigation reservoirs drop and turn turbid. Ute is known for quality, not quantity, of fish caught. It produced the current New Mexico record smallmouth, which tipped the scale at over 7 pounds. The best fishing starts mid-April and continues through June until the hot days warm the water and drive the fish deep. Until then it's possible to sight

In low water, the smallmouth tend to congregate in riffles where the oxygen content is the highest.

Fractured rock in this New Mexico reservoir holds smallmouth food. An effective way to fish this structure is from a small boat.

fish for shallow-water smallmouth. Much of the water is bordered by private land, so a boat is a good idea. Ute Lake State Park has several campgrounds, some of which are open all year.

Primary forage is rusty crawfish and bigscale logperch, a native New Mexico forage fish. Logperch are skinny, small fish that live in the substrate much like sculpin. They rarely exceed 4 inches, sport dark vertical bars that run the length of their body, and have dark backs and light bellies. Ute smallmouth also feed on young-of-the-year gizzard shad during summer and early fall before the quick-growing shad get too big.

East Fork Gila River

As it runs south before meeting the Middle and West Forks, it may not look like a smallmouth bass river, but the East Fork Gila River holds smallmouth up to 4 pounds. Don't expect to see a lot of other anglers on the river due to its remoteness. Do keep your eyes peeled for black bear, mule deer, and elk. The other forks of the Gila, as well as the main stem, have smallmouth, although two years of forest fires and resultant degradation of the watershed have reduced their numbers for the time being. Once the river crosses into the San Carlos Apache Reservation, a permit is required. If you are in the vicinity of where NM 15 and 35 intersect, try Sapillo Creek. It has smallmouth in the reach from Lake Roberts to the Gila River confluence.

The East Fork is best fished by those able to take a few days, willing to drive rough roads and camp at self-contained sites,

Look for smallmouth feeding on shad around the drowned brush and crayfish in the broken rock.

Umpqua River bedrock fingers run perpendicular to the shore. Early in the season, the bass are in tight to the shore. Once the water warms, they move out into deeper water.

If smallies refuse the fly, trim the rubber legs. Umpqua River smallmouth prefer short legs and have an affinity for purple-bodied flies.

because the East Fork is pretty much an all-day buggy ride from most anywhere. The nearest town of any size is Silver City to the south. The upper reach can be accessed by miles of dirt and gravel road that take you through some wild and scenic country off NM 60 west of Socorro. Make sure you have plenty of gas in the tank when you leave Socorro.

OREGON

Oregon is blessed with outstanding smallmouth fisheries across the state, most of which receive little fishing pressure as anglers target trout, steelhead, and salmon.

Umpqua River

The name formerly evoked memories of Zane Grey, leaky canvas tents, and stories of steelhead and salmon told around smoky campfires. The steelhead and salmon are still there, but they've been joined by smallmouth bass that entered the river when a high water event blew out a fish pond in the 1960s. The bass have spread throughout the main stem and South Fork. The cold water of the North Fork has repulsed their advance. Set in a mix of evergreen and deciduous forest, the river twists and turns through bedrock for more than 100 miles from Roseburg to Reedsport. Numerous boat ramps allow power and

The John Day has so many fish, you can wear out your arm. PETER MAUNSELL

Drawing only a few inches of water, pontoons are the perfect late summer low-water craft.

human-powered craft access to the river with only a few navigation hazards, such as Sawyer Rapids below Elkton. No permits are required on the main stem Umpqua.

The North and South Forks join about five miles northwest of Roseburg at River Forks Park. Upstream on the South Fork, smallmouth range to Canyonville and beyond. An easy access spot for a few hours of fishing is the Douglas County Fairgrounds in Roseburg. Downstream, an easy float can be taken from Umpqua Landing near the community of Umpqua to James Wood or Osprey Ramp. Down below Elkton, a popular run along Highway 38 is Sawyer's Rapids to Scott Creek. Because this area has so many fish and so much fishable water, short runs are the rule on the river. Otherwise you end up in danger of running out of daylight and rowing the last miles in the dark.

The river is known for fast action and small fish, but those who drop crayfish patterns in the deeper holes can be rewarded with fish pushing 6 pounds. The recent trend has been an increase in the average size of the fish. The river runs clear, so it's possible to see those big fish inspect and all-too-often reject your offering. Action starts as early as March when a five-fish day is a good day, because they will all be 3 pounds or more. The fishery heats up as the water warms in June, gets better in July and August, then tapers off in the fall.

John Day River

A free-flowing snowmelt river running north through Oregon's high desert to the Columbia, the John Day is a river runner's paradise. The wind- and water-eroded Columbia River Basalt lava flow cliffs tug your attention away from fishing until yet another smallmouth bass whacks your fly. John Day smallmouth were first planted in 1971 and have spread throughout the main river and upstream into the North and South Forks. The most popular sections to float are 48 miles from Service Creek to Clarno (Class II and III rapids) and the 70 miles from Clarno to Cottonwood (Class II to IV rapids). The Clarno to Cottonwood section can be broken into a shorter 43-mile float by paying a fee to use the private launch at Thirtymile Creek. Once you get past Thirtymile Creek, you are committed to float down to Cottonwood. Bureau of Land Management (BLM) river permits are needed on these reaches, and fire and portable toilet restrictions are in place.

The John Day has several rapids ranging from easy Class I to rollicking Class IV. The severity of each rapid varies with water level. At 7,000 cfs, Lower Clarno has huge holes and waves. At 500 cfs and below, Upper, Middle, and Lower Clarno are rock gardens that challenge the best boat drivers. If using a hard-sided boat, BLM recommends a minimum of 800 cfs and, at that level, expect to leave paint on any number of rocks.

The area near Kimberly where the North Fork enters provides good bank access.

Cottonwood Canyon State Park, opened in 2013, provides access to 13 miles of the lower river beginning at Cottonwood. Initially purchased by the Western Rivers Conservancy, the land was transferred to the state for a park, which is the only improved campground on the lower river.

Henry Hagg Lake

Located in the foothills southwest of Forest Grove, Henry Hagg is a top smallmouth bass lake that really turns on when the water temperature tops 60 degrees. The current state record of over 8 pounds and the last five state record smallmouth all came from here. The lake, owned by the US Bureau of Reclamation and operated by Washington County Parks, has boat launches on the west and east shores. The north half of the lake is a no-wake zone. Tanner Creek Arm, the inlet on the northeast side, is known for smallmouth, as is the Sain Creek Arm, which is easily reached from Sain Creek Picnic Area.

Summer's warm weather brings out water skiers and those annoying personal watercraft that fortunately are confined to the south half of the lake. At the same time as the water warms, smallmouth move out of the shallows and into deeper water at the face of the dam at the south end. Before pleasure boats hit the water in the early morning and after they leave the water at day's end, surface fishing can heat up. The closest boat ramp to the dam is off SW Scoggins Valley Road.

The lake is open from the first Saturday in March through the Sunday before Thanksgiving on a sunrise-to-sunset basis. In addition to the boat- and shore-fishing opportunities, there is a 260-foot-long ADA-accessible fishing pier.

Brownlee Reservoir

This 57-mile-long impoundment that forms the border between Idaho and Oregon generates more angling hours than any other Oregon freshwater location. One reason is the outstanding smallmouth bass fishery, which produces both quality and quantity of fish. The typical bass is bigger than those found on either the John Day or Umpqua Rivers. Formal boat launches are sprinkled along the upper reservoir, and small boats can be hand-launched most any place you can get to the water. Farewell Bend State Park at the extreme southern end of the reservoir makes a great base camp for an extended stay. A former Oregon state record smallmouth was taken at Henry M. Hewitt Memorial Park on the Powder River Arm. A cluster of boat launches off Robinson Road (nearest town is Richland) puts boaters into prime smallmouth habitat.

As the water warms with the eastern Oregon spring, bass move into the channels and congregate on steep points and coves. Once the crappie spawn in May, smallmouth feed on the emerging fry, so small minnow patterns are the order of the day. During summer's heat, the bass cycle up and down in the water, going deeper during the day and coming back to the shallows morning and evening. Fishing is best May through October.

A day of hot weather and plentiful snowpack can raise the water level of the John Day River. Make sure to tie the boat securely to prevent it from floating away in the rising water.

Fishing really gets started in late May and extends through June. By July, low water levels restrict floaters to lightly loaded pontoons, but the fishing is exceptional. The Oregon Department of Fish & Wildlife estimates 5,000 smallmouth per mile. For experienced fly fishers, the question is not will they catch fish, but do they want to catch more than 100 in a day. The fish move into the tailouts and heads of riffles to actively feed on all manner of aquatic insects. When adult dragonflies skim the water hunting hatching mayflies and other bugs, the smallmouth launch themselves into the air in a frequently successful attempt to grab the dragonfly. The biggest bass take up positions offering the best combination of food, oxygen, and security. By September, angling attention turns to steelhead, though some anglers fish the lower river for smallmouth as late as January.

Bank fishing access is available wherever a road or highway crosses the river, though the topography from Service Creek to Cottonwood makes hiking along the river a challenge.

Hard plastic poppers float forever without any fly floatant added. In order to get a good hook set, slow down the strike to allow the fish enough time to close its mouth. PETER MAUNSELL

UTAH

Utah first introduced smallmouth bass a hundred years ago, but it wasn't until recently that Utah anglers embraced them.

Flaming Gorge

Wyoming and Utah share Flaming Gorge Reservoir, with Utah having the best smallmouth bass fishing. Illegally introduced burbot have adversely impacted younger smallmouth in the upper third of the reservoir. From Anvil Point boat ramp south into Utah, all ages of smallmouth are present and the fishing is better. If you want quantity of fish, target the southern portion. For quality, stay in the northern portion. There are plenty of smallmouth in the 14- to 16-inch range with few larger fish available. The best fishing months are June, July, and August, particularly on the steep, rubble-strewn shoreline.

In May and June the fish move onto shallow flats and will hold there for a few weeks, even after the spawn. Some of those flats run for miles with fish in water 5 feet deep or less. Generic baitfish patterns (there are no threadfin or gizzard shad in the lake) fished over the tops of weeds will catch plenty of fish. Crayfish patterns are the best choice when fishing rock and cobble structure. By summer, the fish have moved deeper off points.

Antelope Flats, Spring Creek, Dutch John, and Linwood Bay all offer access and fishing.

Jordanelle Reservoir

East of Salt Lake City, Jordanelle, Utah's newest reservoir, has rapidly gained a reputation for trophy smallmouth bass fishing. Located at an elevation of 6,166 feet, this 3,300-acre stillwater fed by the Provo River provides beautiful views of the Wasatch Mountains and bass stretching the scales to the 8-pound mark. That impressive size may be due to the requirement that all bass over 12 inches must be immediately released. That regulation was changed in 2012 to allow retention of one bass over the 12-inch mark.

In the typical year, water temperature is still in the 50s at the end of May. The best fishing is the May prespawn through the third week of June. Forage consists of Utah chubs (silver sides and dark backs) and yellow perch with a few crayfish in the mix.

Modest amounts of smallmouth bass can be found in the Provo River above Deer Creek Reservoir and below Jordanelle Reservoir.

Pineview Reservoir

Some say Pineview, an impoundment of the Ogden River, offers the best smallmouth bass fishing in northern Utah. Certainly it offers the best access, since it lies less than 10 miles outside Ogden in the Wasatch-Cache National Forest at an elevation of 4,900 feet. In Utah, that qualifies as midelevation. Set in pine trees and sagebrush flats, it also has areas of rocky and steep shores. Past years of bountiful water have been good to Pineview smallmouth. A hearty population of several year classes has resulted in fish topping 4 pounds.

Forage for smallmouth are yellow perch and black crappie. Locals favor white streamers and what the gear guys call "firetiger," which combines the dark green, yellow, and orange colors of the yellow perch. Crayfish are absent in Pineview but that doesn't stop smallmouth from hitting crayfish imitations.

The area around the Port Ramp Marina on the west side of the lake is a favorite among locals.

Utah's Lake Powell is great to explore with a rented houseboat. Bring a kayak or pontoon boat for day excursions.

Lake Powell's unique geology draws one's attention and makes it difficult to concentrate on fishing.

Lake Powell

This lake is a largely untapped fishery, in part due to its size (186 miles long at full pool), remote location, and limited access for boaters. There are only four spots where trailered boats can be launched. Wahweap from the southwest, Hall's Crossing from the east, and Bullfrog from the west, both two-thirds up the lake, and Hite at the north end all have marina areas, but a quick look at a Utah road map shows no direct routes between them. Small boats can be hand-launched from several single-lane tracks that lead to the water from the east and west. Power boat rentals are available at the marinas.

Smallmouth fishing has really come on in the past few years with both the quantity and quality of fish improving. Forget the dinks of the past—5-pound bass are showing up with increasing frequency.

Once you gain access, the bass fishing is worth the effort. The best fishing is from Bullfrog Marina up to Hite, and the fish quality is better than ever. An invasive plant species, tamarisk, has taken root along the lake during low-water years. Forage fish try to hide in the now-flooded tamarisk and smallmouth follow the food. Success is ensured by finding and fishing the tamarisk. Threadfin and young gizzard shad are the target forage.

Lake Powell has 1,960 miles of shoreline and 96 flooded canyons, and it is mostly filled with fish from March through November. Canyons with tributaries attract the most fish, as the incoming water supplies nutrients that in turn attract forage fish that attract bass. Smallmouth move into shallower water by April and stay shallow through May, affording sight-fishing possibilities in the clear water, except during runoff when the tributaries turn dark. Crayfish and forage fish patterns are the rule here. Spring and fall are the best times to fish if you want to avoid the power boat and personal watercraft scene.

October through December can be outstanding fishing. The weather has cooled to tolerable levels, and the wind is rarely an issue. Even better, smallmouth follow the remnants of the 2- to 3-inch-long shad into the shallows. Baitfish patterns can result in dozens of fish landed each day, many exceeding 3 pounds. According to Wayne Gustaveson, Utah's Lake Powell expert, smallmouth hang out along the shallow, rocky edges of the canyons and reap the benefit of shad herded into the canyons by striped bass. The stripers set up a picket line in deeper water, preventing the shad from escaping so that no matter which way the shad turn, they run into predator fish.

Anyone planning on fishing Lake Powell should go to www.wayneswords.com to get the latest scoop on the water from Wayne Gustaveson, who knows more about that lake than anyone.

WASHINGTON

In the land of steelhead and salmon, smallmouth are making waves as fly fishers expand their fishing horizons. The state record was caught on a fly rod.

Smallmouth coloration often reflects the substrate of their home water. Lake Powell smallmouth typically are tawny-yellow and lack dark tiger stripes.

This section of the Yakima always holds fish through the postspawn period. It has a mixed-cobble bottom and modest current flow.
MICHAEL T. WILLIAMS

Yakima River

The Yakima River emerged from under the smallmouth bass fishing radar a few years back when I wrote articles for several fly-fishing magazines. My Banana series of flies and D-Dub's Marabou Minnow were developed on the Yak.

Each spring, as many as 30,000 Columbia River smallmouth migrate into the Yakima, running upstream as far as Prosser to spawn. The upstream smallmouth migration collides with the downstream migration of fall chinook fry and mayhem results when bass key on the salmon fry.

May can provide outstanding fishing, especially during low-water years. The river fishes well from April through September and offers an excellent chance to catch the smallmouth of a lifetime. Seven-plus-pound fish are caught each year.

With the exception of Horn Rapids Dam, there are no navigation hazards on the river, which is best fished from pontoons, rafts, or drift boats. The Washington Department of Fish & Wildlife (WDFW) maintains water access sites with boat ramps at Benton City, Snively Road, Hyde Road, and Duportail Road. Light boats can be hand-launched at several locations in Horn Rapids Park. There are concrete ramps at Wye Park and Horn Rapids Park as well. Incidental fly-caught species include spring and fall chinook, carp, channel catfish, and suckers. No permit is required for this day-use river.

The two most popular single-day floats are Benton City to Horn Rapids Park and Snively Road to Hyde Road.

Potholes Reservoir

At 32,000 acres, Potholes can be intimidating to the uninitiated. Those who take the time to learn where the smallmouth live are rewarded with fish topping 5 pounds. A boat can provide access to the area known as the Dunes at the north end of the reservoir. Bank fishers can work along the face of O'Sullivan Dam, the arm where Frenchman Hills Wasteway enters the lake, and Lind Coulee, a long narrow arm on the east side.

In 2005, the Central Washington Fish Advisory Committee began a 20-year program designed to create underwater sanctuaries for juvenile fish. Patterned after the Lake Havasu program, the Committee builds habitat boxes and drops them at specified locations in the lake to create artificial reefs where little fish can go to escape predation.

Potholes Reservoir State Park makes a great base camp. Plusher accommodations can be found at Mardon Resort.

The high bank covered with vegetation means boats are necessary to fish the Yakima River. The river level varies with irrigation flows and the fish move with changing water levels.

The Yakima River is dotted with islands. The smallmouth congregate upstream of the islands and again on the downstream side where the currents join. MICHAEL T. WILLIAMS

Potholes Reservoir is part of the Columbia Basin Irrigation Project. In recent years, the water level has remained high through the spawning cycle and the smallmouth population has benefitted.

Horsethief Reservoir and the mighty Columbia viewed from Horsethief Butte.

Columbia River

The Columbia bisects Washington, then flows west to form the border between Oregon and Washington. In decades past, the Columbia supported prodigious runs of steelhead along with chinook, silver, chum, and sockeye salmon before the nine dams and destruction of spawning and rearing habitat took their toll. The coldwater fish loss turned into a warmwater fish gain as smallmouth have spread throughout the river from Chief Joseph Dam to the tidal-influenced water near Kalama. There are those who believe the Columbia provides the best smallmouth fishing in the country due to its structure, food base, and relative lack of fishing pressure.

The Columbia is big water, subject to significant daily water level fluctuations when the dams generate power and the strong upstream winds that make Hood River a wind-surfing mecca funnel through the Columbia River Gorge. A power boat is necessary to fish the main river when the wind is up. Fortunately, the river offers abundant nooks and crannies where human-powered craft can work the edges, back sloughs, and protected coves. Shore-bound fly fishers can access the water at numerous places off Washington Highway 14. Fishing starts in April and runs through mid-August when the fish move back out to the rock humps in the main river. Permits are not required to float the river.

The Columbia River is filled with smallmouth and receives little fishing pressure. The reach from I-82 to I-5 provides the best access.

Railroad bed on the Washington side of the river provides bank access along the Columbia River for anglers willing to walk. Keep a watchful eye and an ear attuned to trains. Q. LINDSEY BARRETT

Rock Creek Cove, one of several backwaters of the Columbia, has several islands, shallow rock piles, and rotted pilings. All hold small-mouth.

Some knowledgeable anglers predict the next world record smallmouth will come from the Columbia. There are anecdotal reports of 10-pound fish electroshocked near Grand Coulee Dam and an 11-pound fish taken in a research station fish weir.

The sheer size of the river can intimidate those new to its waters. Here are places to get you started: Near Brewster, the mouth of the Okanogan River holds fish. The Hanford Reach between Vernita and Richland requires a boat but gets little pressure in the middle section. Below Burbank, after the Snake River joins, both boat and bank access can be found at Casey Pond. Further downriver, near Plymouth and all the way to Paterson, fish are caught most everywhere along the rocky shoreline. Other hot spots as the river heads west are Crow Butte, Sundale, and Maryhill State Park. For more spots, grab a map and look for any place where a river or creek runs into the Columbia for the next hundred miles, all the way to the grain elevators at river mile 75 near Kalama.

Box Canyon Reservoir

Box Canyon Reservoir is a 55-mile-long impoundment of the Pend Oreille River between Albeni Falls, Idaho, and running north to Box Canyon Dam at Metaline Falls. Built in 1955, the dam slowly converted what had been a coldwater fishery into a largemouth bass fishery. Over the past few years, smallmouth have replaced largemouth as the dominant gamefish. Northern pike, illegally introduced into Montana's Flathead River, passed through Lake Pend Oreille, over Albeni Falls Dam, and invaded the Pend Oreille sometime before 2004. As their population exploded, the Kalispel Tribe and WDFW initiated efforts to reduce the numbers substantially, and bass will benefit from that effort. No permit is required for the river, though a Kalispel Tribal permit is required on reservation waters.

Even though it's labeled a reservoir and subject to water lever fluctuations, Box Canyon has attributes of a river with substantial current. It's best fished from a boat. Pontoons, rafts, drift, and power boats can be launched at any of the numerous WDFW water access sites, city and state park ramps, or gravel launch sites located throughout the reach. Pioneer Park, just north of Newport, to Gregg's Road is a good float. The public ramp at Usk to the WDFW water access site at Ruby is a long run filled with interesting sloughs to explore. Fish the sloughs, then move fast to the next one, or you'll end up rowing in the dark.

For those with power boats, Boundary Reservoir, downstream from Box Canyon Dam, has excellent smallmouth fishing as well. If launching near the dam, get on the water before 9 a.m. to avoid the hydraulic created when the dam starts generating power.

Primary food sources are small forage fish and crayfish. For some reason, the biggest fish, topping 6 pounds, can be taken on topwater spun deer hair bugs.

WYOMING

Where the Great Plains meet the Rocky Mountains, fly fishing for smallmouth among sagebrush and antelope may be the quintessential Wyoming experience.

Fontenelle Reservoir

Southwestern Wyoming is home to Fontenelle Reservoir, a desert canyon filled by the Green River. In May and June, the smallmouth stack up in the bays on the northeast side just uplake from Fontenelle Dam. After the spawn, the fish move into typical smallmouth habitat, so anglers should target cliff faces with substantial underwater rubble. The primary food is crayfish with some Utah chubs and white suckers as well. Clouser-type flies in silver or gray are the best to imitate the forage fish.

The lake experiences a summer bloom of blue-green algae, which restricts visibility in the upper 10 to 12 feet of the water column. Timing of the bloom depends on the amount of water flowing into the reservoir. In 2011, a high-water year, the bloom didn't start until mid-August; 2012 was a low-water year with an earlier bloom. Use splashy topwater sliders and poppers, or dredge the bottom with weighted crayfish patterns during the bloom.

Keyhole Reservoir

Tucked into the northeast corner of Wyoming, Keyhole Reservoir (4,068 feet) is on the western edge of the historic Black Hills. In 2012, after several dry years, this Belle Fourche River

The Pend Oreille River sloughs have smallmouth, largemouth, and northern pike. All feed on yellow perch, so a perch fly pattern is a good choice.

Fontenelle Reservoir is one of Wyoming's best smallmouth waters. Its remote location means little pressure on the bass.

Fish crayfish patterns along the broken rock at Fontenelle Reservoir. Don't be surprised if you share the water with a herd of pronghorn antelope getting a drink.

reservoir filled and water flowed over the spillway for only the third time since the reservoir was built. Fish populations responded to the high water levels in both quantity and quality. The smallmouth exceed 4 pounds, and anecdotal evidence exists of fish pushing the Wyoming state record. Pay close attention to the rocky areas on the north shore.

Smallmouth have plenty to eat. The forage fish include emerald and spottail shiners, young-of-the-year freshwater drum, walleye, crappie, and carp. Wyoming fish managers re-established the gizzard shad population in 2012 after an absence of several years. The water around the rocky shores, points, and cliffs hold plenty of crayfish as well.

Float tubes, pontoons, canoes, and other small craft can be launched most anyplace you can get to the water. The best fishing is May and June, then again in September and October when the water cools.

Belle Fourche River

Below Keyhole Reservoir, the Belle Fourche River flows northeast through spectacular Devils Tower National Monument toward Montana, then breaks southeast before running into South Dakota. It is one of the few flowing waters in Wyoming that holds smallmouth bass. Best access is below Keyhole Reservoir, around Devils Tower, and near Colony for walk-and-wade fishing.

Greyrocks Reservoir

Built in the 1980s to provide cooling water to a local power plant, Greyrocks Reservoir has a growing population of smallmouth bass up to a couple pounds. An impoundment of the Laramie River, the reservoir sits at an elevation of about 4,000 feet and covers 2,000 acres. The reservoir only fluctuates about four feet annually and has been filled to capacity after suffering several drought years. Fishing should continue to improve with the abundant water.

Baitfish—gizzard shad, spottail shiners, yellow perch, and young walleye—along with the ubiquitous crayfish, provide food. Shad adults are too big to be part of the mix, but they are prolific breeders and their young are available throughout the feeding season. Fishing gets started in April—early by Wyoming standards—though the water doesn't reach 70 degrees until July. Early season efforts are concentrated in the shallower upper portion of the reservoir. Fishing is pretty much over by the end of September, most likely as attention is drawn to hunting.

CHAPTER THREE

Understanding Smallmouth

Most westerners cut their fly-fishing teeth on trout. My father, a trout fisherman, taught me to fish, first on the desert creeks of eastern Oregon, then later on the McKenzie River. He grew up in Oregon reading the trout and steelhead stories of Zane Grey and shared his own fishing stories with his children. I'm certain that in his nearly nine decades he never made a cast in coldwater for anything other than trout. He passed that narrow fishing focus on to all his children.

My mother's father, Granddaddy Ty, who left Missouri during the Dust Bowl years, introduced me, as well as my brother and sister, to warmwater fish. Back in his home state, going fishin' meant going after warmwater fish. The still-swimming mess of catfish in the washbasin on his back porch was the first fish other than trout I'd ever seen. Granddaddy Ty, my brother, sister, and I'd go fishin'. Crappie and the rare largemouth bass sufficed on warm spring days before the real fishing—trout— began. Come Opening Day, my dad stepped in to teach his sons and daughter how to fish for *real* fish. Once trout season opened, going fishing meant going after trout. Pretty much my thinking—until my first smallmouth bass.

Western smallmouth grow fat and sassy. Understanding habitat will improve the chance to catch trophy fish. JAY NICHOLS

A midriver rock pile held this trophy. It ate a D-Dub's Bleeding Minnow.

After a stint in the navy, I was living in Oakland, hankering for a trout at the end of a line. The local newspaper told of an East Bay creek flowing with trout and bluegill. One sunny morning in early spring, I headed for the creek and started fishing. I caught a few bluegill, then in one deeper run where the water flowed over a cobble bottom, a fish hit. Blew the doors off any trout I'd ever caught. That was the start of an ongoing love affair with smallmouth.

The first lesson trout fishers learn when smallmouth join the mix is that the best-fighting trout, even the famed McKenzie River redsides, are no match for the brute power of an equal-sized smallmouth. Not to disparage trout, which are widely available, great fun to catch, and beautiful to behold. But the sheer strength of that smallie started me on the path of discovery. I wanted to be a successful smallmouth angler, so I began to learn about the fish, what it eats, and where its food lives. My answers to those questions—answers that are still evolving as research, field experience, and talking with other smallmouth fly fishers reveals more about these fish—make fishing ever more interesting. It's a joy to fish a new river or lake and puzzle out where the fish are—and catch a few. After hooking a smallmouth, it's satisfying to turn to my fishing buddy and say, "That fish was exactly where it was supposed to be." It's great fun to take a newbie smallmouth fisher, and witness their first experience of the raw power of this exciting gamefish.

Swarm of bass fry schooling together for safety. They'll soon disperse.

Before getting deep into understanding smallmouth, though, let's take a brief look at the other species within the black bass genus.

The Other Black Bass

The genus scientists collectively call black bass contains as many as eight species of North American fish: Guadalupe, Suwannee, redeye, spotted, shoal, Bartram's, and the more widely known largemouth and smallmouth. There is logic behind the collective name, since all bass fry look black. There is much discussion and confusion among biologists and anglers when it comes to distinguishing between bass species. Even the experts make mistakes when dealing with immature fish. The US Fish & Wildlife Service mistakenly dumped smallmouth into Montana's Flathead River, thinking they were largemouth. The differences between largies and smallies become clear by the end of their first year.

Westerners generally don't need to learn all the distinguishing features of the other black bass, as only the redeye and spotted bass live here. The Guadalupe bass occur only in Texas on a lofty perch as the state fish. Suwannee are found in but a few Florida and Georgia rivers. Redeye bass swim throughout the southeast, with limited western populations in California, Nevada, Colorado, and New Mexico. In Georgia, locals refer to the redeye bass as "shoalies," even though shoal bass are genetically distinct. Georgia, Alabama, and Florida have shoal bass. And it turns out that the redeye bass in Georgia's Savannah River aren't redeyes at all. They actually are Bartram's bass—a distinction likely perceptible only to biologists.

Fish biologists who study black bass DNA and genetics say spotted bass are the smallmouth's closest relative. Spotted bass share similar coloring with the largemouth, though rather than a continuous dark lateral band, the band is more a conglomeration of spots. The mouth of a spotted bass does not extend past the eye. They are not widely distributed in the West, with limited populations in California, New Mexico, Nevada, and Colorado.

More Bass

Pint-sized rock bass are the smallest of the western bass. They share the red eye and color of a smallmouth, with a stocky, scrunched-up body more akin to that of crappie. They are a kick to catch on light gear.

White bass take their name from their silver-white sides and lighter belly. Instead of a single, wide lateral band, they have several thin, dark lateral stripes. According to the United States Geologic Survey (USGS), white bass are found in all western states save Oregon and Idaho. The Washington Department of Fish & Wildlife (WDFW) disagrees and does not list white bass in the state.

The striped bass looks like an elongated, albeit much larger, white bass. Stripers are found along the West Coast, in the Colorado River and isolated populations in New Mexico and east-

Early morning topwater striped bass by-catch on Lake Powell. Once the sun hits, they drop down in the water column.
WAYNE GUSTAVESON

ern Colorado. In some western waters, hybrid striped and white bass, known as wipers, have been successfully introduced.

Geographical Distribution

Smallmouth were heartland fish, limited by the Appalachians on the east and the plains on the west. They ranged north into the middle Canadian provinces and dipped south toward Dixie.

Smallmouth bass, perhaps heeding the words of Horace Greeley, went west in the late nineteenth century, reaching the Golden State in 1874 and the Silver State in 1888. They also went south, north, and east into all states, save Alaska, Florida, and Louisiana. Of the 11 western states, Arizona was the latecomer to the party; smallmouth were first planted in 1941. One reason for the westward spread was railroad camp cooks who wanted a source of protein for hungry track crews. More impetus for transplanting this fish stemmed from the railroad bosses who wanted to test their mettle against its undeniable qualities as a gamefish. Bronzebacks have since crossed international borders into Mexico, traveled the Atlantic ocean into the Old World, and crossed the Pacific into Asia.

In the west, smallies live in a variety of habitats from sea level in the drizzly Pacific Northwest to the dry pine forests of the Great Basin, at 6,000 feet and into the unpleasantly hot western desert. They swim in rivers controlled by dams, in rivers fed by snowmelt, and in rivers that run to the sea. In the state of Washington, they live in 61 lakes in 21 counties across the state. Other western states have similar distributions.

The boggy shoreline makes bank fishing impossible on this Washington bass pond. A float tube or pontoon is the best option.

Working a crayfish pattern up along the submerged rock is a good way to find fish. Match the weight of the fly to the depth of the water.
STEVE BOHNEMEYER

Shallow broken rock and drowned brush will have smallmouth bass in spring and again when the water cools in the fall.

Rocks make it bass country. Drop the fly next to the rock, then let it tumble down the rock face.

Western desert rivers have seemingly endless curves with fish around every bend.

Deep canyons create deep shadows. The fish follow the shadow-line into shallow water in search of food.

The massive water projects throughout the 11 western states created miles and miles of smallmouth habitat. Lake Powell, formed by Glen Canyon Dam, juts 186 miles from northern Arizona into southern Utah. Rufus Woods, a Columbia River impoundment, reaches 55 miles upstream from Chief Joseph Dam to Grand Coulee Dam. Just across the border in Idaho, Dworshak Reservoir extends 57 miles upstream from the dam. Smaller reservoirs dot the arid West. Built primarily for agricultural irrigation, they hold plenty of smallmouth. This wonderful gamefish lives not far from every fly fisher.

Smallmouth, like other living organisms, have three basic needs, for which they compete with those other fishes living in the same water. They need an adequate food supply. They need shelter—to grow and reproduce. They need security—of a habitat that will offer protection from predators so they might grow from fry to adults capable of reproducing. When those needs are met, smallmouth flourish.

Smallmouth Life Cycle

Water temperature is the primary factor driving the daily and annual life cycle of smallmouth. During the dark days of winter when the water may drop to barely above freezing, small-

mouth typically hunker down in the deepest holes in the river or suspend 60 feet or more below the surface of the lake or reservoir. In the cold of winter, their metabolism drops to near zero and they feed infrequently. When the warmer days of spring begin to heat the water, the bass begin to stir. River and lake bass begin to feed more when the water temperature broaches the 45-degree mark. By the time the water hits 50 degrees, the bass are on the prowl for food.

Prespawn males awaken to spring first. When the water reaches 55 degrees, they begin to hunt appropriate nesting sites, which may be near their winter haunts or far away. Spawning sites vary by water body, though they share common characteristics of depth, substrate, and temperature. Nesting water depth ranges from 4 to 12 feet; the clearer the water, the deeper the nest will be. The preferred substrate is broken rock or cobble. Water temperature runs from 59 to 64 degrees. The male fans the silt and sand from the nest. Using its nose and sometimes even its mouth to move rocks, the male excavate a depression 2 to 4 inches deep and several feet in diameter, then invites a ripe female to share the nest. The largest male builds the best nest and has the most successful hatch.

Male smallmouth become sexually mature at two to four years old. Females ripen at three to four years. The fish engage in serial monogamy. The female drops part of her clutch on a nest. The male fertilizes the deposited eggs as the female floats off to another nest where she repeats the process until her eggs are expended. Females carry somewhere between 2,000 and 7,000 eggs per pound of fish. Once she's gone, the male invites another female to his nest and repeats his cycle until his milt is expended. Each female and male mate with as many partners as possible so that the population as a whole successfully reproduces.

Smallmouth males are typically darker than females.

After she drops all her eggs, the female drifts into deeper water to recover from her rigors. She's done her part and takes no further role in the procreation or fry-rearing process. She'll either suspend midway in the water column or settle on the bottom. Recovery takes up to two weeks. Males take on the job of aggressively guarding the nest against dragonfly nymphs, crayfish, minnows, and other warmwater fish, which do their part to keep the smallmouth bass population in check by eating the eggs and disturbing the nest. Males guard the eggs for several days, and may fan the nest to aerate the eggs in turbid water, until the tiny black fry, only one-quarter inch long with bulging yellow eyes, hatch. When they've doubled in size, the fry swim up from the gravel. They spend several more days under the protection of the male. On reaching an inch in length, they break into smaller groups. At some as yet unknown signal, the fry disperse in order to avoid becoming dinner for dad. Their former protector is now an extremely hungry predator.

The protected period before dispersal is critical to smallmouth survival. High water events or excess turbidity can eliminate an entire year's spawn. Water temperature for the next few months is a significant factor in survival as well. Higher water temperature means more food production, which translates into higher smallmouth survival.

During the spawn period, bass are highly susceptible to anglers who locate and target the nesting fish. The most recent

Prespawn females are the biggest fish. Take care in landing and releasing them. MICHAEL T. WILLIAMS

research indicates that even if a fish is released at the site where it was caught, the spawn cycle can be adversely affected. Predators sneak onto the nest to eat the eggs while the male tries to escape the hook. Additionally, if played by the angler to exhaustion, the male's expended store of energy leaves him unable to protect the nest from attack. Research also indicates that perhaps only 25 percent of sexually mature males will spawn in any given year, so the loss of a nest to predation may bode ill for the overall population in that water.

Anglers needn't stop fishing during the spawn. Not every fish will spawn, and those that do will not spawn at the same time because various parts of the lake or stream reach the magic spawning temperature at different times. Specific knowledge of the water body allows anglers to fish throughout the spawning period without disturbing females dropping eggs or males guarding the nest. North-facing shores, shallow bays, and wind- and wave-protected areas warm up first. When the fish are spawning on north shores, fish the south shores where the fish are still in prespawn. By the time south shore fish head for the nests, the north shore fish may have recovered from their postspawn funk.

Smallmouth life span is inversely related to growth rate. The faster a fish grows, the sooner it dies. Growth rate is directly related to the availability of forage and water temperature throughout the year. All other things being equal, fish that live in warmer water year-round grow faster because they feed all through the winter. Just when you think abundant forage and rapid growth is all good, know that there is a down side to never leaving the chow line. Fast-growing fish living in warm water may die of old age at seven years, while their slow-growing coldwater cousins live twice as long.

How does angler harvest fit into the smallmouth survival equation? The WDFW enlarged the bag limit on the Columbia River and eliminated all size and bag limit restrictions on the entire upper Columbia River system in an effort to reduce smallmouth numbers. The WDFW privately concedes that even with the relaxed regulation, angler harvest will have little appreciable effect on the population. For more on the topic of harvest and smallmouth population health, take a look at chapter 11.

Chow Time

Fry's first food is zooplankton and tiny crustaceans. They soon graduate to aquatic insect larva, and by the time they break free of the nest, some will have started eating their newly hatched brethren. The fingerling diet consists of aquatic insects, smaller fish, and young-of-the-year crayfish. At 4 inches, the fingerlings shift from feeding high in the water column to close to the bottom—where fish fry and crayfish live. By the time they are palm-sized, smallmouth turn to "meat and potatoes," that is, crayfish and forage fish with a side order of large aquatic nymphs, including dragonflies and damselflies. They prefer soft-rayed fish, such as minnows, shiners, shad, and trout. Spiny-ray prey eaten most often are those living close to the bottom, such as yellow perch, redear sunfish, and darter.

The adult smallmouth is a top carnivore that favors whatever food is most abundant and easily accessible. Typically that means crayfish, forage fish, terrestrials, and large aquatic invertebrates, with a smattering of leeches, tadpoles, small birds, and other foodstuffs. As if to demonstrate how widely varied their diet can be, in one Washington desert lake, chironomids made up 80 percent of the adult smallmouth diet.

Diet changes with the seasons because the food that is abundant and available changes. In spring, bass may feed on the newly hatched forage fish and wiggly tadpoles. As the water warms, add young-of-the-year crayfish to the menu as well as aquatic insects, like dragonfly and damselfly nymphs, that have grown large enough to satisfy. In waters where threadfin shad make up much of the forage base, smallmouth always have them for dinner until late fall when the shad succumb to cool water. Threadfin shad typically spawn in spring and again in early fall. They may spawn up to three times a season in waters like Lake Powell.

Some western rivers and lakes have sufficient hatches of *Hexagenia* mayflies that bring smallmouth, never willing to let a full meal deal pass by, toward the surface where they slurp the emerging nymphs and fully formed adults. These huge mayflies, nearly 2 inches long, emerge at dusk after several days of hot weather.

By fall, the smallmouth diet is primarily forage fish and crayfish as the tadpoles have metamorphosized into fast swimming, high jumping frogs, and the invertebrates have grown into airborne adults. Smallmouth try to eat dragonfly and damselfly adults as they hover over the water's surface, but their success rate likely doesn't exceed the calories expended in their devil-may-care leap out of the water. Winter's cold water slows down the fish's metabolism and need for food. The winter diet is restricted to the occasional crayfish, bottom-dwelling forage fish, and winter stoneflies.

Smallmouth Anatomy

Not all bass are created equal. At one time largemouth and smallmouth were lumped into the "black bass" category with little distinction made between the two, except by biologists who still can't seem to agree on how many distinct species of black bass exist. For our purposes we need simply to distinguish between largemouth and smallmouth, having already taken a cursory glance at a few other species. Those new to the bass game should know which is on the end of the line.

The two most significant distinguishing largemouth features are the size of its mouth and its deep belly. The upper jaw extends past the eye, giving rise to the nickname "ol' bucketmouth." Their extended, almost bloated-looking belly earns them another nickname, "sowbelly." They also have a distinctive dark, almost black, lateral band extending along each side from the gill plate to the tail. A deep notch between the front and rear dorsal fin also indicates a largemouth. Typically, their color ranges from dark to light green along the side and white toward the belly to very dark brown in waters with dark mud bottoms. Another distinguishing feature is found in the scale pattern.

Largemouth have no scales on the bases of their soft dorsal and anal fins, and their scales match their size; the current world record is over 22 pounds.

The beginning point distinguishing a smallmouth from its largemouth cousin is an upper jaw that ends before reaching the eye. The smallmouth's front dorsal fin has 9 to 11 hand-puncturing spines, a shallow interdorsal notch, and a back dorsal fin with 13 to 15 soft rays. Pelvic and pectoral fins are soft; the anal fin has 3 spines and 10 to 11 soft rays. Instead of the dark lateral line of the largemouth, smallies wear war-paint-like copper-colored tiger stripes, which begin at the bronzed gill covers and radiate along the body. The large, subtriangular-shaped head slopes into a robust, chunky body. Completing the body color is a creamy or milky white belly.

Not all smallmouth sport tiger stripes. In fact, smallmouth vary widely in coloration depending on the chemical composition of the water, habitat, food source, age of the fish, and other environmental and seasonal factors. Those that live in cloudy water or around grass tend toward backs and flanks of pale or light green, which may account for the nickname "green trout." Cobble-bottom lakes and rivers, like Washington's Yakima River, produce gorgeous fish of deep bronze, earning another nickname, "bronzebacks." No matter where they live, many smallmouth sport clearly distinct and unforgettably vibrant red eyes. And to confuse things, other smallmouth caught from the same location completely lack any hint of red.

The overall coloration of the golden bronze smallmouth acts as camouflage, allowing it to blend with its home territory, which consists of gravel, sand, and rocky substrate. When viewed from above, the dark back blends with the bottom, making the fish less visible to avian predators. Conversely, when viewed from below, the light-colored belly disappears into the brightly lit sky, allowing the bass to escape an upward-looking predator.

When fry emerge from the nest mostly black-bodied, they are slender, bearing little resemblance to the chunky adult fish. At the end of their first year, fry range up to 3 inches long, though most are half that size. By their third birthday, the body dimensions clearly have taken on adult characteristics and coloration. Adult length is roughly three times body depth, which, in turn, is twice body width.

Smallmouth have tiny bristle-like teeth on their upper and lower jaw, although in larger adults, the bristles can become stiff and pointy. More like coarse sandpaper than the sharp, finger-shredding teeth of a brown trout, the bristles help smallmouth catch and hold their prey.

Smallies have a swim bladder, an air-filled sac that allows them to maintain a neutral buoyancy. They rise or fall in the water column by filling or emptying that bladder. Smallmouth, especially those that live in moving water, have longer, leaner bodies than their largemouth cousins.

In an oddity of scientific history, French naturalist Bernard Lacepede labeled smallmouth *micropterus dolomieu*—

Smallmouth colors vary widely depending on where they live. JAY NICHOLS

Red eyes are a distinctive smallmouth feature; however, not all smallmouth have red eyes.

dolomieu in honor of his good friend Compte Dolomieu, a fellow scientist, *micropterus* meaning "little fin." Little fin is a misnomer, as the fish categorized by Lacepede had a damaged dorsal fin with several broken spines and the appearance of a bisected dorsal fin, so it was not a good specimen. The taxonomical error was never corrected, and smallmouth have lived with the misnomer ever since.

Senses

Smallmouth necessarily perceive the watery world through their senses. This allows them to successfully detect food and escape becoming food for other predators.

Sight—The Most Important Sense

From the moment fry emerge from the gravel to the day they die, sight is the most important sense to smallmouth bass. Sight is the primary sense the fish use to find food sufficient to satisfy caloric needs and to avoid being part of the food needs of others. Eyesight's importance to smallmouth is typically a function of its clear water environment; anything that decreases water clarity decreases the importance of eyesight and increases the importance of the other senses, primarily hearing.

The location and mechanics of the eyes play a large role in the success of smallmouth. A human being, looking straight ahead, can see slightly more than 90 degrees to the side from either eye. A smallie can scope 180 degrees on each side of its body without moving the eye. It's almost like having eyes in the back of its head that allow it to ambush prey and evade danger without having to constantly rotate its eyes or move its body. Add a forward field of vision with intersections of binocular vision, where both eyes can focus on an object, and it becomes clear why smallmouth are sight feeders. With normal eye movement, the field of vision becomes full circle, eliminating any blind spots.

Much research has been done as to what fish see. While the full answer may never be known, it's certain that smallmouth are not color blind. Within the fish world, they have above-average ability to differentiate colors, a fact that makes it much more enjoyable to experiment with color when creating fly patterns. Some colors work better in certain light conditions and water conditions than others. Absorption, scattering, and reflection of light rays as water deepens is of less importance to fly fishers than gear anglers because most fly-caught smallmouth are in the upper 15 feet of the water column. Water, at 800 times the density of air, absorbs light quickly.

Scattering of light rays in water is the physical process by which the rays are forced to deviate from their straight line trajectory by something in the water such as sediment. Reflection is what causes glare, and the reason anglers wear polarized sun glasses.

Conditions such as spring runoff, algae blooms, or heavy rains that decrease water clarity also decrease the depths to which light rays penetrate and fly colors are transmitted. Briefly, here's how water and light rays interact. Water absorbs longer light rays, the ones toward the red end of the spectrum, first. As depth increases, shorter blue/green rays predominate. As depth increases and water absorbs more and more light rays, every color, whether is be a vibrant red or brilliant yellow, is seen as black.

The human iris reacts to light much like a photographer changing the aperture setting on a camera. The iris opens and closes in momentary response to the amount of light streaming into the eye. Shining a light in the dark allows us to instantly see. Not so with smallmouth. Their eyes have a fixed iris and no eyelid to block light. The eyeball cannot quickly react to the amount of light penetrating the water. Instead, the fish either changes depth or moves into the shadows in an effort to reduce the amount of light striking the iris. Conversely, in low light, it moves higher in the water column or out of the shadows. Understanding light penetration and how smallmouth react to light gives clues about where to fish and at what depth.

Hearing—Lateral Line and Ears

A Dictionary of Zoology defines lateral line as "a system of receptors, often embedded in special grooves in the skin of an animal, that is capable of detecting vibrations (and therefore movements) in the water surrounding the animal. In most fish, the lateral line runs along the side of the body, but usually it forms a number of branches on the head." Tiny hair-like receptors telegraph data gleaned from water movements and vibrations to the fish's brain. The brain interprets that data and invokes the food, fight, or flight response. Smallmouth have ears located on both sides of their head behind and nearly at the same level as their eyes. Even though there are no external openings, water-borne sound is easily transmitted to the inner ear through skin, muscle, and bone.

In low-light conditions and in off-color water, smallmouth depend more on their acute sense of hearing and lateral line for both food detection and predator protection. A big, bushy fly that pushes a lot of water can be effective under such conditions. Conversely, loud banging in a boat, sloppy casting, or thrashing about while wading send bass scurrying for cover. When night fishing, a noisy fly will draw more attention than a subtle presentation because as the amount of available light decreases, smallmouth rely more on their sense of hearing to locate prey.

Polarized sunglasses cut the glare off reflective water. No glare makes it easy to spot fish and avoid nests. PETER MAUNSELL

Smell

Nares—openings located on the head in front of the eyes—don't have a respiration function. Instead they are packed with chemoreceptors that play an important role in allowing small-mouth to detect scent in the water.

Water flushes through a passageway lined with olfactory epithelium, a membranous tissue festooned with cilia—tiny hair-like receptors like those found in the human ear. When activated, the cilia send signals to the smallmouth's brain for interpretation. Those scents likely serve as a final fail-safe test before a smallmouth swallows food. If the potential edible doesn't pass the smell test, then the smallmouth may reject it. Objectionable smells such as cologne, insect repellent, and sunscreen transmitted from the angler's fingers to the fly may cause fish to reject even the best-looking and feeling fly.

Smallmouth share the same waters as another highly sensitive fish. The smell test is well developed in common carp, which use their extremely sensitive olfactory sense to detect, then reject, fake food. Experienced carp fishers have been known to forego head cement on their flies, believing that residual odor will cause the fish to spurn the fly. Much of carp fishing involves stalking and scouting for tailing fish. While looking for those fish, it makes sense to keep your hands away from the fly to minimize imparting unnatural scent to the fly. It might make sense to adopt this approach when fishing for hard-pressured smallmouth bass.

Tiny receptors in the skin along the lateral line telegraph sensations. Innovative fly patterns incorporate glass rattles. The noise triggers the lateral line and alerts bass that food is near.

Nares are the small openings between the eyes and mouth used to detect scent. JAY NICHOLS

The makers of fish attractants would have the angling population believe that dousing a favorite lure or fly with fish scent is the key to catching the biggest and most fish in the water. Certainly there are fish, such as some catfish, which use their olfactory sense to find food. Not so with smallmouth. The sense of smell is the least important sense available to smallmouth as food-finding aid. Fish attractants might, however, serve to mask otherwise offensive odors transmitted from the angler to the fly. In states like Washington, adding scent to a fly turns it into bait, according to the fishing regulations so it no longer counts as fly fishing.

Taste

Thousands of taste buds line the smallmouth's lips and mouth. These taste buds are used to help the bass decide whether to eject or swallow a potential food. It is a good idea to avoid contaminating the fly with any offensive tasteables like tobacco smoke, petroleum, insect repellent, or sunscreen.

Touch

Smallmouth are also thought to use a sense of touch in deciding whether an object is food or foe. The smallies touch sensitivity is greater than that of trout, which makes smallmouth much more quick to reject any unnatural-feeling fly. Natural hair poppers, gurglers, and sliders have an advantage over hard plastic versions because smallmouth can jettison plastic before the hook is driven home. Soft, lifelike materials such as rabbit and marabou are favorites that can be used to fashion hard-to-reject crayfish and baitfish patterns.

Conditioning

For decades, scientists used the word *instinct* to describe many animal behaviors that they have since come to discover are not instinct. Instead, the actions are the product of learned behavior. Professional bass anglers talk about bass learning to avoid the most common baits and about how the frequency of use directly increases the rate at which the bass learn to avoid getting caught. Evidence suggests that on highly pressured waters, the smallmouth's naturally occurring aggression or curiosity is mitigated by conditioning. The result is that smallmouth are becoming harder to catch on those waters unless anglers change tactics, techniques, and flies. Research shows that as pressure on a given water increases, the catch rate decreases, even when fish density remains unchanged. Natural selection is at work as well. Dumb fish, those unable to learn, get caught more often. The more often they get caught, the more likely they will get harvested or suffer some other form of mortality, leaving only the smart fish in the water.

The constant innovation in lure and fly design and consequent claims of a new design being a better mouse trap actually have some basis in science. With the increase in fly fishing warm western waters, more and more smallmouth get educated to the usual and ordinary flies and how they are fished. The result is that catch rates will decline. The cure to combat conditioned fish is to break out of the usual way—be the leader of the pack. When bass catch on to the new way, it's time to figure out the next new way, which may, in fact, be a return to an old way. Solving the puzzle is what makes fishing so much darn fun.

Feeding Style

Smallmouth feeding style depends on several factors, including water temperature, water clarity, food source, time of year, and type of water. River smallies are more likely to be ambush feeders—lying in wait in the soft water while the current acts as a conveyor belt, bringing foodstuffs to waiting mouths.

Lake smallmouth adopt searching behavior, gathering and herding baitfish schools into shallow water, or using structure to cut off escape routes. During fall on Lake Powell, smallmouth stay along the edges of coves and nail the threadfin shad forced into the shallows by a picket line of striped bass. When the shad are in open water in the summer months, smallmouth grub shattered rock piles for crayfish.

Size

The world record smallmouth, a single ounce shy of 12 pounds, was taken from Dale Hollow Reservoir in 1955 by David Hayes. In fact, Dale Hollow Reservoir, formed by damming the Obey River on the Tennessee-Kentucky border has produced five of the seven largest smallmouth on record, all over 10 pounds. The longer growing season, coupled with abundant threadfin shad contribute to this string of huge fish.

For years, western waters lagged in the big fish race, but Idaho's Dworshak Reservoir keeps putting out bigger and bigger fish. Idaho's most recent state record is a few ounces under 10 pounds. WDFW electroshocking has turned up smallmouth around 10 pounds, and anecdotal evidence points to a near-world-record fish caught in a Columbia River fish trap. The South has the longest growing season, but the northwest states of Oregon, Washington, and Idaho have longevity of fish, an abundant food supply, and limited fishing pressure.

The quality and relative abundance of food determine growth rates of fish. Not all food is created equal in terms of calorie content. In human terms, each gram of fat contains nine calories, while each gram of protein and carbohydrate contains only four calories. Crayfish are a relatively low calorie food, when compared to forage fish with high levels of fat, or high-calorie terrestrials like crickets. The calorie difference in foods could easily explain why as Columbia River fish grow in size, they switch from crayfish to forage fish.

Fish must also weigh the cost of calories expended with caloric value of the gathered food. In order to grow from fry to adult, each fish must solve a simple equation. It must consume more calories than it expends in gathering food. A river with a relatively low abundance of high-quality food like forage fish may grow bigger fish than water with a high abundance of low calorie food like crayfish.

The maximum fish size for any water is directly related to the forage base, growing season, water quality and flow, fishing

Fish the soft water first. In late summer when oxygen levels are low, concentrate on the riffle water.

pressure, and habitat. Those factors vary from water to water and year to year, however some generalizations can be made. Lake fish will grow larger than river fish that consume the same amount of calories. River bass have to expend energy swimming in order to maintain their position in the river, and, during spring snowmelt, fighting the current. Bass living in natural lakes experience a stable environment where deep water to escape extreme weather or a predator is only a few tail wags away. Smallmouth that live along lake margins grow faster than fish living in open water. The reason is simple. Food is easier to find and catch in a shallow-water environment. However, western irrigation reservoirs experience boom or bust cycles. In low-water years, reservoirs lose much of the water and forage that the fish depend on. Even worse are the long-term drought years when the reservoirs go completely dry. In high-water years and for a few years thereafter, fishing can be terrific because the plentiful water allows the forage base to successfully spawn and expand. Smallmouth respond by growing big and fat on the dramatically improved food supply.

Relative abundance of forage is primarily dictated by water temperature. Cold water, under 45 degrees, produces less forage per growing season than does 65 degree water. The less food there is to eat, the fewer fish a body of water can

support, and each fish grows slower than does its cousin in warmer water. Think of forage in terms of farming. A longer growing season allows a farmer to harvest two or more crops each season. In warm water, a forage species may undergo more than one reproductive cycle in a growing season, thereby creating an abundance of food for growing predator fish. Conversely, a shorter growing season will curtail both the number and size of forage.

Waters in mild climates with a longer growing season produce bigger fish. The temperate climates of Washington, Oregon, California, and Idaho are reflected in heavier state record smallmouth for each state, when compared to the harsher climate and shorter growing season experienced in the other western states. Waters with an abundant, high-calorie forage base have bigger fish. Columbia River smallmouth dine on fall chinook and American shad fry in addition to resident forage fish and crayfish. The average fish size reflects this cornucopia.

In rivers and lakes where the local ethic is catch and kill, the chances of those places growing a trophy fish are slim. One Columbia River tributary that my fishing buddies and I hit when the upriver wind whips the main river into unfishable and dangerous whitecaps provides plenty of sport but few big fish due to the stringers of bass removed by bait and gear anglers.

Importance of Water Temperature

Smallmouth prefer cool water and can't tolerate warm water, right? Wrong. The cool water preference theory is bunk, as it was based on faulty conclusions, then unthinkingly repeated again and again as if true. No question smallies live where the water is cold, but they don't really get active until the water tops 60 degrees. As the water temperature continues to increase, so does smallmouth activity level.

Some western stillwaters sport a winter icecap for several months, and many of the rivers get thoroughly chilled over winter and when filled with spring snowmelt. Some of those same waters, certainly those in the western desert states, heat to bath water temperatures when daytime highs hover in triple digits for days on end. Fishing gets crazy good because smallmouth metabolism keeps pace with the warming water temperature, turning those fish into full-time eating machines. All other factors being equal, the warmer the water, the more fish need to feed and the more fish get caught because they are eating all day long.

Below 50 degrees, smallmouth metabolism slows and their food needs are minimal. When the water temperature crests that 50 degree mark, the fish begin to feed in preparation for spawning. Postspawn, when the mark tops 65 degrees, the fishing gets better and continues to improve until the thermometer tops out in the mid-80s. How good? One mid-August day on Washington's Grande Ronde River, when the air temperature was well into triple digits and the water temperature registered 79 degrees, I raised over 60 fish in two hours. And those numbers pale when compared to the John Day River at the same water temperature.

Water temperature determines migration patterns. In rivers and streams, smallmouth generally migrate from the shallows, sometimes great distances, to spend the cold of winter in deep, slow-moving pools. Similar migration patterns are followed by lake fish as they move from shallow water into deep water. In Lake Washington, the smallies spend the winter on rock humps or suspended more than 60 feet deep.

Effects of Weather

No question that a cold front adversely affects lake fishing. In a cold front, the leading edge of a cooler mass of air replaces warmer air, forcing it upward. Storms that form along that fast-moving leading edge produce dramatic weather changes. Air temperature may plummet, matched by barometric pressure drops as the front approaches, hits the low point, then increases as dense, cold air blankets the area. The pressure changes affect bass behavior in two ways, as illustrated by an experience I had in Utah.

A cold rain hit the Wasatch Mountains in early October when I was on a research trip that would end at Lake Powell. Lake Powell fishing was on fire as the front approached. I arrived at the lake two days after the front. Wayne Gustaveson, Utah Division of Wildlife Resources (DWR) Fisheries Biolo-gist, and I hit the water before the sun rose. Each cove we fished that had been filled with smallmouth a few days before the front now was quiet. Wayne took only a few striped bass from a depth of more than 30 feet. The smallmouth had reacted to the front. They moved out of the shallow water where they had been eating threadfin shad and dropped onto rock piles 25 to 30 feet deep. Getting a fly that deep was possible only by using a combination of a T-14 shooting head matched with a sinking line and plenty of patience. On the second day, the smallmouth started to move back into the coves, and we found some in water only 5 feet deep. The stripers had moved shallow as well, following the shad.

Here's even more evidence of the cold front effect on the fish. Utah asks anglers to retain stripers caught on Lake Powell in an effort to maintain viable fish diversity. When cleaning the fish caught on the first day, only one striper had any food in its stomach. The stripers taken on the second day had resumed feeding, as their stomachs were filled with threadfin shad. Low pressure in the days before a cold front hits can ramp up fish activity. Again the Lake Powell cold front illustrates the point. According to the Utah DWR fish checker, anglers reported outstanding topwater catches the day before the cold front hit, in the same area where Wayne and I only found a few deep fish two days after the front passed.

Look for post-cold-front smallmouth on the deepest edge of points, reefs, humps, and river channels or whatever structure they were using before the front arrived. Slow down the retrieve and do what winter steelheaders do—put the fly repeatedly in their face—because they won't chase.

In early spring when bass are hungry after a long winter fast, a few days of warm, calm weather can raise the water temperature a degree or two and spur fish into feeding. The same can occur in late fall.

Trout anglers decry the dog days of summer when the water "gets too warm" and the fish won't hit any fly. By and large, there are no dog days in smallmouth bass fishing. The warmer the water, the better the fishing. Some bass fishers claim that too many days of bright sunshine drive the bass deep because their eyes are sensitive to bright light. It's true that bass don't have eyelids to block light. It's also true that the bass iris is fixed, meaning that it cannot narrow or widen in relation to the amount of available light. But I don't think bass morphology fully explains depth changes. My take on any changes is that the fish are merely following the food. If the food is shallow, so are the smallmouth. Conversely, if the food goes deep, so do the fish and so should you.

Salmon anglers have a pithy saying, "If you can see the bait, you're too late," meaning that the coming of daylight drives baitfish down and salmon follow their food. In freshwater lakes filled with mysid shrimp, the fish that feed on shrimp move up and down in the water as the shrimp move, in direct correlation to the amount of ambient light. On bright days, the shrimp go deeper than they do on cloudy, overcast days. Mostly what that tells the inquisitive angler is, the more you know about the behavior of creatures the fish eat in the water being targeted, the more likely you are to fish where the fish are.

CHAPTER FOUR

Habitat

Across the river and downstream 300 yards from the boat ramp where the edge of the flat drops into a deeper run, I will hook a smallmouth a few feet below the tree that marks the beginning of the run. Barely 15 feet long and discovered by fortuity, the run is a perfect example of western river habitat. Once learned though, discovery become more a process of understanding smallmouth habitat.

Structure

Smallmouth are structure-oriented fish, meaning they relate to the tangible and intangible objects around them, much like people relate to the items of furniture and open spaces in their homes. Here's my definition of structure: any area that is different than the area around it. Structure may be huge, like an island, though more likely the island will feature several different structures along its banks and at either end. In a slow-moving stream, the downstream end of the island will likely feature a weed bed over a silty bottom. The upstream end will be gently sloping cobble.

A visible rock that alters the current is structure, as are submerged rocks that create bulges, current seams, eddies, and such. Smallmouth orient or relate to those tangible objects. Other examples of tangible, visible structure are gravel bars, bridge pilings, islands, large woody debris, docks, and weed beds.

The list goes on to include beaver and muskrat runs, where their comings and goings erode the bank, creating a trough. The trough creates a microcurrent differential attracting small food items, which attract larger food items that end up attracting smallmouth.

Foam lines, whether created by the current or wind, are structure. The foam lines collect and hold bits of food. Small forage fish feed in the foam, only to find themselves the target of smallmouth, or the bass may forego the small fish and eat the food trapped in the foam line.

Smallmouth and broken rock stucture go together like peanut butter and jelly. Work the fly around the rocks because that's where smallmouth food lives.

Docks provide shade for ambush predators like smallmouth.

Pockets of foam are always worth investigating. Baitfish and topwater flies both get results.

Shadows cast on the water by waterside trees, rock walls, and other objects are an example of intangible structure. These are used by smallmouth to great advantage. To understand how a smallmouth uses shadow, here's an analogy. Imagine you are hiding in a dark closet, the door slightly ajar, allowing you to peer into a lighted room. You can see everything and everyone in the lighted room, but they cannot see you in the dark. You are the smallmouth, waiting in the shadow, waiting to dash out and slurp up any unsuspecting baitfish venturing too close to the shadow line. Knowing this about shadows is an incentive to get on the water early before the sun rises so high that the shadows disappear. The same is true about hitting the water later in the day when the shadows reappear.

I like spun deer hair patterns when fishing into the shadows formed by rock walls that drop cleanly into the water. The cast should be made so the fly lands as close to the wall as possible—sometimes I'll bounce the bug off the wall so it plops into the water—then wait for the take. My hair bugs have silicone rubber at the tail and along the body, so any twitch of the fly makes it jiggle irresistibly. The take is always without warning—one moment the fly is on top of the water; the next moment the bass materializes out of the shadows with mayhem on its mind. No wonder I like to fish smallmouth.

Moving Water Bass

I've talked with many accomplished fly fishers who don't fish moving water; instead they spend all their fishing time on flatwater. When asked why, their uniform reply is, "I don't know where to find the fish in a river." Of course, there are just as many moving water fishers who feel completely at a loss when trying to figure out lake fishing. Finding where bronzebacks live in rivers and streams is easy: instead of looking at the entire river, think in terms of the water's component parts. Fisheries biologists like to talk about the number of catchable-sized fish per mile of river. That statistic is really only meaningful when comparing one body of water to another. More fish per mile means you have more opportunities to catch fish on the river that has more fish. However, that doesn't tell you anything about where the fish are within any given mile. Most assuredly, the fish are not uniformly distributed within every mile. Certain places offer better combinations of the three key elements of food, shelter, and security, and that's where the fish will be. Without comprehending those three elements, a person could spend hour after hour flogging here and there and only occasionally cast where fish live. I know because when first learning about smallies, that's what I did. If you want to learn by

It pays to get on the water early to fish the shadows with topwater flies. The takes can be explosive.

Western rivers flow through columnar basalt canyons that were home to Native Americans for thousands of years. These pictographs are on the John Day River, but watch out for the rattlesnakes that live in the broken rock near the basalt.

flogging, skip ahead. Of course, if you want to accelerate your climb up the learning curve, then read on. Once the secrets of moving water habitat are learned, that knowledge can be applied to any new water.

Let's break down an outstanding smallmouth river into its components. Oregon's snow-fed John Day River, born in the Blue Mountains, is a true western river dropping 9,000 feet of elevation before entering the Columbia River. Unsullied by dams, at 281 miles it is the third-longest free-flowing river in the Lower 48. During spring snowmelt, the river rips through the canyon at flows reaching 30,000 cfs, before dwindling to less than 50 cfs in late summer. At low water, the river forms braids that make floating a challenge. The upper reaches are cold water shared by spawning steelhead and salmon and resident trout. The lower and warmer 150 miles, which flow through a patchwork of ranchland, abandoned homesteads, and dark basalt canyons, are ruled by smallmouth.

Over the eons, the river has cut through the numerous lava flows that make up the Columbia River Basalt Group, flows covering much of northeast Oregon, southwest Washington, and western Idaho. In some ways, the lava explains why smallmouth do so well in the Golden Triangle—the thousands of square miles drained by the Columbia River and its tributaries, including the John Day. That's because the primary bottom substrate throughout the region is broken rock of random and mixed sizes all the way from pea gravel to huge midstream boulders and outcroppings.

When fishing a damselfly or dragonfly nymph, adding a strike indicator helps control the depth of the fly and aids in detecting strikes.

The geography of each bank reveals clues about water depth. The steep bank on the left indicates deep water. The flat bench on the right means shallow water. Fish will be in the deep water.

The John Day fits that pattern, with a mixed-size broken rock bottom, instream boulders like the one than forms Basalt Rapid, and rocky shorelines broken by flat benches or terraces found on the inside bends of curves. These prime camping spots formed during high-water events from lighter soils that dropped out as water flows diminish.

All that broken rock mixed with moving water creates prime fish holding features. The one truism for smallies is they want to gain the maximum intake of calories with the minimum expenditure of energy. With that thought in mind, let's look at some of these physical features.

Bulges and Bends

When water runs into a boulder, the obstruction slows the current and forces it back upstream, creating a slight bulge or soft cushion in front of the obstruction. One or more fish make that soft cushion their preferred feeding station, as it gives them first crack at the food without having to compete with the fish hanging out in the downstream eddy. Often the fish in the prime upstream real estate will be the biggest of the bunch.

The biggest challenge to successfully fishing bulges is getting the fly to the fish before the current sweeps it away. Cast a weighted forage fish or crayfish pattern far enough upstream to allow the fly to sink near the bottom, then guide it on a short line into the bulge. The strike will come quickly; these fish are conditioned to make snap eat/don't eat decisions.

Curves

Several western desert rivers, including the John Day, serpentine around lava dikes, turning the river into a series of curves. The inside edge of every curve is shallow, slowing the current. The bottom consists of smaller rock and sand substrate. The outside bend is always deeper and faster and has only large rocks and boulders because the faster current scours out the finer particles. The current may also undercut the outside bend bank. Smallmouth use the large rocks and boulders as shields to break the force of the current while awaiting food brought by the current. During periods of low-light or increased turbidity, smallies move into the shallows to pick off forage fish and crayfish.

Smallmouth feed on crayfish in the riffle water. They will also be looking for dislodged nymphs such as stoneflies. Q. LINDSEY BARRETT

Inside edges are best worked with a floating line and floating flies or with lightly weighted flies that imitate small baitfish and crayfish. Deeper outside edges call for a Sink-Tip and flies with more weight. Try a quartering upstream cast so the fly gets to the bottom where the fish live. Instead of blind casting, try to place the cast so the fly drifts close to visible underwater structure.

Riffles and Runs

Riffles are the shallow, cobbled areas at the head of runs. Riffles are home to small forage fish and aquatic insects like stoneflies. Trout move into the shallow riffles to grab stoneflies and other aquatic insects as do smaller bass. Bigger smallmouth wait just below the riffle where the water deepens and the current slows. In low light, the big boys and girls move up into the shallower water. During periods of low dissolved oxygen in the water, typically in late summer low flows, more bass move into the riffle as it contains a higher concentration of dissolved oxygen.

Fly fishers who learned how to fish on trout will spend way too much time fishing riffles thinking that smallmouth are nothing more than stout trout, and then wonder why they catch only small fish. Smallmouth are not trout, so it pays to relearn how to fish moving water.

Take a few moments to study the riffle to look for current seams or breaks. If any are spotted, focus on getting the fly into each. Even better are those seams or breaks that run into the deepest water. The rocky riffle bottom is home to aquatic insects and small forage fish. A favorite tactic calls for swinging a slider so it floats broadside in the current, looking much like a dazed or injured baitfish.

Runs are intermediate zones—not fast-water riffles, not slow-water pools. The occupancy level depends on the depth of the run and the bottom structure immediately below. If that bottom is composed of silt and sand, then smallmouth will be in the run because that's where the food will be. Conversely, if that bottom is broken rock and cobble with moderate current, smallmouth hang back during the day and will advance into the run to feed during low light. As water temperatures rise in the summer, bass spend more time in the run, as it offers more oxygen than slower water above or below.

If the run is shallow enough to spot the underwater structure, then work the fly over that structure. Otherwise, divide the run into slots about two feet wide and run a cast down each slot until the fish are located.

Swing the fly behind the exposed rock and work the transition zone.

Clear water and variable rock structure make for ideal bass fishing. A stealthy approach will improve the odds of catching fish.

Pools and Rapids

Slow and deep, in comparison to the rest of the river, that's what defines a pool. Pools are the sometime winter sanctuary for smallmouth and the summer rearing area for young-of-the-year. Pools hold the largest number of fish and the largest fish as well. For those reasons, fly fishers should learn how to fish them.

Not all pools are the same, nor do all portions of the pool hold the same number of fish. In a sense, pools are a microcosm of the entire river. As fish are not evenly distributed throughout a river, fish are not evenly distributed in a pool. Pools have a beginning, middle, and end. The beginning, or head, of the pool will hold the most actively feeding fish. That makes sense because that's where the food drifting on the current enters the pool. During the low summer flows, the head carries the most oxygen as well. Look for fish holding in the current seams, the line where the fast and slow waters meet.

The middle of the pool has the deepest water and the slowest current, offering the most protection from predators, while still allowing smallmouth to grub the bottom for crayfish and sculpins or snatch a dragonfly nymph on its way to the surface.

At the bottom or tailout, the pool starts to shallow and the current velocity increases as the water flows over a uniform cobble substrate. Whatever fish are in the area are actively looking for food, so don't pass it by without fishing. If one portion of the tailout is deeper than the surrounding area, fish it thoroughly; that's where the biggest fish will be. More fish move into the

In bright light, the best fish will usually be in the deepest water in the middle of the pool. Angle the cast so the fly has enough time to sink to their level.

The boat driver should maneuver so the angler can cast into the soft-water pocket behind the rock. Another tactic is to drop into the softer water below the rock and cast upstream.

tailout early morning and late evening, as the fish feel more secure in low-light conditions, plus crayfish are more active and available then.

If river conditions and remaining daylight allows anchoring the boat, do so to spend time thoroughly fishing each pool. They hold the greatest collection of fish of all western river structure. On the John Day when the water is at summer low and the bass are concentrated in the deeper pools, the challenge is getting the fly down to the bigger fish before it gets whacked by the hordes of hungry smaller bass. Fish a topwater fly until the small fish get smart and stop feeding, then switch to a deep-water crayfish to get the big boys (and bigger girls) to bite.

If the water is too deep or fast to anchor, softer water can usually be found on one side or the other at the head of pool where the boater can eddy out and fish the rest of the pool.

Heavy water rapids like the John Day's Class IV Lower Clarno are hazards to be negotiated to reach the better fishing areas below. Those kind of rapids are not worth the effort of getting a boat into position to fish the one or two pockets that might hold fish. Exposing the angler, the boat, or the gear to whitewater hazards for a fish or two makes no sense.

On the other hand, smaller rapids, sometimes characterized as rock gardens, can be super fun to fish. A competent boat driver can maneuver the boat so the angler can make short, precise casts into the soft-water pockets behind rocks and the bulges they create. Casts must be short, otherwise the conflicting currents catch the excess fly line and rip the fly out of the sweet spot. Spun deer hair topwater bugs are a kick to fish in rock gardens. The takes are swift and violent as current speed forces the fish to make snap decisions. If a bass hesitates, the food item is swept past, an opportunity lost; too many of those and it goes hungry.

A word of caution here. It's all too easy to get caught up in the fun of run-and-gun fishing and not pay attention to the rocks in the garden. If the raft or drift boat bangs a rock, it will likely bounce off and spin in the current without any significant damage. However, the sudden deceleration of boat slamming rock can launch the angler out of the boat and into the water. Both angler and boat driver should be wearing their personal flotation devices. If the boat driver's handling skills are not up to rock garden maneuvering, move on down the river. Pass on this fishing style, as there are plenty of fish in less turbulent water.

Breaks and Chutes

A current break is an area where the current in a river is diverted by an in-river obstruction. This creates slack water near the obstruction. It differs from an eddy because little or no significant upstream current is created. The break-produced slack water is one of the best fish-holding spots on the entire river. It allows the smallmouth to hunker down without expending energy until an edible floats past in the current. The smallie ambushes the food and immediately returns to its holding area. Maximum calories in; minimum calories out. Make the cast upstream so the fly, floating or subsurface, drifts in the current and sweeps past the slack water.

Current that passes between two obstructions, like rocks, forms a chute when compressed into a tongue or downstream-facing V by the force of the river gradient. The middle of the chute is usually deeper and the current faster than the surrounding edges. Chutes serve as travel corridors for fish moving from one holding area to another. They also serve as feeding areas on the edges where the bottom transitions from deep to shallow—the bass stay in the deep water while keeping an eye for forage fish that stray from the shallows.

Seams and Eddies

When differential currents—one faster than the other—flow alongside each other, they produce a seam of slack or reduced flow current that attracts fish much like a current break does. When the fish are in that zone, they use less energy, yet they are able to feed on tidbits brought to them by either current.

Look for seams wherever structure causes the main current to split, braid, hesitate, or alter course. The downstream end of the structure, perhaps an island, where the current splits to form an eddy then comes back together produces a seam. More subtle seams are found below smaller types of structure. Dry-fly trout anglers skilled at getting a drag-free drift understand that moving water travels at different speeds and have the ability to discern seams. Those new to the game need to learn to read current speed. Once they do, seams and the fish that hold in them will be revealed. When a seam is spotted, cast the fly so it runs down the seam right next to the slow water.

Ever wonder what causes a portion of the river, an eddy, to flow upstream? That upstream current is created by an obstruction like a rock, ledge, or small island. As the water flows downstream around the obstruction, a depression is formed in the

The boater is running the main current and missing the eddy in the foreground. The fish will be in the eddy, facing downstream into the upstream current.

A hillside vantage point revealed an abrupt underwater ledge. Fish parallel to the ledge with a full sinking line.

surface, which gravity fills with water flowing back upstream to fill the depression. Eddies may be as small as a few feet or as large as several hundred yards. The strength of the current and the amount of upwelling determines whether the eddy is worth fishing. If the upstream current and upwelling are too strong, the fish expend so much energy maintaining position that they choose better feeding locations. The Lower Salmon River has some of the longest eddies on western rivers. Roily eddies should be avoided because the strong upwelling of current makes the smallmouth work too hard in exchange for the food; instead fish the softer ones. Any fish in the eddy will be facing downstream, awaiting food to be carried to them by the upstream flow, so they are best fished from downstream. Since the fish are facing downstream into the current, the cast should be made to the downstream end of the eddy with slack to allow the current to carry it up the eddy.

Undercut Banks and Ledges

Find an undercut bank with a soft-to-moderate current flushing food into it, and it will be filled with smallmouth because this variety of structure provides everything—food, shelter, and security—a bass wants. The current drives food into the waiting fish. The overhang protects bass from attack by avian pred-

ators. It also allows the bass to hang back in the shade where it's difficult to be seen by unsuspecting forage fish and crayfish. Undercuts with current running parallel are nearly as good, though they will likely hold fewer fish because the current drives the food past, instead of into, the undercut. Both should be approached cautiously to avoid warning the fish, then thoroughly fished. Start at the head of the undercut and work all the way down.

Short ledges with water either breaking around or pouring over them are another fish magnet. Exposed bedrock fingers lying perpendicular to the channel are an easy structure to spot, though they may be a challenge to effectively fish depending on current speed. Years of water flowing over the ledge often undercuts the ledge, affording protection for the bass while they await the food presented by that same current. The frothy water adds to the sense of security, allowing a closer approach. During the prespawn, the fish will be at the shallower end of the ledge. By midsummer they will have moved to the deepest edge of the ledge, where they'll stay through late fall.

The best fish hold where the water first drops over the ledge. Regardless of whether the cast is made from upstream, downstream, or parallel to the ledge, the fly needs to work through the froth and drop into the deeper water. To accomplish that, the fly may need to land upstream and tumble off the ledge. It's critical to maintain line control so the strike will be detected.

Smallmouth cruise between parallel perpendicular bedrock fingers. They will be shallow early in the year and move deeper as summer wears on.

In the bright sun, the fish will be in the deep water off the rock face. Only small fish will be found over the light-colored sandy bottom.

Short casts work best to avoid having slack line on the water. Sink-Tip lines, short leaders, and weighted crayfish or baitfish patterns are my favorite way to fish ledges. Another option is a floating line and weighted fly under a strike indicator. The indicator makes it easier to detect strikes, and the resistance it creates in the water aids in hooking the fish.

Gravel Bars and Flats

Gravel bars are consistent food producers and for that reason attract smallmouth. Schools of forage fish frequent the shallow water around the bar, while smallmouth lurk on the edge where the water changes depth, ready to slash up to chomp any baitfish that stray from safety. If the transition zone merges into a bottom that includes good-sized rocks, boulders, or logs, those objects break up the current and provide holding areas. The more structure, the more likely bass will be present throughout the day. A transition zone lacking structure may only hold fish early and late in the day, when the light is low. If the bar contains organic materials, including silt and mud, crayfish can be added to the food menu.

Flats are somewhat amorphous as they may have a substrate composed of cobble and gravel mixed with mud, sand, or silt. They may include sunken woody debris or be bounded by willows, small trees, or grasses. The most definite feature is that they lack any clearly defined structure above or below the surface. What flats lacks in visible features, they make up for in the variety of smallmouth food found there. Woody debris and vegetation hold aquatic insects and harbor forage fish attracted by the bugs. The soft bottom is home to dragons and damsels; both nymphs are big enough to attract the attention of smallmouth. Crayfish hunt the flats and, in turn, are hunted by smallies. Shallow flats, 1 to 3 feet deep, are more likely to have fish during early morning, late evening, and at night. If the flat is deep enough to provide a sense of security from predators, smallmouth will be present all day, even during bright sunlight. Both bars and flats can be fished with floating or unweighted baitfish flies cast into the zone where the water depth changes. If dragonfly and damselfly adults are present, go with a topwater fly because the fish will be looking up to feed on top.

Weed Beds and Grasses

The topography of the John Day with its tremendous differential flows and relatively steep gradient means not many weed beds form. Of those that form, even fewer are underwater and

Smallmouth cruise the edge of the tules. When hooked, they often charge into the bushes with the angler chasing. The fish usually wins the battle.

available to hold food and attract smallmouth during late summer low flows. Wherever weed beds are found—midcurrent or along the bank, in bright sun or fully shaded—they attract smallmouth. Weed beds are the beginning of the food chain that ends with smallies at the apex. The weeds provide protection from the current so small food items gather in the shelter. They attract predacious dragonfly nymphs, crayfish, and small baitfish, all of which bring smallmouth to the table. Trout fishers who fish nymphs understand the bounty of weed beds as the trout nose into the weed bed, seemingly to shake the weeds, then drop back to eat the dislodged bugs. Smallmouth are lazier—they set up station on the edge of the weed bed and wait for food to come to them.

At low water, patches of bright green grass sprout around now-exposed rocks, which at other flows are inches or feet underwater. The grass patches are the vertical equivalent of the horizontal weed beds as they offer the same food chain and the same selection of foods, albeit on a smaller scale. Damsels and dragons migrate to the grass beds and use the stems to pull themselves out of the water. Once out, they begin the molting process. Try an unweighted nymph on a floating line during the migration.

Feeder Creeks and Deadfalls

Feeder creeks or tributaries are yet another fish magnet because of what they bring to the river. The water they bring is generally a different temperature—warmer in winter and cooler in summer—than the main river. That temperature differential attracts food items that attract smallmouth.

The creeks bring additional and, depending on the nature of the drainage, different nutrients into the system. A creek that drains through one of the wheat fields or grazing lands that abut portions of the river will pick up different solids than one draining a remote sagebrush-filled canyon. Both types of creeks add to the food web that ends with smallies on top.

Tributaries bring more highly oxygenated water, an important feature in the late summer low flows when bass seek areas that have current and consequently, more dissolved oxygen. Desert thunderstorms are usually brief and violent affairs that dump vast amounts of precipitation in a short period of time. In John Day canyons, the rain falls on steep surfaces with little absorptive capacity, turning seep creeks into sediment-carrying gushers. These bring more suspended solids into the river, creating a mudline that dissipates as the waters blend. Small forage fish are attracted to the food in the mudline. The turbid water acts as another form of structure. The sunlight penetrating the water is diffused by the suspended solids and the resulting reduced visibility makes it difficult for unsuspecting forage fish to escape ambush by the smallmouth.

Laydowns, or deadfalls, are trees that have died or been uprooted and that fall into the river and end up alongside the riverbank. The combination of sparse desert vegetation and high stream gradient makes for few deadfalls on the John Day—those trees that fall either get stranded high above the waterline when the river is at a fishable flow or they get swept all the way

downstream to the Columbia River. When deadfalls are encountered, they add another element providing fish-holding structure of shade, current deflection, and perhaps protection from overhead predators.

Riprap and Stream Armor

The days of dumping car bodies into the river to deflect the current from washing out the bank and flooding a rancher's field have gone the way of the buggy whip. Where western rivers run alongside a road, portions of the bank may be armored with riprap. Riprap is rock or other material used to protect shoreline from erosion by wave and current action. Riprap made of materials such as sandbags or sprayed concrete is best ignored, for it lacks the interstices where fish food can live. Rock or broken concrete riprap, on the other hand, has plenty of holes where crayfish and forage fish live.

The best time to fish riprap, at least on rivers with crayfish, is when the light is low and the crayfish start moving in search of food. When smallmouth move in tight to the shore, it's important to land the crayfish pattern within inches of the rocky bank, otherwise you'll be fishing behind the smallmouth with their noses pointed toward the bank.

Water Temperature

Water temperature, from barely above freezing in the depths of winter to the mid-80s in summer's heat, dictates what a stream smallmouth does and where it lives. Washington's Yakima River is a good example. Trout fishers know the Yakima as Washington's only Blue Ribbon trout stream. When the river emerges from the last canyon, it broadens and slows and smallmouth replace trout. Each year in late spring (the exact timing is determined by water temperature), up to 30,000 sexually mature smallmouth leave the cool water of the Columbia River and head into the warmer Yakima River to spawn alongside the resident population. The upstream migration crashes head on into the downstream outflow of fall chinook fry. Small baitfish patterns trigger several weeks of outstanding fishing as the smallmouth key on baitfish flies, even after the real fish have been swept downstream.

The migratory bass spawn, then disburse throughout the lower 40 miles of the river. As the water cools toward fall, they drift downstream to winter in the deeper water of the Columbia, leaving the resident fish to spend winter in deep pools. These water temperature–driven migration patterns are repeated in tributaries throughout the Columbia and Snake River drainages.

Dissolved Oxygen

Smallmouth bass are restricted in their habitat by the amount of dissolved oxygen in the water. They can survive in levels as low as 1 to 3 milligrams per liter, but need at least 6 milligrams per liter for normal growth. Fry production is diminished when

Smallmouth migrate from coldwater rivers like the Columbia and Snake into warmer tributary streams to spawn. They stay in their adopted water until the cold water triggers a return downstream. MICHAEL T. WILLIAMS

dissolved oxygen levels reduce. In pool-and-drop smallmouth rivers, knowing the oxygen requirement gives the angler a hint about where to look for fish during each season. The warmer the water is, the more likely the bass will be concentrated in the highly oxygenated drop areas.

Depth

River bass generally live in depths between 2 and 20 feet. As rule of thumb, the warmer the water is, the shallower the fish will be. There is also a correlation between the amount of light and water depth: the brighter the light, the deeper the fish.

Bottom Composition

The perfect smallmouth stream has a broken rock and cobble substrate interspersed with larger boulders. More rock means more forage means higher densities of fish. At first glance, boulder fields might appear to be the best habitat, but they, like unbroken bedrock, offer little forage.

An Idaho Fish & Game survey on the Snake River proved that all rock is not created equal. Biologists studied two areas of bedrock. The expanse of unbroken bedrock looked good to the

eye but proved to hold only a few resting fish. Similar-sized areas of broken bedrock held plenty of bass because crayfish and small baitfish—primary smallmouth food items—lived in the wide interstices. The broken rock also provided shade and ambush sites for the smallies.

Sandy and silty areas are likely to be devoid of smallmouth and can be hazardous to wade. The particles settle over the bottom and asphyxiate many of the small food organisms that support life in the river. Silt that settles on the smallmouth nests after the eggs are dropped can smother the eggs. Suspended silt reduces visibility for both the fish and the fisher. Murky water and good smallmouth fishing rarely coexist.

Current

Western smallmouth streams like Oregon's Umpqua and John Day Rivers are free-flowing snowmelt rivers that undergo huge annual swings in flows. In high water years, the John Day rips along at 30,000 cfs, but by summer's end, it reduces to barely a trickle. Even rivers that have flood control, power, irrigation diversion, and flow-through dams suffer episodes of high current velocity.

Prolonged high current speeds can be disastrous to the smallmouth population. The current scours nest sites before the

Broken rock and cobble bottom makes for good smallmouth water. A big rock formed a nice current seam. Nine consecutive casts landed in the seam and resulted in nine smallmouth.

The current delivers the food to river. Add a little jigging action to the fly to trigger a strike.

eggs hatch, sweeping newly hatched fry downstream, or eroding the forage base.

Current also acts as the food delivery mechanism to awaiting hungry smallmouth. As the current flow changes, smallmouth amend their position within the river as a result.

Migration

Early research, since debunked, concluded smallmouth spent their entire lives varying but a few feet upstream or down. In actuality, river fish travel substantial distances to find appropriate and unoccupied spawning habitat.

Resident river fish have been shown to make annual pilgrimages to suitable winter quarters. Migration distances are positively correlated to the severity of the winter. In the harshest weather, smallies may travel more than 60 miles from their summer range, then return to the same area the following year to spawn.

Stillwater Bass

For the "I only fish rivers" crowd, this section will demystify stillwaters. Most western stillwaters are irrigation or flood control reservoirs. Lake levels fluctuate with the demands of irrigation and the amount of precipitation received in the drainage. For example, some Utah reservoirs that would have been on the "must fish" list went dry in 2013. As lake levels dropped, the forage base either dried up or moved to a new location. The smallmouth moved with the food. Another aspect of lower lake levels is increased turbidity when the wind-driven waves churn the shallow, silty bottom. The fish head into deeper water, making themselves less available to fly fishers. When they are in the shallows, they fail to spot your offering unless it bonks them on the nose. One positive aspect of the low water is that you can take note of lake structure. Return to fish that structure when water level returns to normal.

Now here's some great news. A quick review of the state record smallmouth for the 11 western states reveals what you might expect. For the most part, the biggest fish live in stillwaters. Without having to fight moving water, stillwater smallmouth spend less energy than their river cousins. That means for every calorie consumed by a lake fish, more goes into growth. I suspect management strategy also plays a part, as the reservoirs are managed on a mixed-species basis, assuring smallmouth an adequate forage base. And some more good news is that several states not traditionally thought to be smallmouth factories are producing a new state record fish every few years. Idaho and Nevada are two examples.

Cast a topwater fly parallel to the sides and end of the dock. Work around the lily pads and along the shoreline toward the dock on the right.

Western stillwaters spread across an area roughly one-third of the continental United States, ranging from the moist Pacific Northwest to the arid Southwest. The natural lakes, such as Lake Washington, are deep, glacier-scoured, steep-sided trenches with few flats. Reservoirs are either relatively shallow flow-through waters, such as Nevada's Rye Patch Reservoir, or flooded deepwater canyons, such as Lake Powell. Despite the geographical and topographical differences, it's possible to make specific statements that hold true for the different types of water bodies. Understanding those common threads allows the new-to-lakes angler to improve the odds of cracking the still-water code.

Flow-through reservoir currents may be accelerated during periods of heavy irrigation or power generation drawdowns. The wind, so often prevalent in the west, creates waves that act as a form of current. The lake environment is static compared to a river. Instead of fish holding in one spot, reaping food brought by the current, lake smallmouth act more like hunter-gatherers. They follow schools of threadfin shad, cruise along the sloping points of land grubbing for crayfish, and venture into the shallows to forage for aquatic insects, leeches, and small fish. Research has shown that the bigger the bass, the more distance it covers in its search for food.

Like river fish, lake smallmouth orient to structure. Lake structure includes flats, steep banks, humps, rock piles, drop-offs, points, springs, docks, and other manmade objects. In reservoirs add riprap on the edges of dams to the mix. Locating the structure is the first step to finding lake fish. Google Earth is a good source for preliminary armchair investigation. Topographic and commercially produced maps are available. The best source of information, however, is spending time on the water, plotting waypoints on a GPS, noting structure and fish location, or committing notes to paper. Your written notes should include water temperature, air temperature, time of day, amount of sunlight, and other pertinent information.

Flats

A flat is any gently sloping bank that gradually transitions into deep water. Just as rock walls are visible indicators of deep water, low-angle, above-water terrain hints at shallow water

Smallmouth can be found along the sloping point and in the flooded brush. The blue heron is a clue that baitfish are present, so tie on a baitfish pattern.

below. The best smallmouth flats will have deeper water nearby. The fish can move onto the flats to feed, then scurry to safety in the deep water if necessary to avoid a predator. The best fishing for the biggest fish on the flat will be at the edges where the flat drops into deeper water. If the flat is very large, shorebound anglers may not be able to reach the best water. Boat anglers who spend their time shooting toward shore, not understanding the importance of deep water, miss the best fish as well.

Steep Banks

These are the intermediate areas, the medium-angle banks that fall between rock walls and flats. The best steep banks are close to another form of structure, such as a nearby flat, a point, or where a river or stream enters the lake.

Humps

Although the surface of a lake is flat, the bottom is filled with the same type of features as above-water terrain. Humps, also called saddles, are underwater islands, land masses big and small that are higher than the surrounding areas. Humps hold fish because they attract food. The top of the hump gets the most attention from fishers, but produces few fish. The sides of the hump have more fish with the biggest concentrations on the down-current side. The fish, acting like river bass, will face into the current. The best way to fish a hump is to target fish near the top first, then work the down current side with a cast made toward the top and retrieved down the side. Humps are most easily located using fancy electronics, topo maps, and, if shallow, noting dark patches against the water surface.

Rock Piles

Similar to rock structure in rivers, the rock piles, which may be nothing more than a few isolated boulders lying on a substrate of different material, attract fish. The bigger the pile, the more fish it can support.

Drop-Offs

Rather than separate and distinct structures, drop-offs are areas where the bottom falls away from other structure. On flats, water depth may abruptly change from knee-deep to 30 feet or more. When fish move out of the depths to feed, they will stop or hesitate at the breaks or transition areas. In trench lakes and flooded canyon lakes, drop-offs can resemble chasms. Lake Washington is over 200 feet deep while Lake Powell drops more than 500 feet. Winter fish on Lake Washington hug rock piles 60 feet or more down, effectively taking them out of reach of fly fishers.

As the water warms, the fish move into fishable depths, going shallow to feed, then retreating into the drop-off zone.

Wading anglers have to fish from deep to shallow. Boaters can work either way, though shallow to deep generally results in fewer snags and more fish. A crayfish pattern tied on a jig hook can be cast into the shallows, then bounced down the drop-off.

Points

Long, sloping points of land that run like an arrow into the water are prime smallmouth spots deserving full attention. Some fish hold along the spine of the point. Follow the descending spine, as more and better fish will be in the deeper water, 10 feet or more, and along each side of the spine. Where threadfin shad make up much of the forage fish base, they follow clouds of plankton driven against points by the prevailing wind and current, only to run into waiting smallmouth. When the bass are crashing shad, throwing a topwater slider into the mix triggers some of the most fun a fly rodder can have. Crayfish patterns are always a good option along points when the sun is off the water.

Springs

Like most underwater structure, springs are tough to spot; however, once located, they should be marked because they will always hold fish. In summer when the water has warmed to the point where the dissolved oxygen is low, cool water from the spring allows the bass to breathe easier. When winter has chilled the lake to barely above freezing, warmer spring water attracts all the foods that a hungry smallmouth might eat.

Docks

Smallmouth use dock pilings as nesting sites, then return later in the year to feed when the young-of-the-year forage fish hide under docks. They also use the shadow created by the dock as an ambush site.

Road and Riverbeds

Western reservoirs are flooded canyons and coulees where roads and rivers used to run. Smallmouth use underwater river and stream channels as travel corridors to get to and from spawning and feeding sites. Flooded roadbeds are another prime smallmouth location. When Banks Lake, an irrigation storage reservoir in Washington, was built as part of the Columbia Basin Project, it flooded an asphalt roadbed. Think of the road as a ledge, with deeper water on either side of the bed. The sun warms the water on the ledge and smallmouth come out of the deeper water to feed on the forage attracted by the warm water. Bass will also use broken chunks of asphalt as spawning cover. Topographic maps are the best source for locating flooded roads and rivers.

Riprap

The riprap anchoring the sides of concrete or earth-filled dams can offer good smallmouth habitat that is best fished shallow to deep by casting toward the riprap from a boat.

Sunken Woody Debris

Unlike the prototypical southern reservoir filled with flooded timber, laydowns, and stickups, western stillwaters have limited amounts of sunken woody debris. The flow-through and irrigation reservoirs were built in desert or shrub-steppe canyons with few trees before they were flooded, and what was there has long since rotted away. Smallmouth will spawn and feed near woody debris, so take the time to fish it.

Offshore Reefs

Reefs are the shallow-water version of rock humps and should be fished much the same. Start on top and work down the sides. The number of fish that frequent the reef is directly proportional to the composition of the reef. The greater the disparity in the size of the rocks making up the reef—from baseball to Smart Car size—the more fish will be found. The spaces between the rocks offer both food for smallmouth and protection from their predators.

Hybrid Water

The Columbia River, a huge fish factory and producer of the Washington state record, is a hybrid water. It's part river with current, part lake when backed up behind one of the huge hydroelectric dams, and part tidal basin with tidal effects felt more than a hundred miles upriver from the Pacific Ocean. Anglers familiar with flowage reservoirs will recognize the variables at work on the Columbia. Anglers who are also sail boarders or wind surfers will factor in the strong upriver winds, which create swells of 5 feet or more.

Water levels in the Hanford Reach above Pasco and Wallula Pool above McNary Dam may fluctuate as much as 10 feet a day upstream of the hydroelectric dams during periods of high electrical power demand. The increased water volume running through the generators also increases the current velocity and water level below the dam. The smallmouth must adjust to these sometimes radical changes, and so must the anglers and boaters.

As in rivers, smallmouth do not live in unbroken, direct current. To find the fish, you need to find some form of structure

Smallmouth use rotting pilings in shallow water as nesting sites. The pilings also provide food for smallmouth as the pilings attract insects and forage fish that feed on the insects.

The biggest fish are in the deeper water along the edge of the roadbed.

that breaks the current. Outside the deepwater navigation channel running from the Pacific upstream to the Snake River confluence, the Columbia abounds in structures like rock humps, big and little islands, back-bays, riprap, pilings, and more. The single most important factor to keep in mind about all this structure is that the fish will be found on the down-current side.

By now, you understand that smallmouth and rock go together, but all rock is not created equal in its ability to attract and hold smallmouth. There are seasonal variations. For example, spawning smallmouth seek mixed gravel and cobble rock while early summer fish may favor riprap along a dam face. But what do you do when faced with a stillwater like Lake Powell and its expanses of seemingly unbroken rock? You could drift and fish along the shoreline, hoping to find a fish, or

you could look closer to discern the differences in the rock. Look for those areas where wind and water carved out chunks of rock that fell into the water to create a fan, like a scree slope on an alpine mountain. A big chunk of rock lying in the water off a point of land at the entrance of a canyon will hold fish; two or three such rocks will hold more fish, and a sunken boulder field still more.

A close look along unbroken rocks faces reveals what might best be described as microstructure. Look for places where the rock juts out a few inches, a small section has broken off, or the rock folds inward to create a soft pocket. It takes close examination and an eye for distinguishing details to locate the places that hold fish, but once that skill is learned, it can be applied on every new water.

CHAPTER FIVE

What Smallmouth Eat

It's easier to list what smallies *don't* eat than what they do, as these opportunistic feeders consume most anything smaller than themselves. They feed on whatever food is most abundant and available. They may be sipping Tricos on the John Day, emerging caddis on the Yakima, slashing shad on Lake Powell, or busting crayfish on Fontenelle Reservoir. They are able to survive and, in most cases, thrive on a varied diet. The smallmouth's diet is determined by several factors, including the fish's age, size, the relative abundance and availability of food sources, and the presence or absence of predators, and other species competing for the same food. Fish biologists assert that smallmouth outcompete most other species to come out on top.

Before we get into detail about the main food groups, let's look at when adult smallmouth head for the food trough. Some anglers put peak feeding times at first light and last light. Others narrow it to the 45 minutes before and after sunrise, sunset, moonrise, and moonset. Still others ignore diurnal cycles and

Big flies catch fewer but bigger fish. Make sure the fly rod and line are balanced to handle the larger fly.

look at a bigger picture. They point to the moon cycles and opine that one quarter of the moon cycle fishes better than another quarter. And there are those who claim fishing is terrible during the day near a full moon, while others take the opposite stand. One study noted that three times as many big western smallmouth were caught during the first and second quarters of the moon than in the third quarter. But those raw numbers ignore all other variables such as water temperature, wind, ambient temperature, and angler effort in each moon phase. If those other factors combine to keep anglers off the water during the moon quarter, the number of fish caught in that quarter will be skewed. Biologists measure fishing success in catch per unit effort (CPUE) in order to eliminate some of the variables. What's missing from these opinions is hard data accumulated over a long period of time so all the variables that affect catching fish get filtered out or otherwise adjusted.

The results from one such study on the Columbia River shows smallmouth feed throughout the day, with peak feeding times roughly at 7 a.m., 11 a.m., 1 p.m., and 9 p.m. In other words, hours perfect for summer fishing. Get up early, have that morning cup of coffee and get on the water; fish through the afternoon bite, and come off for a leisurely dinner; then get back on the water as the light fades.

Take into consideration how much food a smallmouth eats as well as the frequency of consumption. Stomach samples reveal that by the time the Columbia warms in July, small-mouth consume five times as much food as they do in the cool water of April. That consumption amount holds steady through summer until the water temperature begins to drop in early fall. That data make biological sense. As the water warms, the metabolism of the smallmouth speeds up and food is processed faster. As food is processed faster, a greater volume of food is necessary to live.

Smallmouth have a reputation as gluttons—feeding when they can't possibly be hungry. I've noticed when fighting a bass that it will disgorge bits and pieces, even whole prey, clearly demonstrating it had recently eaten. One smallmouth had a 4-inch tube and 5-inch plastic worm in its mouth, another had a 3-inch crayfish resting on its tongue that it hadn't bothered to swallow before smacking my fly. Some fish have eyes bigger than their stomachs. I was surprised to learn the Columbia River data revealed that smallmouth eat less than one prey item per day. Equally surprising is the size of the prey items. Standard wisdom is that flies used for smallmouth are small, much smaller than those used for largemouth. I suggest rethinking that, as the sampled smallmouth had eaten several species of forage fish, including largescale suckers and chiselmouth over 9 inches long.

Smallmouth anglers know that smallies love crayfish, and the Columbia has plenty of crayfish for bass of all sizes to eat. The stomach samples in the Columbia River study showed a definite correlation between smallmouth size and food

The fish will be in the deeper water along the transition zone. A Sink Tip or full sinking line may be required to present the fly to the fish.

Lake Powell smallies grow fat on crayfish during the cool water winter months. Use crayfish patterns until the new crop of threadfin shad appear in the spring.

preference. The results controvert the conventional belief that crayfish are the preferred food of bass across all size ranges. While smaller bass eat plenty of crayfish, the Columbia River data showed the larger the fish, the fewer crayfish it ate. As fish grew in size, their food preference turned to forage fish, and the Prickly Sculpin fly topped the list. By the time the bass reached 17 inches, crayfish, by prey item, made up less than 10 percent of their diet.

Time of day, time of year, water temperature, availability of prey items during the sample period or any number of other factors could have skewed the sample. But my Columbia River fishing experience, over a period of years and many miles of river, closely matches the research data. Nearly all of my large Columbia River smallmouth, those over 3 pounds, have taken a big brown or olive rabbit sculpin pattern, such as my Boo Radley or D-Dub's Prickly Sculpin.

As in real estate where location determines value, location on each body of water determines what forage is available for the fish in that location. The type of substrate that supports *Hexagenia* on California's Lake Almanor is different than the rocky shore toward the face of the dam where forage fish and crayfish live. Consequently, the smallmouth in each location will feed on the food that is abundant and available at that location. In fertile waters that support a variety of abundant and available foods, the fish may exhibit more selectivity than waters with a more limited selection. Fertile-water fishers need to match the hatch closely to catch fish and continue matching the hatch when the bass switch to an even better or bigger food source.

Predictably, basic food preferences change as smallmouth grow from fry to trophy-sized adults. As fry, their diet is 95 percent small crustaceans. Young-of-the-year smallmouth, those born in spring, add small aquatic insects, newly emerged fry, and crayfish to the diet. Those that survive the first winter, now 150 mm long, leave little food behind for big stuff—forage fish, crayfish, leeches, and the like.

In most western waters, smallmouth are the apex shallow-water predator. Their varietal diet allows them to eat whatever is abundant and available at any given time of year. In some waters, such as Lake Powell, smallmouth and stripers both target threadfin shad, but do so in a symbiotic relationship. The stripers come up from deep water to attack shad schools, while smallmouth come at them from the shallows. Another example of species sharing the same water and food are carp and smallmouth. Both eat crayfish and insects. When a carp grazes along the bottom, disturbing the substrate in search of edibles, it will frequently be shadowed by one or more smallmouth reaping the benefit. Smallmouth gain an advantage in the relationship by reducing the number of competitors; they dine on carp fry and young-of-the-year while carp leave smallmouth fry alone.

Munching Minnows

To a smallmouth bass, a forage fish is any fish it can eat. Like humans, forage fish have three basic body types: long and slender (western silvery minnow); bulky head with rapidly tapering body (sculpin); and robust, pear-shaped body (threadfin shad). Prey fish live at different levels of the water column. Like crayfish, these food items share common movement—a quick darting motion—when faced with the prospect of getting eaten by a smallmouth. Sedentary sculpins spend most of their life hiding on the cobble bottom. When disturbed they flit a few inches, and then drop back motionless on the bottom, relying on their natural camouflage to blend with the rocks. Threadfin shad occupy the opposite end of the spectrum, living in large schools, traveling miles of open water in a day, and feeding on plankton in the top few inches of the water column. When the school is attacked by bass, individual shad dip, dive, and dart in a frenzy to avoid being eaten. Smallmouth typically select their prey based on the size, then on species.

Resident forage fish, those living in the same water as smallmouth, are primarily spring spawners. Males develop bright color patterns to attract females. Some, like threadfin shad, may have a secondary spawn in late summer or fall. When that occurs, both 3-inch adults and juvenile shad will be available for consumption.

Several western rivers enjoy runs of American shad. Until the shad fry run back to the ocean, the smallmouth add them to the menu.

Smallmouth benefit from the out-migrating salmon fry and smolts. Contrary to the big-fly, big-fish rule, small baitfish patterns work better during the migration.

As its name implies, the western silvery minnow is a slender-bodied minnow sporting bright silver sides, white belly, and yellowish olive back. It grows up to 7 inches long, though most are smaller. An early summer spawner, it feeds on bottom ooze containing organic materials and invertebrates. Western silvery minnows are school fish that may gather with other forage fish, like flathead chubs, and share similar body shape and color. The other minnows, shiners, and chubs eaten by smallmouth share similar body type and coloration. They can be found in tailouts, at midlake reefs, alongside and among weed beds, on shallow flats, and tight to the bank. Fly patterns imitating this body type should cover a range of sizes while retaining a slender profile.

Usually found in clear, clean water, sculpins occupy the bottom of the water column, living and feeding on organic materials among the rocks and gravel substrate. Predominately mottled dark gray, olive, or brown across the back and sides, they easily blend in with their surroundings. The large, fan-shaped pectoral fins accentuate the triangular head and narrow body that is wider than deep. Most adults are less than 5 inches. My Prickly Sculpin fly has a fur collar around a rabbit strip body to achieve the wedge-shaped head.

Threadfin shad sport a silver-white body with a gray to blue-black back. The body is deep but narrow, tapering to a deeply forked tail. Shad depend on light for foraging so they stay high in the water column, traveling in schools inches under the surface. They are pelagic, feeding on plankton in the open water during the day, then heading toward the shallows and shoreline cover at night, only to repeat the process the next day. Crappie, bluegill, and other sunfish have a similar body type. D-Dub's Marabou Minnow is a good generic imitation of this body type. Match the hatch to specific forage fish by changing the color of marabou used for the back.

Almost all forage fish live from two to four years with the adults being available, if not necessarily abundant, year-round. Threadfin shad are the only forage fish known to be intolerant of cold water and will die if the water temperature drops below 45 degrees.

In river systems like the Columbia and Sacramento, smallmouth are the beneficiaries of migrating salmon, steelhead, and shad offspring. Salmon and steelhead run to sea in May and June, followed by shad in August and September. Smallmouth, particularly the 6- to 14-inch fish, make a significant dent in those populations.

There is nothing delicate about how a smallmouth attacks a baitfish. It targets the fish, attacking from behind, then when close, the bass opens its mouth and inhales the food by forcing water through its gills, much like sucking a soda through a straw. Common belief holds that smallmouth suction baitfish that have spines, like sunfish or three-spine sticklebacks, head-first so the spines are compressed and don't catch in their throat. The baitfish is swallowed whole, then squeezed and moved into the foregut where digestion begins.

Since smallmouth don't have fly-shredding teeth like brown trout, when tying baitfish flies, I prefer soft materials like marabou, rabbit, and arctic fox over bucktail. I believe the softer materials pulse, shimmer, and wiggle and generally look more lifelike in the water than the harder, more durable bucktail. When fishing stillwater where there is no current to provide action to the fly, soft materials win hands down.

Crunching Crayfish

Crayfish are an important food for smallmouth in almost every western water from when the bass are only 3 inches long. Crayfish continue to be important throughout the smallmouth's life, though, at least on the Columbia River, they decline in importance as the bass grow larger.

One or more species of crayfish is present in every western state, and they share similar life cycles. Regardless of the crayfish variety, size, or color, they all share common characteristics. They live in the substrate, are most active in low-light conditions when they crawl about scavenging for food, and quickly scuttle backward when trying to escape a predator. Relatively short-lived, only full-sized adults are available to smallmouth until late spring when the eggs, which may have spent the entire winter attached to the female, hatch. The young remain attached to the mother until they molt twice, then leave home. Crayfish molt or shed their exoskeleton several times during their life and are quite vulnerable to predation until the new shell hardens. Ranging in color from light tan to burnt orange to dark olive, they take on the color of the substrate where they live. The underside is always several shades lighter than the back and sides.

Protecting that lighter underside is important to a crayfish because it is unable to defend itself when upside down. It has an interesting organ that allows it to detect which is right side up. Tiny hairs in the statocyst, which is packed with grains of sand, act as motion sensors and allow the crayfish to right itself when flipped by the current or a smallmouth. Knowing that crayfish immediately right themselves is important when designing and constructing an imitative fly pattern. The finished fly, when fished, should ride right side up so it acts more like the real thing rather than rolling and rotating like an out of balance gyroscope.

Fly designers who want to run counter to conventional crayfish design wisdom might design a fly that tumbles out of control in the current. Here's why. The statocyst is attached to the crayfish atennules and is shed along with the rest of the hard carapace each time the crayfish molts. Until the new shell hardens and the crayfish packs the statocyst anew with grains of sand, it has no equilibrium control or ability to defend itself. In that stage, it is a defenseless and tasty treat.

Crayfish activity centers around food, both finding their own and avoiding becoming food for their predators. Unlike most smallmouth foods, crayfish are not free to swim about the country. When foraging, they slowly move along the bottom, reacting quickly to danger by propelling themselves backward. Understanding where they live and their movements give positive clues about where to fish and how to retrieve crayfish patterns. Nocturnal creatures, crayfish spend their days living under rocks and vegetation, venturing out to feed at night on living and dead plants and animals, which they rip apart with their claws. They are most likely to get eaten while foraging.

When confronted by a predator, a crayfish raises its claws in a defensive posture while scuttling backwards toward safety. Because of those intimidating claws, smallmouth prefer juvenile crayfish, 1 to 3 inches long. Smallmouth inhale crayfish using the same suction technique used on baitfish. Fish aim for a rear attack in an effort to avoid those claws.

When a crayfish senses danger, the fight or flight response kicks in. Opting to stand and fight, the crayfish tucks its tail and raises its claws—presenting daunting obstacles. D-Dub's Fighting Craw adopts this posture by adding weight near the hook eye and closed-cell foam on top of the shank over the hook point. Battles between smallmouth and large crayfish, while usually won by the fish, demonstrate the effectiveness of those claws. The smallmouth tries to grab the crayfish, only to let go when the crayfish clamps a claw across its snout. Any fly tied with hard materials or materials that have been lacquered in an effort to realistically imitate claws are less likely to get eaten and, if eaten, less likely to get a good hook set. I use soft rubber legs and marabou that suggests claws but doesn't dissuade smallmouth from getting a good grip on the fly.

Crayfish patterns are either imitative (realistic) or suggestive. Imitative flies replicate all the body parts, often with hardened materials that may cause the fly to wobble or move unnaturally in the water. The suggestive patterns get eaten by fish because they closely resemble the shape, size, movement, and color of the real deal. I greatly favor the suggestive flies constructed with soft, wiggly materials, such as marabou, rabbit, and rubber. An important consideration when tying any crayfish pattern is adding sufficient weight so that the fly maintains contact with the bottom, where crayfish live. Weighting options include bead chain, dumbbell eyes, coneheads, metal or glass beads, rattles, wire, or dubbing made from aluminum fibers.

An exposed crayfish in smallmouth waters is not long for this world. Bounce crayfish imitations along the bottom like the natural. Smallmouth may "taste" the fly before firmly striking. Resist striking until you feel firm resistance. JAY NICHOLS

A Chartreuse Caboose, its color unlike any natural food living in smallmouth water, is an excellent pattern. The color may allow fish to see it from a greater distance.

A crayfish pattern can be dead-drifted along the cobble or broken rock bottom as if it were foraging for food. I tie all my crayfish, like the Chartreuse Caboose and Crawdad Candy—even my Rabbit Bugger—with all the weight, including any lead wire, on top of the hook shank. The weight acts as a counterbalance to the hook point so the flies ride with the hook point up. This tying style decreases the chances of snagging the bottom and may increase the rate of hooking fish.

Cast the fly upstream so it has time to sink to the bottom, then track the movement of the fly downstream with the rod tip. It's important to maintain both a natural drift and a tight line, as the takes can be surprisingly subtle for such an aggressive fish. Water depth and current velocity dictate either a floating line paired with long leader or go with a Sink-Tip or full sinking line and short leader to get the fly down where crayfish live.

When smallmouth are holding along the bottom in deep runs and pools, dead drifting is a great method to get fish. Trout anglers used to high-sticking nymphs will easily master this method.

Those who run nymphs under a strike indicator will appreciate the technique of drifting crayfish flies in shallow water using the same system. The distance between the fly and the indicator should be 1 to 1.5 times the water depth.

I carry crayfish patterns covering the spectrum of size and color, including one color not found anywhere in nature. My Chartreuse Caboose is a mainstay pattern wherever smallmouth are found. Match the size of crayfish to the season. Early in the year all crayfish will be adults that survived the winter. Only after the water begins to warm will the newly hatched crayfish be available. By the end of summer, the young-of-the-year will have gone though several molts to reach adult size. Armed with this knowledge, use larger flies early and late in the season and smaller ones midseason.

Ingesting Insects

Smallmouth prefer bigger, meaty food items like baitfish and crayfish, but they eat what is abundant and available. In many waters that includes aquatic invertebrates like dragonflies, damselflies, stoneflies, and mayflies. Some mayflies are tiny, seemingly barely worth the effort. Others, like the *Hexagenia*, are the giants of the mayfly world, attracting attention from smallmouth wherever they hatch. And there are exceptions to that general rule that bigger is better, like when the John Day fish focus on tiny Tricos before dragons and damsels hit the water or when the Yakima fish slurp emerging caddis when they should be pounding fall chinook fry.

Either completely lacking or present only in such small numbers as to not be of significance to western smallmouth are two foods common to the Midwest and East: hellgrammites and *Ephoron leukon*, or white miller mayfly. Hellgrammites, the larval form of the dobsonfly, are missing in action because they are either rare in relation to other forage or simply not present in western waters. The Aquatic Invertebrate Biologist for the WDFW says there are no hellgrammites anywhere in that state's waters. White millers apparently occur only east of the Mississippi.

Stoneflies and mayflies are most often available when the nymphs leave the bottom and begin their migration to the surface to hatch. A nymph like a Pat's Stone, Hare's Ear, or Casual Dress, dead-drifted under a strike indicator is a good bet.

Damselflies get snapped up when they undulate toward the surface, where they haul themselves out of the water onto rocks, streamside vegetation, and other objects. A marabou damsel on a floating line and light leader retrieved using short, slow strips or a hand-twist method garners strikes.

This smallie was feeding on the abundant and available midges. It couldn't resist when presented with a large Woolly Bugger.

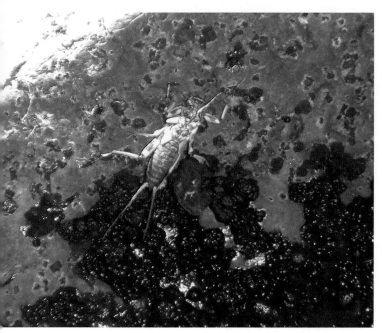

Stonefly shuck is evidence that the nymphs live in fast current. A representative pattern such as a Pat's Stone or a general pattern such as a brown Woolly Bugger can be fished through riffles and pool tailouts.

Dragonflies are a smallmouth favorite. Nymph patterns catch fish but adult imitations are great fun to fish.

Dragons, damsels, mayflies, and stones make up the usual aquatic invertebrate fare. Each is big enough to satisfy the cost/benefit equation when they are abundant and available. Stomach samples of John Day River smallmouth taken from April's cool water revealed aquatic insects to be the primary food source. Rather than a clear dietary preference for the bugs, this reflects the fact that forage fish have not yet spawned and crayfish are still inactive.

Dragonfly nymphs spend most of their life crawling around or hiding in the bottom of lakes and rivers eating most anything smaller than it. They are capable of short bursts of speed by expelling water through their body, much like squid. Since nymphs live on the bottom, that's where the fly needs to be, so either a Sink-Tip or sinking line works best. Crawl the fly slowly along the bottom, with the occasional short, quick strip to simulate the water jet action. The dragonfly life cycle is primarily spent underwater where the nymph may live four years, growing larger until it's ready to leave the watery world. During the underwater period, the larger nymphs may grow to more than 2 inches long, big enough to attract the attention of smallmouth.

There are three families of dragons, known colloquially as crawlers, sprawlers, and burrowers. Long and slender, the crawlers are active predators that are always on the move in search of prey. Sprawlers are short, flat-bodied, ambush predators hiding in the substrate, waiting for food to come to them. Short and squat burrowers are sit-and-attack predators hiding in the silty bottom. Crawlers, the biggest family, are the most available nymphs. All nymphs take on the color of the substrate where they live, with olive or brown predominating.

Dragonfly nymphs emerge in late spring or early summer by climbing grass stems, tules, or other structure sticking out

Adult damsefly patterns take fish once the daytime temperature warms enough for the natural adults to start hunting insects floating in the surface film or flying barely above the water.

of the water. They split their shell, unfurl and dry their double wings, then fly off. Adult dragons are efficient and highly effective predators hunting and killing other flying insects with astonishing accuracy. When they return to the water in a few weeks, their mating and egg-laying activities take place barely inches off the surface, once again drawing the attention of bass. Nymphs are easily imitated by a Casual Dress or olive Carey Special.

The damselfly lives much the same, though it has a shorter life than dragonflies. Most spend one year underwater with a few spanning two years. Damsel nymphs are slender and more delicate than dragons, with distinctive three-part feathery gills on the tail. As nymphs, they molt up to 18 times, each time getting bigger and darker in color. During the late spring or early summer emergence, nymphs swim toward shore where smallmouth await to intercept. Electric blue in color, adult damsels trigger surface feeding activity during the mating and egg-laying cycle of late summer. Nymphs are imitated by a Marabou Damsel, adults by the Stalcup Adult Damsel or an Electric Blue Gurgler

Adept clingers and crawlers that hug the rocky bottom or vegetation of western streams and rivers, stonefly nymphs, or naiads, are available every month of the year. Like dragonfly nymphs, stonefly nymphs may spend four years underwater before navigating toward shore and pulling themselves out of the water to hatch. They are most available when dislodged by the current from the riffles where they live or when they head for shore. Stoneflies, both in their nymph and adult forms, are well known to western trout anglers. When fishing a nymph, the key to success is getting the fly down to where the insect lives. A Pat's Stone drifted under a strike indicator is a simple, effective impressionistic pattern.

Mayfly species abound in western rivers and lakes, but only one, *Hexagenia*, is big enough to consistently attract the attention of smallmouth. This nymph spends up to two years living in a burrow in soft substrate. It becomes available for smallmouth on leaving home and heading to the surface to emerge as an adult. The adult waiting for its wings to dry provokes splashy surface rises. Primary emergence of these big nymphs is triggered by several successive hot days in mid-July. They begin their ascent in the evening, with most popping out around 9 p.m. The best way to fish the hatch is to have two rods rigged, one with a sinking line and nymph, the other with a floating line and adult pattern. The Hex Nymph is a good subsurface pattern while the Hexagenia Quigley Cripple works on the surface.

Terrestrial insects are land-based bugs that frequently find themselves in the water, the result of an ill-advised hop or a gust of wind. Grasshoppers, crickets, and beetles are the most likely fare. There are over 8,000 grasshopper varieties around the world, roughly 500 in North America and much fewer, maybe less than 100, in the West. Taxonomic identification is

Damselflies and dragonflies use patches of grass (as seen on the left in this photo) to pull themselves out of the water. A Marabou Damsel fished with a hand-twist retrieve and a floating line near the grass will catch fish. Swarms of damselfly adults bring even the cagiest smallmouth to the surface.

Hexagenia—a mayfly species large enough to attract bass. Smallmouth eat both the nymph and the adult.

Some mouse patterns sport ears, eyes, whiskers, feet, and a slender tail. That level of detail likely catches more fly fishers than fish.

not important, but size is. The large flying hoppers rarely become bass food. Strong flyers, they rarely get blown onto the water. Mostly it's the smaller ones—about an inch long and can only hop—that find themselves in harm's way. Field crickets, those mostly black, round-bodied grasshopper relatives, share the same streamside vegetation and frequently find themselves in the water where they become a target of opportunity for smallmouth. Grasshoppers and crickets are easily imitated by a Blitzen Hopper in tan for hoppers and black for crickets. A Hi-Vis Foam Beetle is a good choice when beetles are on the water.

Large and small insects bring forage fish to the surface to feed, which in turn bring smallmouth into the shallows to feed on the forage fish. Don't ignore small surface feeding fish; big smallmouth lurk nearby and can be caught by the right size and shape baitfish pattern.

Leeches

There over 700 varieties of leeches around the world, 14 in Washington and plenty in other western states. Leeches are segmented worms that reproduce in the spring. The young become abundant and available in summer. Leeches tend to live and move near shallow substrate to avoid predation. Most are brown, black, olive, or tan in color. Compressed, their body is 2 inches long, but can elongate when swimming up to 6 inches. These tasty critters move in two ways: along solid objects they move like inchworms; in water they elongate their body and

swim like an eel. When inching along, use a slow 3-inch strip retrieve. When swimming, try a hand-twist retrieve.

Woolly Buggers are the usual leech imitation. For a different approach in spring when smallmouth have taken over the shallows prespawn, run a size 8 wet fly hook through a 3-inch piece of brown rabbit strip "wacky style," then fish it under a strike indicator. Keep a tight line, and jiggle the indicator to imitate a live leech.

Frogs

Stillwater smallmouth see more frogs than river fish, but every smallmouth knows what to do with a swimming frog or a nice, soft tadpole. Deer hair spun in bands of yellow and green festooned with rubber legs is a perfect topwater frog pattern. Tadpole flies, such as the Black Tadpole, have a bulky head and skinny tail. Tadpoles rarely leave shallow water, so the fly should be tied without weight and fished on a floating line.

Other Menu Items

Smallmouth will eat almost any living thing that intentionally or accidently enters its watery domain. Small birds, salamanders, worms, snakes, mice, and other small furry creatures fall prey to a hungry or curious smallmouth. Spun deer hair flies are a reasonable facsimile for mice. My Boo Radley fly with its long rabbit tail can imitate a worm or water snake.

CHAPTER SIX

Thirteen Top Tips and Techniques

Smallmouth bass fishing, like all other fishing, is part art and part science. Ignoring the debate as to whether art is innate or learned, science clearly can be taught. The best fishers spend time learning about their quarry, what it eats, where the food lives, how the food moves, when the food is available—the list of study topics goes on and on. And the learning never ends because the more knowledge gained, the more seemingly unrelated facts, observations, and experiences begin to fit into a cohesive, yet ever-expanding whole.

Wow, that was pretty metaphysical for a book about learning how to catch a fish with a brain the size of a grain of jasmine rice. Not rocket science. Not brain surgery. But learning is part of the ongoing pleasure of fishing. A longtime guide friend once said if he ever stopped learning about fish he might as well stop guiding. The thrill, however subtle, of learning something new each time he took client on the water was part of what kept his work from being just another job. What follows are tips and techniques that keep my days on the water from being just another job.

Tip No. 1: Learn how smallmouth food moves.

Smallmouth bass eat other fish, and the more you know about the fish smallies eat, the more likely you are to select a fly of the right shape, size, and color. Not all baitfish live in all western waters. You won't find a Sacramento pikeminnow in a Montana river, but you will find them in California's Russian River. Not all baitfish have the same body type, even if they live in same stratum. The western silvery minnow is a bottom feeder like a sculpin, but it doesn't look much like one. Not all baitfish live at the same water depth. Those same sculpins spend their days hiding under rocks while threadfin shad swim in the top few

The supple materials in this fly mimic the motion of smallmouth foods. The easy-to-see color makes the fly stand out from other possible foods.

The odds of catching more fish increase when you're paying attention.

inches of lakes and reservoirs. Not all baitfish are available at the same time of year or even the same time of day. Gizzard shad are plentiful right after they spawn in the spring, then they grow fast and quickly become too large to be smallmouth food.

Smallmouth, being primarily sight feeders, key on movement of potential food. The erratic swimming of an injured baitfish, the skittering crayfish, or the jet-propelled dragonfly nymph all trigger strikes. Knowing that motion garners attention, it's all too easy to fall into the trap of applying a one-size-fits-all technique of creating motion by using the same retrieve regardless of fly type. Certainly you'll catch some fish that way. However, learning to retrieve the fly in a way that more closely imitates the food smallmouth eat goes a long way toward increasing the number of fish hooked. Crayfish differ from baitfish, which differ from nymphs, which differ from leeches, and so on. Fishing a crayfish pattern so it acts like a real crayfish will attract fish more often than fishing that same pattern as if it were a threadfin shad.

So how does a crayfish move and how fast? That depends on whether it's moving forward—in that case it's slowly crawling—or moving backward—when it tucks its tail and jets for safety. In the first instance, dead drifting the fly in moving water or slowly retrieving it in still water is the right approach. A quick strip-and-pause retrieve best imitates the backward motion.

Learn where the forage lives in the waters you fish. Crayfish are easy because they are bottom dwellers. Dragonfly and damselfly nymphs share the same level as crayfish. Baitfish cover the entire water column, with sculpins hugging the bottom and threadfin and gizzard shad swimming barely under the surface. Shiners can be found at all levels, depending on the species.

For a better understanding of smallmouth foods, make a point to get to know your local fish biologist and ask questions about the forage base in the waters you intend to fish. I've talked with fish biologists and program managers in all 11 western states, and without exception, every one was willing to take time to answer my questions and happily share their knowledge. Plus, that netted several invitations to go fish with these local experts.

Knowing that smallmouth are sight feeders and that movement is a key to detecting food should give some clues about materials used to construct smallmouth flies. Materials that breathe, flex, and flow in the water garner more attention and thus more strikes than rigid, lifeless products. Marabou, rabbit, webby hackle, and rubber legs predominate in my flies because they act alive in the water. The hard-shelled crayfish is not an exception to the rule. If you watch a crayfish in the water, the antennae and other body parts are rarely still. I want my flies to have movement just like the real thing.

Tip No. 2: Be engaged.

We've all caught fish when we were fiddling with a piece of gear or watching the clouds, doing anything but paying attention to the fly in the water. I've caught two fish on one cast—the rod in one hand, a peanut butter and jelly sandwich in the other. Dumb luck to be sure. We'll catch more fish more often when we pay attention. Watch for fish-eating birds diving or feeding on the water, as they are eating the same food that attracts smallmouth. That requires you to correctly distinguish cormorants and mergansers from pintails and mallards. Understand what causes *agua nervosa*. When fishing stillwater, use the countdown method so you'll know how deep the fish was that you just caught so you can replicate the cast. Try to figure out why the last cast caught a fish while the previous 20 went untouched. Was it depth, speed of retrieve, placement of the fly into different structure, or another reason? Analyzing the process may reveal the answer, leading to more fish on the end of your line.

That may sound like a whole lot of mental gyrations when the object is to have fun on the water while catching smallmouth. Try it to see if it works for you. If so, it will soon become second nature, almost intuitive, so little brain power is actually needed. If after trying it, the process sucks the fun out of fishing, then stop. If we're not having fun, we're not doing it right.

Continue to do what's working and stop doing what isn't. Practice doesn't make perfect if you are doing it wrong; it only ingrains the bad habit. Many fly fishers spend way too much time changing flies when they should be changing how they are fishing the fly. I've never caught a fish when my fly wasn't in the water. Lefty Kreh is said to have caught over 87 different fish species on the Clouser Deep Minnow, proving both that it's a really effective pattern and that it can be fished in a variety of ways. Instead of going through the fly box tying on yet another fly, alter the speed of the retrieve or alter the depth by going deeper or starting shallower.

Part of the process of being engaged is taking frequent breaks to disengage. Put the rod down and take up the oars so your buddy can fish. Grab the camera and shoot a few images—there's always something interesting happening on the water or along the shore. Look for bugs in the water, watch the birds on the bank, or do whatever gives your brain a respite. It's much easier to put your brain back in gear after a rest period than to try to stay engaged for long periods of time.

Tip No. 3: Learn streamcraft.

Learn how to read the water so you can more accurately predict where smallmouth, particularly trophy smallmouth, live. The more easily you distinguish water features such as current breaks, eddies, rock humps, and all the other types of structure—and understand how the smallmouth food moves around

Before making that first cast, take a few moments to observe the water. Note the current seams, the rock structure, and other stream features so that first cast can be placed in the most-likely fish-holding spot.

Observe how the current curls around the rocks and swirls behind the grass. These are clues for where to find fish.

Carefully fish the foam line and the broken rocks. You may need two different patterns—a baitfish in the foam and a crayfish down among the rocks. MICHAEL T. WILLIAMS

The smallmouth are all in the shadows. Carp were in the sun.

that structure—the more fish you'll catch. It's totally satisfying to assess a water feature, determine that it should hold a fish, make the cast, and hook a nice smallmouth.

Learn how different water conditions alter where the fish live. As a general rule, they avoid heavy current and will move to the edges where the current is gentler. When the water is off-color, like in spring runoff or summer desert thunderstorms, the fish again move to the edges where visibility is greater. Conversely, when flows diminish and dissolved oxygen levels drop, fish move into the heads of riffles where the flows are strongest because here the oxygen is the greatest. In lakes, the fish move into the shallows in spring, drop into cooler water in the summer heat, then return to the shallows for a fall feeding frenzy.

The second part of streamcraft is learning how to safely be on the water in a floating device. Realistically evaluate your skills against the river hazards likely to be encountered. Consult the available river guides before getting on the water. Make sure your boat is in good repair. The best boat driver I know (and one I'd float anywhere with) brushes up on his skills and learns new ones by occasionally attending a whitewater guide school. That's the best way to flatten a steep learning curve and increase the likelihood of a safe trip down a western river.

Another part of streamcraft is teaching yourself to always fish the near water first. The temptation is to make the first cast toward the sweet spot in a riffle, run, or rock hump. Don't do it unless the sweet spot is the near water. It took several instances

of spooking big bass out of the shallows by barging into the water, focused only on a particular spot, before I learned this tip. If there are fish in the sweet spot, they will still be there-after you catch all the in the near water. Make the first cast while still standing away from the water's edge, then gradually move the cast out until you've covered the entire area. And be quiet on the water. Sound travels four times faster underwater than through air.

Tip No. 4: Be a better caster.

Notice I said better, not longer. Distance is overrated and accuracy too often ignored. It is a rare fly fisher who can throw 70 feet of fly line; it is even rarer to hit the mark at that distance and still rarer to be able to hook a fish at that distance. Like the golf adage of "drive for show, putt for dough," you'll catch more fish with short, accurate casts that put the fly where it needs to be, control the rate of retrieve, and minimize slack. Do so and you'll have the thrill of seeing the fish take your offering.

Learn how to bend it like Beckham around obstructions to get into those hard-to-reach places overlooked by others or, if noticed, rejected as being too difficult to hit. There's no reason why you can't sidearm a cast under a low-hanging branch or skip a fly under a dock. If the gear guys can do it, fly casters can as well. Teach yourself to cast with your nondominate

Wind is a fact of life on western smallmouth waters. Getting on the water before the wind starts is a good idea. Learning how to cast in the wind without hooking yourself or your fishing partner is a better idea.

Overlining the rod helps to defeat the effects of wind and makes for more accurate casts. Distance is generally improved as well.

hand—after 50 years of fly casting, the shoulder of your dominant hand will thank you, and your brain will learn new ways to cast. Learn how to punch tight loops into the wind, a skill especially useful when the wind howls upstream on western rivers. When casting into the wind, adjust tippet diameter as necessary to maintain accuracy. Learn how to avoid casting tippet-tangling tight loops when fishing two flies. Slow the stroke to open up the loop. You should be fishing two flies whenever it's legal to do so. One pattern might work while the other is ignored, and there is nothing like hooking two fish simultaneously.

I get better casting results by overlining the rod by one or two line weights. For example, I'll use a 7- or 8-weight line on a 6-weight rod. The heavier line loads the rod with only a few feet of line beyond the rod tip, and I can shoot plenty of line if necessary. If your budget allows for buying specialty lines, go for a bass bug taper that loads the rod quickly with minimal false casts.

Smallmouth that have been caught and released multiple times learn avoidance behavior. In popular waters fish become more adept at avoiding sloppy casts and detecting fraudulent presentations. The ability to make accurate casts and precise presentations increases in importance. Make the first cast to each location the best cast.

Tip No. 5: Intend to catch fish.

Fish every cast with the intention that it will catch a fish. Make it clear that you know the difference between casting while on the water and fishing. There is nothing wrong with casting for casting's sake, but fishing implies a purpose. Fishing is casting with intention, and the intention of each cast is to catch a fish. Be mentally prepared to catch fish; have your head in the game and good things happen.

If you focus each cast with the purpose of catching a fish, then when you do hook a fish, you'll know what worked. You'll know where you landed the fly, how it related to visible structure, how deep you were fishing, the speed of retrieve, and where the fly was when the fish hit. You'll be able to replicate the cast and hopefully repeat the result. Plus, when you pay attention to those factors, you can take that information and apply it at a different time or in a different setting. That takes some of the guesswork out of the game. And don't forget, it is a game. Have fun.

Tip No. 6: Fish where the big fish live.

Bass are school fish, so if you are only catching small fish, go elsewhere. Try fishing a different type of structure, like moving from a gravel and weed bed bottom to a broken cobble substrate. The little guys are in the less favorable habitat because they can't compete with the big fish for the better feeding or spawning habitat.

Fish the prime habitat at the prime time and fish a big fly. All the red paint has been knocked off this Chartreuse Caboose from being bounced along the bottom.

Everyone wants to fish poppers on the John Day River, and those who do will catch small bass, one after another, all day long. No question it's a kick. There are so many fish that the smaller fish get to the fly while the big guys and gals are still making up their minds. However, if the goal to catch big fish on that river, the best bet is to go deep. That's where big fish live and eat, and the weighted fly quickly passes through the smaller fish zone. In my experience, the big fish on the Umpqua act the same way—they want their food to be on the bottom.

Some fly fishers, afraid of losing flies if they dredge the bottom, never catch the big fish. Don't be afraid to lose flies—they are cheap in comparison to the rest of your gear. It makes no sense to spend hundreds of dollars on the best rod, the best reel, and several of the best lines, and then get cheap about the relatively minor cost of a few store-bought flies.

Just when you've been convinced by the preceding paragraphs that you must fish deep for the big ones, here's the other side of the coin. The five largest smallmouth I've taken on the Pend Oreille River, including one over 6 pounds, all have taken the Hamster, my spun deer hair topwater fly.

I love traveling through the West and fishing new water. There is something quite satisfying about coming to new water; analyzing the structure, water levels, and all the other factors that determine where a good fish lives; then being rewarded with a tug on the line. However, that's not the best way to catch the big ones, because it is only through sheer fortuity that the big fish habitat can be located on a first outing.

A better way is to take a page from the trout guides who spend day after day on a particular water. Repeated exposure allows them to thoroughly learn that water and learn where the big fish live. If your target water is a lake, take pictures when the water is down and you can see the exposed structure—old stream channels, rock piles, and the like. The same can be done

When first learning a water, float a short section, then shuttle back upstream and run it again using the information gained on the first run.

Carry plenty of water and have it handy to drink.

on rivers at their late summer lows. Look for deep slots in the weed beds, undercut banks, and other big fish holding or travel lanes. Once you learn the likely spots, then you can fish them with confidence any time of the year.

Tip No. 7: Be nice to your body.

Western smallmouth fishing is mostly done in hot, dry, windy, and often high elevation conditions, all of which combine to extract moisture from your body. Professional athletes have learned that peak performance requires proper nutrition and hydration. I'm not suggesting fly fishing for smallmouth is comparable to three sets at Wimbledon or running the New York Marathon. I am suggesting that you'll be more engaged, make better casts, and have more fun on the water if you keep your body fueled and hydrated.

My favorite water bottle for lake fishing or river floats is a half-gallon plastic milk jug with a molded-in handle and screw top. I run a carabineer or short strap through the handle and attach it to the boat. When the day heats up to triple digits, I drop the jug overboard to cool in the water. Walk and wade fishing means a smaller bottle carried in the back pocket of my vest.

When I was a 20-something, I'd have a cup of coffee and a donut for breakfast, then not eat again until I came off the water after dark. A more sensible approach is to eat a decent breakfast and carry food to eat during the day. Try different energy bars until you find one that you like, then make sure you stick one or more in your vest for a late morning or afternoon refueling.

Tip No. 8: Try it at night.

I love night fishing. My brother hates it. No question it's different after dark, so start night fishing on familiar water, and get on the water while there is still some light. As the light fades,

your eyes will gradually acclimate to the growing darkness and your comfort level will increase. I love the night sounds—the coyotes yipping, the breeze rustling the streamside cattails, the distant owl calling. . . . The darkness makes me more aware of my surroundings, things which go unnoticed in daylight, and that in turn enhances the fishing experience.

Why fish at night? In low-light conditions, smallmouth leave the security of their daytime haunts and sneak in close to shore looking for baitfish and crayfish that have left the security of their hiding places. Every tug on the line is the start of an adventure. You never know how big the fish is until it comes to hand. Plus, on those few western waters that get heavily pressured, nighttime fishing means little competition from your fellow anglers.

Short casts, tight to structure is the rule. Unless you are an exceptional caster, night fishing is the exception to my two-fly rule. Take a headlamp or flashlight, wade only water that you've scouted in the daylight, and avoid being on stillwater at night unless your boat has running lights. Be prepared to hook some big fish. Keep a log of weather and water conditions as well as the time you hit fish to see if a bite pattern develops.

Tip No. 9: Give them options.

Fish two flies where legal. Go big and small, light and dark, floating and sinking, or any other combination that you think might work. I fish two flies more than 90 percent of the time, and, as I've said, it is a total kick to hook two multipound smallmouth on one cast. The second part of this tip is you'll need to alter your casting stroke. Open up the loop to minimize tangling.

Those who fish two flies usually put the largest in front and the smallest at the tail. Nothing wrong with that—I do it that way sometimes, too. A variation that takes advantage of the aggressive nature of smallmouth is to reverse the order. Try a

Crayfish imitations are excellent night flies. Smallies will key on these nocturnal creatures.

Fishing two flies takes advantage of the smallmouth's aggressive nature. Mix different colors and sizes.

Experiment with the speed of the retrieve until you find the one that works. Keep using that retrieve until the fish stop biting. Then begin the experiment anew.

small dragonfly nymph in front, then a larger baitfish pattern in back so it looks like the baitfish is pursuing and about to consume the nymph. That combination can goad neutral smallmouth into striking.

The strongest two-fly connection is a direct line; tie the second fly to the bend of the first fly. That said, it's a challenge to land two because when the second bass grabs the second fly, it creates just enough slack for the first fish to escape. The odds of hooking and landing the second fish increase if one fly is attached by a short length of leader to a perfection loop tied in the main leader so that it runs perpendicular to the leader. A problem arises if the fish, once hooked, decide to go their separate ways. Even if one fish breaks off, it's a thrill while it lasts.

When giving presentations to fly clubs, I always get the question, "How do you fish the fly?" My answer is, "I fish the fly exactly how the smallmouth tell me they want it," and then explain what that means. As part of the process of giving options, I experiment with various retrieve methods and speeds by casting upstream, by swinging with an upstream or downstream mend, by letting the fly hang at the end of drift—a variety of techniques. All the variations are intended to get the smallmouth to tell me how they want the fly that day and, even more precisely, at that time of day. Whichever way you cast, make sure to keep the rod tip pointed where the fly line enters the water in order to maximize detecting strikes and driving the hook home.

When casting upstream, my best results come from retrieving the fly slightly faster than the current so the fly gives the impression of being alive and tasty. When casting across the current, trout fly fishers tend to throw an upstream mend in the line in order to gain a dead drift. That makes sense if fishing a nymph. But more often, after making the crosscurrent cast, I'll toss a downcurrent mend. That creates a belly in the fly line, which causes the fly to present a broadside profile. The downcurrent mend is particularly effective when the bass are keying on migrating baitfish. The sideways profile differentiates the fly from the tightly packed school of baitfish, making it more likely to be seen and eaten by a fish facing into the current.

Varying patterns also offers options. Fly fishers love to look at other fly fisher's fly boxes. Some boxes are neatly arranged with fly after fly, each an exact replica of the next, like soldiers on parade. My boxes look more like a motley crew: no two flies exactly alike, some with disparate colors, all more impressionistic than realistic. That's partly due to the fact that Mother Nature does not spin out perfect copies. Some bugs are malformed. Some baitfish are weak, sick, or injured. Some crayfish have only one claw or none at all. These less-than-perfect copies are all prime targets. The other reason is I am always tweaking my flies in an effort, haphazard at best, to make them more effective. Who says a black Woolly Bugger has to wear black hackle? Mine have chartreuse, olive, brown, grizzly, red-dyed grizzly, purple-dyed grizzly, and yes, a few sport black hackle.

I buy glass beads at the craft store in the rainbow variety pack. My Woolly Buggers sport red, yellow, blue, green, orange, and other bead colors. If the smallmouth get selective (yes, it happens) or get into a lock jaw state of mind, I've got a fly they've never seen before, which may snap them out of their funk.

What this tip is intended to communicate is, don't hesitate to experiment. Fishing for smallmouth is a lot like folding socks. There's more than one way to catch fish. Don't get stuck in a rut of thinking there is only one way or doing it only one way. I don't eat the same dish for dinner every night, night after night, and I believe smallmouth are much the same.

Tip No. 10: Use the right retrieve.

Dead-drift retrieve

As the name implies, this cast is made upstream and the fly is allowed to settle while the angler follows the progress of the fly with the rod tip as the fly moves downstream. A strike indicator can be used to control the depth of the fly and as an aid in detecting strikes. This is an extremely effective technique for fishing crayfish patterns or other bottom-dwelling foods like stoneflies. Instead of a weighted fly, try an unweighted fly with a split shot crimped 12 to 18 inches in front.

In fast current where more weight is needed to get the fly into the feeding zone, take a page from the gear guys. Instead of wrapping lead around the leader or crimping a split shot in front of the fly, go the other way. Add a short length of monofilament to the hook bend, then crimp a split shot to it so the shot bounces along the bottom and presents the fly in the feeding zone. This method works better than adding weight to the leader above the fly. If the shot below the fly gets wedged between rocks, the worst that can happen is the shot slips off. Not so when the weight above the fly gets caught. Efforts to extricate the weight typically cause it to move down the leader to the nearest knot or against the fly—in either case, the fly is lost if the leader breaks.

Super-slow retrieve

Make the cast, then let the fly settle and rest for as long your patience holds out, then begin to retrieve slowly for a few feet. If no fish grabs it, pick it up and cast again to a different spot. This is an effective method of enticing fish that have seen plenty of lures and flies during the season into leaving the safety of structure and biting the fly. Try this with topwater flies as well as crayfish patterns.

The super-slow retrieve is not for everyone. It requires patience to perfect.

Striptease retrieve

Years ago I read that humans are the only species in the animal kingdom that move at a steady pace. All others move, pause, check their surroundings for danger, then move again. Make the cast, remove the slack, and wait a few seconds before beginning the retrieve. Take a few strips of varying length, pause, then strip again. Vary the number, length, and speed of the strips as well as the duration of the pause to more realistically imitate smallmouth foods. This retrieve works for both subsurface and topwater flies. Varying the length of the stops, pauses, and motion allows you to match the mood of the smallmouth. This retrieve has the added bonus of helping keep your mind engaged in the game. (See Tip No. 2.)

When the water is cold and the fish lethargic, a slow retrieve is the order of the day. Speed can be increased as the water warms and the fish warm as well.

Continuous motion retrieve

This is a perfect retrieve when smallmouth are keying on foods that are in constant motion, such as leeches, emerging damselfly nymphs, and out-migrating anadromous fry and smolts. Leeches move like an inch worm, elongating then compressing their bodies through the water, never still. Damsels wiggle/swim through the water until they reach a solid object that they use to climb out of the water. The out-migrating fish—salmon, steelhead and shad—are always on the move as they may have hundreds of miles to cover before reaching the saltwater.

After making the cast, watch the line carefully to detect any strikes on the drop. Once the cast reaches the appropriate depth, begin the retrieve without pauses. The length and speed of the line strips should be varied until the right combination unlocks the mood of the day. The hand twist retrieve is a variation of the continuous motion retrieve. It's an effective "swimming nymph" retrieve, but I find it tiring when done for very long.

Ripping retrieve

Saltwater fly fishers use a double-hand retrieve. They make the cast and then tuck the rod under their arms while stripping the line as fast as possible using both hands. This panic retrieve triggers aggressive, slashing strikes. The hand strip sets the hook and then the battle is on. The ripping retrieve is a single-hand strip variation where the rapid speed of the vanishing fly triggers the fish strike. This is an effective subsurface forage fish retrieve. When using this method on topwater bugs, toss a mend left or right every few feet to get the fly to alter directions like a disoriented mouse or frog.

Cast across the current, then strip the fly rapidly across the current. If a downstream mend is added, the fly will run broadside across the current.

The long rabbit tail on the Red Ass Ratt wiggles seductively in moving water. To make the fly ride higher, treat the spun deer hair and rabbit tail with fly floatant.

Topwater retrieve

You can fish topwater patterns in two ways. First, you can smack the fly down so it creates an attention-getting splash. Let the bug rest a bit, then twitch and wiggle it across the surface. If the smallmouth are leaping after adult damsels or dragons hovering a few inches over the surface, try casting a wide open loop to lazily float the fly down to the water surface. The wide open loop gives the bass time to fix its sights on the fly. Be ready to strike, as sometimes a bass will grab the fly before it hits the water.

Tip No. 11: Learn to catch conditioned fish.

Research has proved that bass, the most caught and released fish in the sporting world, learn to avoid a commonly used lure or fly. In lab tests, they learn to distinguish between identical targets to strike the one that releases food and avoid the one that gives an electrical shock. This ability to learn is what keeps lure and plastic manufacturers and fly designers in business, trying to stay ahead of the fish.

Heavily pressured smallmouth are most often found on lakes and reservoirs that have gear bass tournaments. The tournament entrants often prefish before the event, then return over the two-day event to catch the fish previously located. That scene is repeated several times over the season as different clubs hold their events.

When faced with educated fish, the most obvious solution is to change patterns. Snip off the currently popular pattern and bend on an old classic. Less obvious solutions, and more likely to get better results, are tweaking the speed and rhythm of the retrieve or changing fly size.

Tip No. 12: Mix and match.

Conventional fishing wisdom matches floating flies with floating lines. Unconventional fishing wisdom matches floating flies, usually forage fish patterns, with sinking lines. When I mention this concept during a presentation to a fly club or at a fly-fishing expo, the quizzical looks from the audience turn into understanding smiles once they grasp the thinking behind it. The sinking line draws the floating fly under the surface where most forage fish live. A quick strip of line makes the fly dive; the pause that follows allows the buoyant fly to rise a few inches, suggesting injured prey and an easy meal for a smallmouth. For even more fun, add a small marabou Clouser behind the floating fly.

Tip No. 13: Strip strike.

Trout fishers learn to set the hook by lifting the rod tip. Saltwater anglers learn the strip strike. The physics of the rod tip strike work against the angler and in favor of the fish because the rod tip flexes toward the fish, creating slack and reducing its power to drive the hook home. Not so with the strip strike, where all the power of a long strip of line combined with a raised rod tip is directed down the tight line connection to the fish. The second advantage of a missed strip strike is that the fly stays in the strike zone, giving the fish another chance to get hooked. The process of learning never stops: Please e-mail your tips and techniques to me at thefishingwriter@gmail.com.

CHAPTER SEVEN

Thoughts on Western Flies

Years ago I attended a meeting of the local Bassmasters fishing club. These were tournament gear anglers who surely cast a jaundiced eye toward the solitary fly fisherman in their midst. During a question-and-answer session, a newly minted bass angler asked, "What's the best bait to use?" (Bait, in bass gear fishers jargon, refers to anything used to catch the fish, including spoons, plugs, and plastics.) Being new to the sport, he wanted to know which crankbait/softplastic/plug/spoon he should buy. In other words, he asked for a silver bullet. The simple answer from an experienced angler on the other side of the room: use the bait you have confidence in. Baffled and befuddled, the newbie left the meeting, not realizing that the silver bullet had been revealed.

Hundreds if not thousands of smallmouth bass flies are available today. Every time a tier sits down at a vice, he creates a new fly, rediscovers an old pattern, or alters an existing fly. Inveterate tinkerers, fly tiers are on the unending quest for the Holy Grail, the one fly to rule them all. Some deny the reality of the Grail. Others recognize its existence, but not all who do call it by the same name. In truth, there are many Holy Grail smallmouth flies, each bearing a different name. The names, sizes, shapes, and colors of those flies differ; however, they all share one commonality. The fly evokes confidence in the user and for that reason the user fishes it better and is more likely to catch fish, thereby reaffirming the confidence.

In short, the best western smallmouth fly is the one that inspires confidence in the user. Some know it as the Chartreuse Caboose. Some call it the Casual Dress. Others know it as the Meat Whistle. The common name for each of these different Holy Grail patterns is "The Confidence Fly."

Over the years, I have developed or modified several flies that I am confident will catch smallmouth bass anywhere. They vary in size, shape, and color depending on the locale where they are used; however, they share similar characteristics. They are quick and simple to tie, constructed from easily obtained

The BananaRama flies can be tied in any color of rabbit. Experiment with the barred and two-toned rabbit strips as well.

The Chartreuse Caboose is one of my favorite flies. Water depth and velocity varies, so tie this pattern in several different weights.

materials like rabbit, marabou, chenille, Estaz, and low-grade hackle, and they imitate a basic smallmouth forage food group. Spun deer hair bugs are the exception to being quick to tie. Packing all that hair nice and tight to get maximum floatability then trimming it carefully so as not lop off any of the interspersed rubber legs takes time.

My tying mantra is "Less is more." I tie my baitfish flies sparsely, more impressionistic than realistic. Marabou typically replaces the traditional bucktail. Since smallmouth teeth are more akin to sandpaper than material-shredding fangs, I don't need the extra durability afforded by bucktail or the synthetic fibers. My supple, flowing marabou flies give more fish-attracting action than even the softest bucktail. That sexy marabou action is critical when fishing stillwaters because there is little or no current to add action to bucktail as in rivers.

The best flies, from bottom-dredging crayfish to topwater poppers, share common characteristics that make them efficient tools for catching fish and a pleasure to cast. Because I almost always fish two flies, aerodynamics, or castability, is right at the top. Whether it's run-and-gun float-fishing on a western river or a day at the lake probing structure, repeatedly casting poorly designed flies quickly lights up the ol' rotator cuff and steals all the pleasure from the day. Yet another reason for sparsely tied flies.

All flies should have lifelike movement when sinking or at rest. When action is imparted by line strips, rod movement, or the current, the best flies spark to life and imitate the natural movement of smallmouth food. Marabou, rabbit, and other soft furs; silicone rubber legs; and similar materials make the best flies jiggle, quiver, wiggle, shake, wobble, shimmy, and twitch. Ultra suede or chamois does a pretty good imitation of the silicone curly tail grubs favored by gear fishers. As in life, the best flies are never static; there is always some movement. All the

more reason to select flies tied with soft lifelike materials and rubber legs.

A well-tied fly is durable, able to withstand being eaten by smallmouth all day long. Some of my spun deer hair bugs have raised a couple hundred bronzebacks and are still going strong. If smallmouth rip off a few rubber legs, I can replace those appendages. Counterwrapping hackled flies, like rabbit buggers and crayfish, with copper wire makes them practically bombproof. The durability of store-bought flies is always an open question, one that typically leads to tying your own flies where you control the quality.

Of course, a fly that's fun to cast, durable, and lifelike goes to the scrapheap if the materials used interfere with hooking fish. I rarely add weedguards to my topwater flies. Instead, I tie the tail and body materials, then trim the hair so the hook rides point up. That way nothing gets in the way of a good hook set.

If you fish where weedguards are necessary, they are simple to add to a fly during the tying stage. Common weedguard materials are hard 20- to 30-pound monofilament and light (0.012) wire. The easiest wire method is to attach a single or double strand at the eye of the hook and extend it at a downward angle, ending just past the hook point. If the wire is too stiff, it interferes with hooking the fish and may deflect the fly out of the smallie's mouth; too flexible and it does little to prevent the fly from getting hung up on weeds.

A mono weedguard, again in single or double strand, is attached on top of the hook shank over the hook point, then, once the fly is constructed, brought forward along the hook point and attached to the shank in back of the hook eye. Mono guards that shield the hook point suffer from the same issues as wire guards, which is why I don't use them.

I favor easily constructed flies using soft materials. My fly box includes plenty of garish color combinations in addition to natural colors.

You can imitate crayfish with a specific crayfish pattern. Brown Woolly Buggers may get mistaken for crayfish as well.

Topwater flies constructed from foam, balsa, or cork offer another weedguard option. A short piece of monofilament can be cemented into the fly body material behind the hook eye to form a loop perpendicular to the hook shank. This arrangement has minimal effect on getting a good hook set because of the gap between the point and the weedguard.

Sharp hook points and mashed barbs go hand in hand. Maybe one day the hook manufacturers will make barbless hooks the order of the day. Until then, when I tie, the barb goes down before the hook goes in the vice. And in answer to the wondered question, no, I don't lose fish because the barb is down. I lose fish on a faulty hook set because the point is dull or as a result of trying to control my pontoon while fumbling for my camera. Slack develops in the line, allowing the fish to escape being photographed. One of my best visual memories is of a smallmouth rocketing out of the water, its bronze body shimmering in the sunlight, and flinging the fly to the side with a violent head shake. I love smallmouth, in part because of their uncanny ability to trigger a vertical airborne release.

I used to believe that long flies, like the venerable Carrie Stevens streamers, required 6X or 8X long hooks. Only tradition dictates a long-shanked hook. Over the years, I've gradually shifted from tying my Banana series on 6X long shank hooks to short shank or stinger hooks like Daiichi 1730 or the 1760-3x version. When smallmouth inhale a baitfish, they attack the head. A shorter shanked hook puts the hook's business end closer to the point of attack and makes for more positive hookups. The shorter shank also means the fish is more likely hooked in the lip instead of deep on the tongue or in the gullet, reducing the risk of killing the fish. And the shorter shank reduces the leverage the fish can apply when it's twisting, dodging, and gyrating, trying to throw the hook.

The array of hook choices can be truly overwhelming, as hook manufacturers have created innumerable and constantly evolving styles. One style that has passed into unfortunate oblivion is the keel hook like the Mustad 79666. To solve the supply problem, I make my own by bending a light wire panfish hook into the keel shape. Even better hookups can be gained by slightly offsetting the point. A good alternative to bending your own metal comes from the Daiichi 1870. The graceful bend of the swimming nymph design becomes a keel hook when weight is added to the top of the shank.

Size, shape, and color. Of these three, color is least important, unless the color of fly knotted at the end of your tippet is your confidence fly. In that case, color is the most important factor—but only to you. The deeper the fly is fished, the less important its color. As light rays are absorbed, even the brilliantly visible D-Dub's Chartreuse Caboose is seen as black in really deep water. In my Banana series, yellow and white work best in clear water. Black and brown show a better profile in turbid water.

Saltwater fly fishers swear that forage fish patterns are not complete until they have big eyes. No question that bulging eyes are the predominate feature on fry but become less important as the fish grows in size. The Murdich Minnow is a highly effective forage fish pattern, though I'm not convinced that the eyes make the fly materially more effective. My take on eyes is they catch the eye of the angler more than the fish. But if eyes turn the fly into your confidence fly, don't leave home without them.

If a pattern trails a small spinner blade off the bend of the hook, has it stopped being a fly? What if the tier adds a glass rattle or sticks a propeller behind the hook eye? There are no universal answers to these questions—only individual ones. There is little question that adding flash and sound can increase

Yellow works on topwater flies as well. The addition of rubber legs and marabou or soft hackle adds appeal. Crush the barb to make releasing the fish easier.

A sparsely tied D-Dub's Orange Banana likely is mistaken for a crayfish. The fly is easy to tie and highly effective.

Hard plastic topwater bugs are easy to cast, and the fish love them. The traditionalist may prefer spun deer hair topwater flies.
BEN ROMANS

the effectiveness of the pattern. The blade and propeller add flash and emit low-frequency sounds alerting fish that food is nearby. The rattle—a couple of metal balls sealed in glass— triggers the smallie's lateral line.

Trout fishers stress over having the exact shade of blue dun hackle for the Blue-Winged Olive or the precise hue of dubbing for the body of Pale Evening Dun. I'm not sure if that stress is caused by selective fish or selective outdoor writers. With smallmouth, and I'm stepping out on a limb, I think presentation trumps color matching every time. A well-presented fly that looks like something good to eat or that triggers an aggression strike will outfish a poorly presented precisely color-matched fly.

The shape of my flies is more a function of aerodynamics and casting ease than an attempt to achieve an exact match of fish forage. Streamlined shapes cast better than those shaped like dinner plates. Here's where I split hairs. When fishing topwater bugs, there is no indication that smallmouth prefer one shape over the other, so it makes sense to use the shape that can be cast all day long. Some multicolored spun hair bugs look so much like the real thing they are truly works of art, but a challenge to cast and should therefore be avoided.

I find myself gravitating to throwing topwater flies even under what are thought to be less than optimal conditions. My biggest smallmouth to date, a more than 6-pound prespawn female, took a Hamster during the cold water spring runoff. Topwater flies include gurglers, sliders, poppers, wakers, and divers—all of which are designed to trigger aggression strikes from smallmouth.

Smallmouth of all sizes eat grasshoppers, crickets, beetles, and other land-based bugs that find their way into the water. From midsummer through early fall, terrestrial patterns should be part of your bronzeback arsenal. Cast the fly so that it lands

with a heavy splat, let it rest a few moments, then twitch it to trigger a strike. Let the fish tell you how much or how little action they want imparted to the fly, then stick with it until the fish tell you something different.

Gurglers, sliders, and wakers are the quietest of the topwater flies. They work well in calm or in clear water where the bass are able to sight hunt. Poppers have a wedge, cupped, or flat face and are made of hard plastic, foam, or spun deer hair. Plastic is quick and easy to tie; foam will float forever—but both lack the aesthetic pleasure of tying and fishing spun deer hair flies. These make a satisfying sound on landing and can be skittered, gurgled, and twitched to drive bass into striking.

The old bass fishing books counseled casting the topwater fly, then lighting and smoking a cigarette while the concentric rings of water spread and dissipated before imparting any action to the fly. I don't have the patience for that, and besides, I don't smoke—plus waiting would only work on stillwater. As with other types of flies, I let the fish tell me how they want it. I'll experiment with retrieve speed until they tell me which they want that day. To get more hookups, keep slack out of the line and the rod tip close to the surface and pointed at the fly.

Topwater fly size matters depending on conditions. In clear, calm water during daylight a large bass bug may scare the fish instead of triggering strikes. The opposite may be true under low-light or wind-riffled conditions when a big bug is necessary to draw attention.

Baitfish come in three distinct body shapes: long and slender (sucker); bulky head with quickly tapering body (sculpin); and robust, pear-shaped body (threadfin shad). When smallmouth are boiling on threadfin shad, give them a shad-shaped fly. If it doesn't work, give them a fly with a different shape.

Match baitfish size to the prevailing food source. Fish can get keyed in to a specific prey size and ignore other equally abundant prey. WDFW biologists did extensive stomach surveys of Yakima River smallmouth at a time when summer steelhead and spring chinook smolts and fall chinook fry were out-migrating. The research revealed that smallies focused on the smaller fry and ignored the larger smolts that would logically seem to be the preferred prey. After reading that paper, I designed several different fry patterns. Hours of on-the-water research proved that fly size, in this case less than 3 inches, was more important than color or shape.

Another common characteristic is texture. Hard is out; soft is in—and here's why. Since smallmouth don't have hands or fingers, the only way they can sample what appears to be food is with their mouths. Flies made with stiff materials (yet another reason to not use weedguards) get rejected faster than

The Hamster quivers, wiggles, and seduces bass into striking. Use a wide gape hook when tying and trim the hair so there is plenty of exposed point.

When casting wind-resistent topwater bugs, trim the leader sufficiently to make casting easier. The explosive strikes can trigger an overreaction from the angler, resulting in broken-off flies.
BEN ROMANS

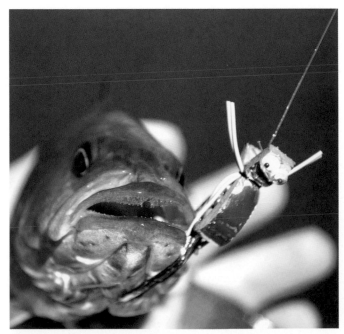

This smallie liked the look of this Violet Gurgler. Topwater creations can be quite fanciful in color and accessories. The eyes on this Gurgler are never seen by the bass that attacks from beneath.

Clouser-style flies can be tied to imitate a variety of baitfish. When tying make sure to create the dark over light color scheme.
JAY NICHOLS

soft-textured flies. The longer a fish holds on to the fly, the greater the likelihood of hooking that fish.

Hard-shelled crayfish are not an exception to the texture principle. Crayfish are at their most vulnerable right after they have molted and before the new calcium-rich exoskeleton has hardened. Like the soft-shelled blue crabs so favored by Chesapeake Bay restaurant patrons, soft-shelled crayfish get slurped up by bronzebacks. The size of crayfish is also at play. Smallmouth prefer smaller crayfish, the under 3-inch variety, instead of the monster 6-inch, fully armored, big-clawed ones. Smaller crayfish are softer, less able to deter attack, and easier to eat.

Chapter 2 covers some of the best places to fish in the 11 western states and lists primary forage. What clearly stands out is how crayfish and baitfish predominate in those waters.

Many of my flies are nothing more than rabbit and chenille or other body material. I'd rather catch fish than spend hours tying flies.

Another example of an easily tied fly. D-Dub's BananaRama is almost all crosscut rabbit.

Small 1- to 3-inch crayfish patterns catch more fish that larger flies. Still, it's a good idea to have some larger flies in your box.

Aquatic invertebrates run a weak third. There are 500 varieties of crayfish worldwide, ranging in size from the Tasmanian giant, tipping the scales at over 11 pounds, to the *Cambarellus diminutus*, stretching barely an inch. Over 390 species call North America home, with most having mailing addresses in the southeastern United States. Alabama claims more than 60 species, but the numbers drop radically (fortunately for those fly fishers who demand exact imitations) in the West. Montana has two native species and two carpetbaggers. Arizona had no native crayfish but now has at least three species that were imported to provide fish food. Washington had only one native species, but fish now consume at least five species.

The importance of crayfish in the smallmouth diet is well documented in fish and game department research publications. Those publications demonstrate several important facts about the predator-prey relationship. As smallmouth mature into adults, crayfish, as a general rule, become more important as prey, both in percentage of diet of individual fish and in percentage of the fish population. The stomach surveys also show a seasonal effect, likely closely related to water temperature. In the early season cold water surveys, smallmouth rarely consume crayfish, because the crayfish themselves may be abundant but are rarely available. Availability changes with rising water temperature as the crayfish become more active.

Washington's native signal crayfish, *Pacifasticus leniusculus*, spawns in the fall with the females carrying the fertilized eggs on the underside of her body through winter. The eggs, or *berries*, hatch in the spring but remain attached to the female for several more weeks before they leave home for good. When the juveniles, now about three-quarters of an inch, depart, the smallmouth take note of these bite-sized protein chunks.

Although growth rates vary among species, all molt several times during the first year of life. During the molt, the new shell is opaque until it hardens. Give light-colored patterns a try for a different look.

When designing crayfish patterns, keep in mind that they are bottom dwellers, so that's where the fly should be fished. Bead chain or barbells tied on top of the hook shank, if sufficiently heavy, will act as a counterbalance to the weight of the hook point so the fly will ride hook point up. The combination

D-Dub's Rabbit Bugger imitates a variety of smallmouth foods. They mistake it for a leech, crayfish, sculpin, or dragonfly nymph. It may be the most versatile fly in your box.

When using a rabbit strip, weight the fly so it rides in the water with the skin side down. This matches the natural dark over light pattern of crayfish and baitfish.

of small bead chain (or barbell) and strips of lead lashed on top of the hook shank is my preferred weighting system. The amount of weight needed will vary depending on the current speed and water depth.

Weighting the fly this way solves two problems. It reduces the chances of the hook point digging in or getting wedged into the rocky bottom. It also eliminates the need for a hard monofilament or wire weedguard, which gets in the way of a good hook set.

In nature, a crayfish, even when scuttling from danger, keeps its belly to the bottom and does not roll or yaw, even in turbid water. Materials used to craft crayfish patterns should allow the finished fly to successfully imitate crayfish behavior. Crayfish flies tied with stiff materials wobble and twist during the cast, causing the leader to twist into knots. Those same stiff materials cause the fly to wobble and spin unnaturally during the retrieve. The most effective crayfish flies are tied with soft materials, avoiding both problems.

When crayfish are on the feed, they walk along the bottom, supported by their eight legs and using their claws to hunt and gather. If threatened by a predator, they retreat, propelling themselves backward with rapid movement of their tail. During the rapid retreat, their claws fold together and the body becomes streamlined. Crayfish patterns tied with pincers constructed of materials too stiff to collapse when retrieved fail to act like real crustaceans. This unnatural movement makes those stiff flies less effective. Yet another argument for using soft materials.

Some anglers debate as to whether the *primary* smallmouth bass forage is crayfish or baitfish. There is no debate that smallmouth feed heavily on baitfish. That leads to the inevitable question of what exactly is a baitfish. The short answer is this: a baitfish is any fish smallmouth eat. The specific type of baitfish varies by time of year, body of water, and where the smallmouth live within a body of water. For example, a lake smallmouth living in open water will more likely be feeding on pelagics, such as shad and shiners. A smallie living near shore on the same lake will focus on cover-oriented species, such as sunfish and crappie.

Primary western baitfish include threadfin and gizzard shad, emerald shiners, spottail shiners, sculpins, suckers, northern pikeminnow, carp, sunfish, and three chub species. Baitfish cover the gamut of body types, coloration, and preferred habitat. Instead of filling multiple fly boxes with every conceivable pattern to match every possible baitfish in the water, try this simplified approach.

Baitfish share common color schemes and characteristics. Regardless of species, their backs are always dark, their bellies always light, and their sides serve as a transition between the two. The series of baitfish patterns developed by Bob Clouser clearly follows the dark over light standard, with flashy material separating dark from light.

Recall that there are three distinct forage fish body types: thin, medium, and chunky. Shiners and minnows are slender, chubs are medium-bodied, and shad and sunfish have more robust shapes. By varying the volume of materials when tying flies, it's easy to craft a few flies that cover all the bases.

Green and yellow Clouser is a standard color pattern. A nonslip loop knot allows for more up-and-down motion during the retrieve.

With few exceptions, all forage fish are spring and summer spawners. Early in the season, before the first spawn, only adults will be abundant and available, so full-sized fly patterns are the rule. As the spawn approaches, males adopt spawning dress; their colors brighten to attract the females. Flies with a touch of red or orange near the throat may attract more attention than the standard pattern color palette. After the spawn, smallmouth begin to target the now-abundant and available fry. Smaller patterns will take more fish.

At any given time of year, smallmouth focus on a fairly uniform length of prey. The very smallest baitfish are too small to attract attention and the largest are too quick or big to be worth the energy expended in the chase. Distilling the commonalities into fly patterns means carrying flies ranging from 1.5 to 4 inches in three different body shapes, all with the common color scheme of dark over light. When fishing the Columbia River, recall that as smallmouth grow into trophy-size, so does the length of their preferred prey. Add a few longer flies if fishing that water.

Further down on the smallmouth buffet table are aquatic invertebrates. Once smallmouth reach more than a few inches long, they graduate from insects to more substantial foods. Large nymphs like dragons and damsels are big enough to satisfy and justify the energy expended. In some coldwater rivers, dragonfly nymphs are the primary food source until the first baitfish spawn provides a different source of protein. The giant mayfly, *Hexagenia limbata*, lives in some western rivers and lakes. Its size, well over an inch long in both the nymph and adult stage, if present in sufficient numbers, gets attention from smallmouth. Of course, every rule has exceptions. In one remarkably fertile eastern Washington lake, chiromomids—small midges—made up 80 percent of the adult smallmouth diet.

Smallmouth love leeches and eat flies that imitate the undulating motion. Woolly Buggers and rabbit leech patterns are among the most effective. With its body compressed, the leech looks like a glob of gelatin but elongates to a streamlined sliver over 6 inches long. Leeches live in a variety of habitats across the West, from Washington desert lakes to Wyoming mountain lakes. They can be found clinging to submerged rocks, woody debris, and vegetation. They can also be free-swimming in low-light conditions, a time when they are most available to smallmouth. The last hour of daylight and on into full dark are excellent times to fish leech patterns on a dry or intermediate line. Black, dark brown, and olive are the primary colors.

Smallmouth are inquisitive, opportunistic feeders. Their diet includes many other foods that live in, near, or fly over the water inhabited by smallmouth. Mice, shrews, voles, and other small streamside mammals find their way into smallmouth gullets. Early in the year, tadpoles are on the menu. Those that survive to metamorphosize into frogs get eaten as well. Water snakes and even small birds become part of the food pyramid. These limited "targets of opportunity" represent only a small portion of the daily calories consumed by smallmouth, but topwater fly patterns that imitate the floating or swimming foods are some of the most exciting to fish.

Trout fishers, especially those who only fish dry flies, may find frustration when first targeting smallmouth. Trout reveal

The red rabbit fur tail pulses in the water, looking much like blood from an injured baitfish. The predatory smallmouth key on the weak or injured forage. TOM QUINN

Don't hesitate to experiment with colors and materials when tying. Bead shops and craft stores are excellent places to find innovative fly-tying materials.

their location by sporadically or rhythmically rising to floating insects. Hooking the rising trout is just a matter of timing the rise, then casting the dry fly into the feeding lane of a active fish. Trout are also more susceptible than smallmouth to being caught because they must feed more often than smallmouth. An insect eater, it needs to feed a lot to gain that feeling of being sated. Every time that trout rises it is vulnerable to being caught by an angler. Not so with a smallmouth that gobbles a nice, juicy frog or mouse that satisfies in a single bite.

With smallmouth, casting topwater flies is a question of knowledge plus faith because smallmouth rarely reveal their location. I've been on western smallmouth rivers during Mother's Day caddis hatches with nary a caddis disturbed by any decent-sized smallie. A month later that may change. By summer, when the dragons and damsels are skimming over the water, scooping food or laying eggs, bass fling themselves in the air in an attempt to grab those meaty morsels. However, the biggest bass will still be feeding under the surface.

Fishing topwater may not be the most effective way to catch the biggest smallmouth, but it certainly is the most exciting. Every smallmouth bass fly fisher should have topwater bugs ready for action. The fly is cast to a place where a smallmouth might be lurking. The water undisturbed, rubber legs wiggling, a promise unfulfilled—until the water implodes and the bug

vanishes or the big bronze shape comes over the top to engulf the fly. Strike too soon and the fly fails to seat, defeat snatched from the jaws of victory. Wait a beat or two, raise the rod tip, and the hook finds purchase.

Assigning a fly to a food category is by its very nature a highly subjective task. For example, is a Woolly Bugger a crayfish, baitfish, or subsurface pattern? What about a Muddler Minnow? Certainly it's a topwater pattern when greased with floatant. But it's a baitfish when fished on a sinking line. And how to classify a Gurgler—a foam-backed floating fly intended to represent a baitfish—designed to be fished underwater with a sinking line, it also fishes quite well as a topwater fly?

The category or label assigned to the fly pattern is not the point. From the angler's standpoint, what is important is to understand the various foods the fly imitates and to present the fly in the best possible imitation of that food. If smallmouth are gorging on grasshoppers, a Muddler Minnow attached to a strong tippet and dry line makes a passable imitation. Conversely, if smallies are scooping sculpins off the bottom, then a short leader and sinking line will get the Muddler down to the bottom.

With that, here are some excellent western smallmouth bass flies, many with comments from the tiers on how to fish these "silver bullets."

Flies

JOE'S SMALLMOUTH SCULPIN

Joe Kristof, Issaquah, WA

Body Hook:	#1/0 Mustad SL53U BL
Stinger Hook:	#6-8 Gamakatsu or Owner
Thread:	Black 6/0
Eyes:	Yellow dumbbell eyes (small)
Stinger:	18" Maxima Ultra (10-pound-test)
Tail:	2 olive and 1 brown schlappen feathers per side (brown on inside)
Body:	Peacock Crystal Chenille (small) with 4 strands Holographic Pearl Flashabou on top
Flanks:	2 olive and 1 brown schlappen feathers per side (brown on inside)
Collar:	Olive, black, and brown rhea bunch tied and distributed around hook shank
Head:	Olive, black, and brown coarse dubbing
Note:	Cut the body hook at the bend after tying the fly. For the stinger, make sure the thread is doubled, hitched, and furled by spinning with forceps, then knotted.

SMP

Gene Trump, Corvallis, OR

Hook:	#2 TMC 511S
Thread:	White 6/0 Uni Big Fly Thread
Body:	White Rainey's Pencil Popper (medium), painted as desired with craft spray paint
Tail:	Red saddle hackle; flash material as desired
Eyes:	Super Pearl Hareline Dubbin Adhesive Holographic Eyes ($7/32$")
Note:	Color combination is the body painted silver while leaving the belly white and then spraying the back black. Other combinations work in different fisheries: silver with copper sides and a brown back, or silver with a green back. The back should always be sprayed a darker color than the belly. Two white rubber leg strands are optional.

A pencil popper is meant to represent a baitfish struggling on the surface and should be presented as such. Use quick strips to create a pop, then let the pattern rest. Repeat. Many strikes occur when the pattern is at rest after popping.

LUKE'S FLIPPING FLY (CRAYFISH)

Jon Luke, North Bend, WA

Hook:	#4/0 Gamakatsu 604
Thread:	Orange 100-denier Ultra GSP Thread
Eyes:	Gold I-Balz (1/4")
Skirt:	Boss Intruder Punch Skirt, Clear Water Craw
Tail:	Orange rabbit
Tail Flash:	Gold Holographic Mylar Motion
Rattle Case:	Orange nylon tube
Rattle:	Glass rattle
Head:	Brown Estaz Grande
Weedguard:	Double strand of hard mono
Note:	In lakes and reservoirs, fish it with a floating line, bouncing it slowly off the ledges of points and banks. If fish are on feeding the flats, it can be stripped fast for some serious action. In rivers, high stick to bounce it along the bottom with the current.

LUKE'S BASS TUBE

Jon Luke, North Bend, WA

Hook:	#4/0 Gamakatsu 604
Thread:	Chartreuse 100-denier Ultra GSP Thread
Eyes:	Mottled-green/blue bead chain eyes (60 lb. mono)
Tube:	White nylon sleeve (1/2")
Tail:	Chartreuse marabou and round silicone skirt; chartreuse or silver flake
Tail Flash:	Chartreuse Holographic Mylar Motion
Rattle:	Brass worm rattle
Note:	In lakes and reservoirs, fish it with a floating line, bouncing it slowly off the bottom to create a jigging motion. In rivers, strip, pause, strip, pause from the bank back to the boat.

WOOLLY BUG

CDR Joel Stewart, San Diego, CA

Hook:	#2-12 Mustad 79580
Thread:	Black 3/0 Uni-Thread
Eyes:	Antique brass bead chain (small)
Tail:	Chartreuse round rubber
Legs:	3 chartreuse round rubber legs
Body:	Olive chenille (medium)
Hackle:	Soft saddle hackle, palmered from stern to bow
Note:	Tie the chartreuse round rubber in a V for the tail. Evenly space the legs along the body. CDR Stewart is the author of *A Fly Rod in My Sea Bag*.

CHUCK AND DUCK

Jimmie Eichman, Lakeside, OR

Hook:	#2-8 Mustad 9671
Thread:	Black 6/0 Danville
Eyes:	Brass (³/16")
Butt:	White chenille (medium)
Body:	Black chenille (medium)
Legs:	3 white round rubber legs evenly spaced along the body
Note:	Fish it on a floating line or 10' Type IV Sink-Tip. When the white legs disappear from sight, I know I have a fish. If the fish are deep, I will use a Casual Dress as the second fly about 12–14" behind the Chuck and Duck. The white legs are the fairly stiff innards from bungee cords. I also tie it with a purple chenille body.

CASUAL DRESS

Originated by Polly Rosborough
Jimmie Eichman, Lakeside, OR

Hook:	#2-8 Mustad 3906
Thread:	Black 6/0 Danville
Tail:	Brown mink
Body:	Light gray muskrat dubbing
Thorax:	Brown mink with guard hairs
Head:	Black mink dubbing
Note:	If the fish are shallow, I use the Casual Dress as my only fly. I sometimes add small rubber legs in a light green shade.

SILVER FOX

Eric Olson, Seattle, WA

Hook:	#8 Daiichi 2220
Thread:	Uni mono (fine)
Body:	Pearl flat Diamond Braid
Wing:	Silver fox with underfur combed out
Head:	Fish-Skull
Note:	For the wing, begin bunches of fur about halfway down the shank, adding bunches but leaving room for skull. I like to fish this around any kind of structure. Let the fly sink, begin stripping in, and hold on. The strikes can be jolting.

BLOOM'S M.R.S. BUGGER

Brian O'Keefe, Bend, OR

Hook:	#4 Dai-Riki 710
Thread:	Red 210-denier Danville
Eyes:	Brass dumbbell (medium)
Tail:	Tan marabou with 4 strands of Pearl Krystal Flash
Body:	Tan chenille (medium)
Wire:	Copper (fine), counterwrapped over body
Hackle:	Brown saddle hackle, palmered
Note:	I like this fly because it sinks fast, has a jigging action, and the marabou tail has great action. It can be tied or bought in fly shops in colors that work as crayfish.

HARA KIRI

IT WORKS

Originated by Bob Wood
Modified by Jim Higgins, Kent, WA

Hook:	#4 Daiichi 1750
Thread:	Olive dun 6/0 Uni-Thread
Tail:	Olive pheasant rump
Body:	Light yellow Hareline Ice Dub UV
Throat:	Olive pheasant rump
Back:	Olive pheasant rump
Note:	To fish this fly, I cast close to structure and allow the fly to sink to the desired depth, then start a strip retrieve. I am trying to imitate a small forage fish, so I vary the strip length and speed of retrieve until I find what the fish want. I also tie this pattern in a weighted version by wrapping the front half of the shank with lead wire.

Sam Matalone, Coppell, TX

Hook:	#4-6 Daiichi 2451
Thread:	Black 140-denier Wapsi UTC
Eyes:	Red dumbbell with black pupil (medium)
Tail:	Green dubbing brush with small piece of closed-cell foam glued at tag end so the tail floats up
Body:	Green dubbing brush
Note:	Construct the brush for the tail with flexible wire. The more movement the better the action. The tail should extend 3–4" beyond the hook bend. For the body, wrap remaining dubbing brush to the front of the hook, taking several wraps around the dumbbell.

This fly is extremely effective and should be on the bottom 90 percent of the time. The retrieve can be varied from extremely slow to continuous movement. This fly will surprise you.

SHAD IMITATION

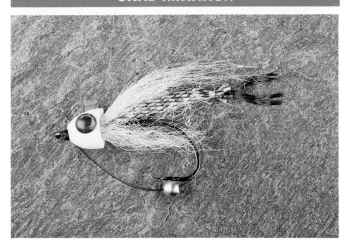

Sam Matalone, Coppell, TX

Hook:	#4-6 TMC 777SP or Gamakatsu SC15
Thread:	Black 280-denier Wapsi UTC
Weedguard:	20 lb stiff mono strung with tungsten bead
Tail:	Brown-dyed grizzly hackle
Body:	Green Mylar tubing, brown-dyed grizzly hackle stem
Wing:	SF Flash Blend Shaded Chartreuse, white craft fur
Head:	Rainey's Pee-Wee Pops
Note:	For the tail, cut the center section out to form a V, then strip the remaining fibers from the stem. Clip a suitable length of Mylar or any other hollow tube material. Insert the stem of the hackle into the tube and secure with half hitches and head cement. For the body, attach the Mylar and hackle stem to the hook at the midpoint of the shank. Using your favorite synthetic material, create an upper (dark) and lower (light) wing that extends beyond the tail, but leave room at the head. The wing color and profile should be representative of the baitfish in your area. Slip a Rainey's Pee-Wee Pops over the hook eye so that it overlaps the wing. Add hologram eyes to head.

This imitation can be fished with a sinking line to get a very deep presentation. I typically use this fly with a floating line in 3–7' of water. The tungsten bead will ensure the fly is at the proper orientation. If fish are suspended, let the fly just sit for up to 30 seconds (yes, 30 seconds) before moving it. Fish the pattern at various speeds.

SHAD IMITATION #2

Sam Matalone, Coppell, TX

Hook:	#4-6 TMC 777SP or Gamakatsu SC15
Thread:	Black 280-denier Wapsi UTC
Tail:	Grizzly hackle
Body:	Silver Mylar tubing, grizzly hackle stem
Wing:	Olive over white craft fur
Head:	Rainey's Pee-Wee Pops
Note:	For the tail, cut the hackle center section out to form a V, then strip the remaining fibers from the stem. Clip a suitable length of Mylar or any other hollow tube material. Insert the stem of the hackle into the tube and secure with half hitches and head cement. Attach the Mylar and hackle stem to the hook at the midpoint of the shank. Using your favorite synthetic material, create an upper (dark) and lower (light) wing that extends beyond the tail, but leave room at the head. The wing color and profile should be representative of the baitfish in your area. Slip a Rainey's Pee-Wee Pops over the hook eye so that it overlaps the wing. Add hologram eyes to head.

This imitation can be fished with a sinking line. This fly works great on suspended fish; experiment with your retrieve to figure what works best.

QUICK SHAD PATTERN

Sam Matalone, Coppell, TX

Hook: #2-6 TMC 777SP or Gamakatsu SC15
Thread: Black 280-denier Wapsi UTC
Tail: Church-window pheasant rump hackle
Body: Mylar tubing and church-window pheasant rump hackle stem
Wing: White craft fur
Head: Hologram eyes (large size for #4 hooks, extra large for bigger hooks)
Note: For the tail, cut the hackle center section out to form a V, then strip the remaining fibers from the stem. Clip a suitable length of Mylar or any other hollow tube material. Insert the stem of the hackle into the tube and secure with half hitches and head cement. For the body, attach the Mylar and hackle stem to the hook at the midpoint of the shank. Using your favorite synthetic material, create an upper and lower wing that extends beyond the tail. The wing material also forms the head. The bottom wing is white and the upper is light gray. Once both wings are in place, trim to the match the profile of baitfish in your area. Add hologram eyes and a black dot with marking pen behind the eye.

    This is a quick and effective pattern to tie. It works on all fish.

QUICK BAITFISH IMITATION

Sam Matalone, Coppell, TX

Hook: #2-6 TMC 777SP or Gamakatsu SC15
Thread: Black 280-denier Wapsi UTC
Tail: Church-window pheasant rump hackle
Body: Mylar tubing and church-window pheasant rump hackle stem
Wing: Olive over white craft fur
Throat: Red craft fur
Head: Hologram eyes, adhered with epoxy (large size for #4 hooks and smaller; extra large for bigger hooks)
Note: For the tail, cut the center section out to form a V, then strip the remaining fibers from the stem. Clip a suitable length of Mylar or any other hollow tube material. Insert the stem of the hackle into the tube and secure with half hitches and head cement. Attach the Mylar and hackle stem to the hook at the midpoint of the shank. Using your favorite synthetic material, create an upper (dark) and lower (light) wing that extends beyond the tail. The wing material also forms the head. Once both wings are in place, trim to the match the profile of baitfish in your area.

    This is a quick and effective pattern to tie. It works on all fish. I have used this basic pattern to tie flies 6–9" in length for stripers/hybrids in Texas. It is an easy fly to cast at 9" with a sinking line.

THOUGHTS ON WESTERN FLIES ■ 121

SMALL BLACK FLY

Sam Matalone, Coppell, TX

Hook:	#4-6 Gamakatsu Octopus
Thread:	Black 280-denier Wapsi UTC
Tail:	Peacock body feather
Body:	Mylar and peacock stem
Wing:	4 black saddle hackles. Add a few strands of green Flashabou on each side.
Hackle:	Large webby black hackle, folded back
Head:	Red hologram eyes
Note:	Determine the appropriate length and size for a tail, then strip the remaining fibers from the stem. Clip a suitable length of Mylar or any other hollow tube material. Insert the stem of the hackle into the tube and secure with half hitches and head cement. For the body, attach the Mylar and peacock stem to the hook at the midpoint of the shank. Smallmouth just cannot resist this small black fly.

WHITMAN CRAW

Devin Petersen, Seattle, WA

Hook:	#6 Mustad 9672
Thread:	Brown 6/0 Uni-Thread
Eyes:	Silver bead chain (medium)
Tail:	Tan rabbit dubbing
Body:	Tan rabbit dubbing
Wing:	Red squirrel tail and pumpkin rubber legs
Note:	Fish this fly on a floating line, bouncing it along the bottom like a real crayfish. It works best in clear water.

DOMINIC SINGH'S SPICY STINGER

Dominic Singh, Ellensburg, WA

Hook:	#6 Daiichi 1760 or 2220
Thread:	150-denier Veevus GSP
Weight:	.025-inch-diameter lead-free wire, brass conehead
Tail/Body:	Crayfish orange rabbit barred Zonker strip
Legs:	Pumpkin orange hot-tipped rubber legs
Collar:	Crayfish orange schlappen
Note:	I originally tied this for large trout in the Yakima River in my hometown of Ellensburg, Washington, but I found it worked surprisingly well in Oregon ponds and lakes near the Deschutes River for smallies on a 3-weight rod. When fishing from the bank, I cast this streamer out about 10 yards and pulse retrieve, occasionally popping, stopping, twitching, or sweeping the fly back. Smallmouth will almost always charge from the front and suck the fly in after about 10 seconds of slow pulsing, making the rabbit ripple in the water. In addition to largemouth and smallmouth bass, I have caught large sunfish on this fly.

REDEYE CRAWBOOGER

Aaron Culley, Redmond, WA

Hook:	#4-6 TMC 5263BL
Thread:	Brown 6/0 Benecchi
Bead:	Black $^3/_{16}$" nickel
Weight:	.025-inch-diameter lead wire (10 turns)
Tail:	Gold Halo Flashabou, gold rubber legs
Body:	Pumpkin or gold sparkle chenille
Hackle:	Ginger neck hackle, palmered
Note:	Cast it over weed beds, then let it sink with a medium fast strip using intermediate sinking line.

CHERNOBYL ANT WITH BODY ARMOR

Hal Gordon, Aloha, OR

Hook:	#10 Mustad 79580
Thread:	Brown or black 6/0 Danville Flymaster
Underbody:	Tan foam, separated by thread wraps into four segments
Body:	Two strips of $^1/_8$" foam, brown on bottom, black on top
Indicator:	Yellow foam
Legs:	Brown rubber (round), two at head, two at rear
Note:	I fish this ant from a pontoon boat with a dry line and 10-pound tippet. It is best fished by floating down the middle of the river and casting into the grass along shore, then stripping it fast back to the boat. The bass hammer the fly several feet from shore.

SMP

Skip Morris, Port Ludlow, WA

Hook:	#6-10 Daiichi 1560
Thread:	Orange 3/0 Danville Flat Waxed Nylon
Eyes:	Lead barbell eyes or bead chain
Body:	Orange shiny dubbing blended with Arizona Sparkle Nymph or Haretron
Wing:	Orange marabou over yellow marabou
Head:	Epoxy
Note:	Bind the wing with turns of thread that crisscross the barbell eye stem, rather than just around the wing and shank, as that will shorten and restrict the wing.

Coat the thread windings holding the wing with epoxy or a few coatings of head cement. I've caught plenty of smallmouth on the original orange-yellow version of my SMP (a fly originally designed for bluegills and other panfish), but when rivers like Oregon's John Day and Umpqua go transparent in summer, I, and the smallmouth, lean toward browns, olives, and other such natural, somber colors.

CASUAL DRESS

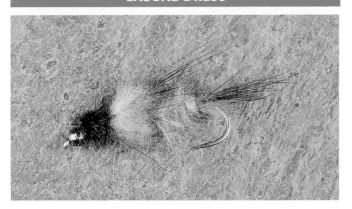

Originated by Polly Rosborough
Dave Hughes, Portland, OR

Hook:	#4-6 TMC 5263
Thread:	Black 6/0 Uni-Thread
Bead:	Black 3/16″ nickel
Tail:	Mink guard hairs
Body:	Light gray muskrat dubbing
Thorax:	Brown mink with guard hairs over the back
Head:	Black mink dubbing

HEX NYMPH

Steve Bohnemeyer, Chico, CA

Hook:	#8 TMC 5262
Thread:	Yellow 6/0 Uni-Thread
Tail:	Brown feather barbs
Body:	Pale yellow yarn
Thorax:	Pale yellow yarn
Wing Case:	Tuft of fluffy tan hen hackle barbs (half the shank length)
Legs:	One wrap of feathers
Note:	Build up the yarn for the thorax—this is the key to the fly. Pull the feather barbs over the thorax for the wing case. Finally, pull one wrap of feathers down to form the legs. Fish this fly on a Type III shooting taper with braided mono running line. Cast it out, and let it sink. Strip with short jerks while kicking slowly in a float tube or pontoon. Begin to fish the fly 2 hours before the adults emerge.

BLACK TEENY EGG SUCKING LEECH

Jim Teeny, Gresham, OR

Hook:	#2-8 2xl
Thread:	Red Size A ProWrap
Tail:	Black pheasant tail fibers
Body:	Black pheasant tail fibers
Underwing:	Black pheasant tail fiber tips
Note:	For the body, tie the pheasant tail fibers in butt-first and wrapped forward. For the underwing, tie the fiber tips off after the body is wrapped and pulled under. Fish this on a floating line, a Teeny Mini-tip or the Teeny T-130 for getting deep. Other colors for smallmouth are ginger, purple, and hot green.

MEGA CRAW

Michael Bennett, Seattle, WA

Hook:	#2 TMC 8089
Thread:	Fluorescent fire orange 210-denier Ultra Thread
Weedguard:	60 lb. fluorocarbon
Eyes:	Wapsi unpainted lead eyes (large)
Antennae:	Orange-black Wapsi Barred Sili Legs
Claws:	Orange grizzly saddle feathers
Body:	Golden brown Hareline Ice Dub
Body Hackles:	Ringneck pheasant rump feathers (natural)
Legs:	Orange-black Wapsi Barred Sili Legs
Shellback:	Orange bucktail
Note:	The Mega Craw was a pattern I developed for fishing smallmouth in Lake Washington in Seattle, but it has been successful on largemouth and smallmouth in a variety of lakes. A fly pattern called the Crazy Dad was the inspiration for the Mega Craw, but the Crazy Dad is a very small fly and I wanted a much larger version with a weed-guard. After a number of revisions, the Mega Craw is the final product. For smallmouth in lakes, I fish it more than any other fly.

Just as when looking for good smallmouth water in any lake, the best place to fish crayfish patterns is on rocky bottoms, especially if larger rocks are also present and form some kind of bottom structure such as a ledge, rock pile, or hump. These are perfect places for slowly crawling the Mega Craw along the bottom.

BENNETT'S BAITFISH PERCH

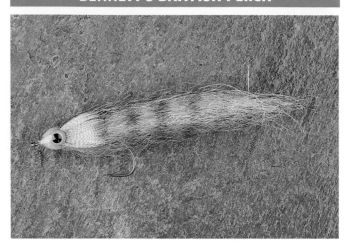

Michael Bennett, Seattle, WA

Hook:	#2-10 TMC 8089
Thread:	Danville .006 clear monofilament
Body:	Deadly Dazzle in colors from bottom to top: Hot Orange, Misty Green, Wild Olive, and Misty Black.
Pectoral Fins:	Wood duck gold mallard flank
Eyes:	Yellow Wapsi Solid Plastic Eyes (6 mm)
Note:	For the body, mark faint vertical par markings along the sides of the fly with a black Prisma Marker. Bennett's Baitfish are general baitfish patterns that can be tied in a variety of colors to imitate a variety of food items like shad, bluegill, and so on. My favorite color variations are perch and smolt. The smolt version is most effective in late spring when trout or salmon smolt are exiting streams into a lake or lower river system where smallmouth are waiting to intercept them. The perch version I find more effective as summer arrives and perch invade shallow water area to spawn.

I usually fish the Bennett's Baitfish patterns on intermediate or fast-sinking full-sink lines, depending on the depth I'm trying to achieve. If I'm fishing this pattern shallow, I'll strip the fly very fast, trying to trigger a response strike. If fishing it deeper, I'll slow it down to keep the fly wandering just above the tops of any weeds.

Figuring out at what depth the fish are on any smallmouth lake is important, and often the outside edge of the weed line is a good place to start. Casting the Bennett's Baitfish parallel to the weed line and fishing the outside edge can be an effective method throughout the year.

BENNETT'S BAITFISH SMOLT

Michael Bennett, Seattle, WA

Hook:	#2-10 TMC 8089
Thread:	Danville .006 clear monofilament
Body:	Deadly Dazzle in colors from bottom to top: Natural Belly, Misty Blue, and Misty Black.
Pectoral Fins:	Wood duck gold mallard flank
Eyes:	White Wapsi Solid Plastic Eyes (6mm)
Note:	For the body, mark faint vertical par markings along the sides of the fly with a black Prisma Marker.

MYSTIC MOUSE

Michael T. Williams, Eugene, OR

Hook:	#2 Daiichi 2720
Thread:	White 3/0 Uni-Thread
Tail:	Leather sewing cord
Butt:	Orange Ultra Chenille Fluorescent
Body:	Spun deer hair, light, then dyed black, then natural brown; bottom half trimmed off
Note:	This fly presents a realistic profile of a swimming mouse. If fly floatant is added, it will ride higher on the water. Use it on bright sunny days if the fish refuse the Red Ass Ratt.

RED ASS RATT

Michael T. Williams, Eugene, OR

Hook:	#2/0 Gamakatsu B10S
Thread:	Red 3/0 Uni-Thread
Tail:	Red rabbit strip
Body:	Spun deer hair
Collar:	Spun moose hair
Note:	Trim off the bottom half for both the deer hair and the moose hair. I originally designed this fly for northern pike and other large, toothy fish, but it has proven itself to be an excellent smallmouth bass fly as well.

WYATT'S WONDER

Michael T. Williams, Eugene, OR

Hook:	#2 Daiichi 2720
Thread:	Red 3/0 Uni-Thread
Tail:	Purple rabbit strip
Body:	Bright Jewells metallic braid
Head:	Spun deer hair, bottom half trimmed off; liberally coat the remaining hair with head cement to make stiff
Note:	The stiff head makes this fly push more water.

PURPLE BUNNY

Michael T. Williams, Eugene, OR

Hook:	#4-6 Mustad 3366
Thread:	Black 3/0 Uni-Thread
Eyes:	Nickel dumbbell (medium)
Tail:	Purple rabbit strip
Body:	Purple rabbit strip, palmered forward
Note:	This fly started out as a steelhead pattern then morphed into a smallmouth pattern. Umpqua River bass love the color purple. Fish it on a floating line and retrieve in a jigging motion.

AT-EM BOMB

Michael T. Williams, Eugene, OR

Hook:	#2 TMC 300
Thread:	Black 3/0 Uni-Thread
Eyes:	White and red Testor's Model Paint, Sally Hansen Hard As Nails
Tail:	Yellow rabbit fur
Body:	Cotton darning thread, silver oval tinsel
Throat:	Red rabbit fur or brown hackle fibers
Underwing:	Yellow marabou
Overwing:	White bucktail
Topping:	Peacock herl
Note:	Paint the eye white using a wood kitchen match. Apply the red pupil with a finish nail. When dry, cover the eye with two coats of Sally Hansen Hard As Nails. This pattern imitates a small yellow perch. Fish it like a wounded or disoriented baitfish.

RED-EYED CLOUSER

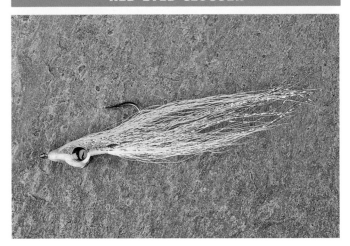

Michael T. Williams, Eugene, OR

Hook:	#4-6 Mustad 3366
Thread:	White 3/0 Uni-Thread
Underwing:	White bucktail
Flash:	Silver Krystal Flash
Overwing:	Chartreuse bucktail
Note:	This creation is the traditional Bob Clouser–style baitfish.

BLITZEN HOPPER

Michael T. Williams, Eugene, OR

Hook:	#8-14 Daiichi 1280
Thread:	Red 3/0 Uni-Thread
Tail:	Moose hair and red hackle fibers
Hackle:	Badger, palmered
Body:	Yellow poly yarn
Rib:	Copper wire (medium)
Wing:	Church-window mottled pheasant body feather
Underwing:	Yellow Krystal Flash
Legs:	Strands of deer hair
Head:	Spun deer hair, clipped to form bullet head
Note:	Grasshoppers float low in the water and get eaten even after they sink, so I don't use fly floatant on this fly. Cast tight to shore on a floating line, retrieve in short, intermittent strips.

DUMB-G-BUG #1

Michael T. Williams, Eugene, OR

Hook: #4-8 TMC 3762
Thread: Black 3/0 Uni-Thread
Eyes: Nickel dumbbell (medium)
Butt: White chenille
Body: Black chenille
Legs: 14 white rubber legs

DUMB-G-BUG #2

Michael T. Williams, Eugene, OR

Hook: #4-8 TMC 3762
Thread: Red 3/0 Uni-Thread
Eyes: Nickel dumbbell (medium)
Tail: Black marabou
Butt: Chartreuse Estaz UV Lights
Body: Purple chenille
Legs: 14 white rubber legs

DUMB-G-BUG #3

Michael T. Williams, Eugene, OR

Hook: #4-8 TMC 3762
Thread: Red 3/0 Uni-Thread
Eyes: Nickel dumbbell (medium)
Butt: White chenille
Body: Rootbeer Estaz
Legs: 14 white rubber legs
Note: These three flies are intended to catch the fish that are feeding on the bottom, so if I'm using a floating line, my leader is long enough to get the fly down. A Sink-Tip and shorter leader works better. The fish will take it on the drop as well as when bounced along the bottom.

CHICKABOU CRAYFISH

Originated by Henry Hoffman
David Paul Williams, Bellevue, WA

Hook: #6 Daiichi 1730
Thread: Brown 210-denier Danville Flymaster Plus
Claws: Brown chickabou
Eyes: Black and white dumbbell tied over hook bend
Body: Brown chickabou
Legs: Brown chickabou
Tail: Brown chickabou
Note: I fish this fly on a floating or 10' Sink-Tip line, making sure to bounce it along the bottom in all the places where crayfish live.

BROWN LEAD HEAD

David Paul Williams, Bellevue, WA

Hook: #4-6 Daiichi 1730
Thread: Brown 210-denier Danville Flymaster Plus
Eyes: Black and white dumbbell tied over hook bend
Tail: Brown chickabou and copper flash
Body: Dark copper Estaz
Hackle: Brown saddle, palmered
Wire: Copper, counterwrapped through hackle
Note: Drag this pattern over bottom structure.

CRAYFISH LEECH

David Paul Williams, Bellevue, WA

Hook: #6 Daiichi 1870
Thread: Brown 210-denier Danville Flymaster Plus
Weight: .025-inch-diameter lead wire (10–15 turns)
Body: Crayfish orange rabbit (crosscut)
Flash: Pearl Krystal Flash
Collar: Pheasant rump
Note: This pattern appeals to smallmouth who can't make up their minds as to whether they want crayfish or leech for dinner. Either way, it works best when fished deep in the water column.

D-DUB'S BLEEDING MINNOW

David Paul Williams, Bellevue, WA

Hook:	#4 Daiichi 1870
Thread:	Red 210-denier Danville Flymaster Plus
Eyes:	Gold w/ Sparkle Silver Montana Fly Company Sparkle Dumbbell Eyes (medium)
Tail:	Red rabbit (straight cut) and silver flash
Body:	Rabbit (crosscut), palmered
Note:	This simple-to-tie pattern imitates an injured baitfish. I fish it on a long Sink-Tip or floating line depending on water velocity or depth. It's a great pattern when the smallmouth are feeding on fry.

D-DUB'S FIGHTING CRAW

David Paul Williams, Bellevue, WA

Hook:	#1/0 Daiichi 4660
Thread:	Brown 210-denier Danville Flymaster Plus
Tail:	Golden yellow/pearl flake Barred Crazy Legs, orange foam on top of shank
Body:	Copper metallic Estaz
Weight:	.025-inch-diameter lead wire at head (10 turns)
Note:	The foam makes this fly ride in a fighting crayfish position. It should be fished on sinking line right on the bottom.

HOBBY LOBBY #1

David Paul Williams, Bellevue, WA

Hook:	#4-8 Daiichi 1870
Thread:	Black 3/0 Uni-Thread
Tail:	Night Fire Deep Eyelash
Body:	Deep Night Gilt Eyelash
Weight:	.025-inch-diameter lead wire (15 turns)
Note:	Fish this pattern made from Hobby Lobby materials like any Woolly Bugger pattern.

HOBBY LOBBY #2

David Paul Williams, Bellevue WA

Hook:	#4-8 Daiichi 1870
Thread:	Black 3/0 Uni-Thread
Tail:	Deep Night Gilt Eyelash
Body:	Night Fire Deep Eyelash
Weight:	.025-inch-diameter lead wire (15 turns)
Note:	Both Hobby Lobby patterns are killer flies for night fishing—where legal. The copper and black color combination is irresistible to most gamefish.

D-DUB'S RABBIT BUGGER

David Paul Williams, Bellevue, WA

Hook:	#6-10 Daiichi 1730
Thread:	Brown 210-denier Danville Flymaster Plus
Tail:	Rabbit (straight cut) tied skin side up, copper Krystal Flash
Body:	Brown chenille
Hackle:	Brown saddle, palmered
Wire:	Copper, counterwrapped through hackle
Weight:	2–3 strips .025-inch-diameter lead wire lashed on top of hook shank
Note:	This pattern imitates crayfish, leeches, and dragonfly nymphs, which form the basis of smallmouth foods. The weight on top of the hook makes it ride point up. Brown is my favorite color, followed by black, rootbeer, and crayfish orange. This pattern catches fish everywhere and is one of my top three producing flies.

D-DUB'S FRY

David Paul Williams, Bellevue, WA

Hook:	#6-10 Daiichi 1730
Thread:	Green 6/0 Uni-Thread
Eyes:	Silver bead chain (small)
Body:	Silver Z-Braid (2 mm)
Gills:	#615 Glissen Gloss Rainbow
Underwing:	UV Minnow Belly
Flash:	Pearl Krystal Flash
Overwing:	Olive sheep wool
Topping:	Peacock herl
Head:	Peacock herl
Note:	I developed this pattern as a variation to Bob Clouser's Deep Minnow. When fall chinook fry are flushing out of the Yakima River, this is an excellent pattern.

BOO RADLEY

David Paul Williams, Bellevue, WA

Hook: #4-8 Daiichi 1730
Thread: Brown 210-denier Danville Flymaster Plus
Bead: Copper ($^3/_{16}$")
Tail: Brown rabbit
Body: Black Flashabou
Wing: Brown rabbit
Flash: Copper
Head: Brown marabou
Note: This fly and my Prickly Sculpin are designed to present a large profile and tapering body, just like the real thing. Fish it on the bottom where sculpins live.

D-DUB'S MARABOU MINNOW (OLIVE)

David Paul Williams, Bellevue, WA

Hook: #4-8 Daiichi 1730
Thread: Green 6/0 Uni-Thread
Eyes: Gold w/ Sparkle Silver Montana Fly Company Sparkle Dumbbell Eyes (medium)
Body: Opal white Z-Braid (2 mm)
Gills: #615 Glissen Gloss Rainbow
Underwing: White marabou
Flash: Pearl Krystal Flash
Overwing: Olive marabou

D-DUB'S MARABOU MINNOW (BROWN)

David Paul Williams, Bellevue, WA

Hook: #4-8 Daiichi 1730
Thread: Brown 210-denier Danville Flymaster Plus
Eyes: Gold w/ Sparkle Silver Montana Fly Company Sparkle Dumbbell Eyes (medium)
Body: Opal white Z-Braid (2mm)
Gills: #615 Glissen Gloss Rainbow
Underwing: White marabou
Flash: Pearl Krystal Flash
Overwing: Brown marabou
Note: These creations are both generic baitfish patterns that use marabou instead of bucktail because the marabou presents more lifelike motion, particularly when fishing stillwaters.

NIGHT RIDER

David Paul Williams, Bellevue, WA

Hook: #6-8 Daiichi 1730
Thread: Black 6/0 Uni-Thread
Weight: 2–3 strips of .025-inch-diameter lead wire on top of hook shank
Tail: Black marabou or rabbit (straight cut), and 4 strands Krystal Flash
Body: Black Estaz Metallique
Hackle: Black saddle, palmered
Note: I tie this fly in three different colors with different body materials. The other materials are olive Estaz Metallique (Morning Madness) and chartreuse Estaz UV Lights (Afternoon Delight). The rabbit tail holds up better and gives a larger profile in the water than marabou. This series of flies will catch fish anywhere and everywhere. I typically fish it on a short Type III Sink-Tip. After the cast, I let it sink, then slowly retrieve it. Although I just started tying these three versions, they are rapidly becoming favorites because they flat out catch fish and are so quick to tie.

CHARTREUSE CABOOSE

David Paul Williams, Bellevue, WA

Hook: #4-8 Daiichi 1730
Thread: Chartreuse 140-denier Danville
Eyes: Gold w/ Sparkle Silver Montana Fly Company Sparkle Dumbbell Eyes (medium)
Tail: 9 chartreuse rubber legs, 4 strands Krystal Flash
Body: Chartreuse Estaz UV Lights
Hackle: Chartreuse saddle, palmered
Note: This fly has gone through a number of iterations. When I first tied it, the dumbbell was at the hook eye, but since I'd never seen a crayfish with eyes in its tail, I moved the eyes back. I leave the head a little ragged to look a bit more like a crayfish. Depending on water depth or current velocity, I may lash strips of lead on top of the shank in order to get the fly down to the bottom where crayfish live. The Caboose is another of my top three flies.

UMPQUA CLOUSER #1

Gary Lewis, Roseburg, OR

Hook: #6 Dai-Riki 710
Thread: Black 6/0 Uni-Thread
Eyes: Brass dumbbell (medium)
Body: DNA Holo Fusion Fibers

UMPQUA CLOUSER #2

Gary Lewis, Roseburg, OR

Hook: #6 Dai-Riki 710
Thread: Black 6/0 Uni-Thread
Eyes: Brass dumbbell (medium)
Body: Yellow bucktail over red Krystal Flash

UMPQUA CLOUSER #3

Gary Lewis, Roseburg, OR

Hook: #6 Dai-Riki 710
Thread: Black 6/0 Uni-Thread
Eyes: Brass dumbbell (medium)
Body: Gold Krystal Flash over yellow bucktail
Note: Tied sparsely, these flies present a slender profile in the water. I mostly fish them on a floating line, casting toward structure and varying the retrieve until I find what works best.

Estaz is a fantastic material for crafting fly bodies. It comes in three thicknesses and multiple colors, and it is easy to work with.

The color combination of the Afternoon Delight shows up well in the water and stands out from other potential food sources. Fish it late in the afternoon when the sun has left the water.

CHAPTER EIGHT

Seasonal Smallmouth

It's perhaps bold to make definitive statements about how fish act or where fish live at different times of the year. But with more than 40 years of smallmouth experience, I'm willing to be bold. We are talking about fish and, like people, not all fish act alike, even under what appear to be similar conditions. If all were known about smallmouth habits, that would mean research had done its job and a lot of fisheries' biologists would be looking for jobs. However, all is not known and what is known is subject to regional differences, watershed differences, and specific lake and stream differences. Toss in environmental changes that occur over time, and the fact that not all biologists reach the same results when interpreting the same datasets.

If we have what the business school professors call *perfect knowledge*, that is, if we know all there is to know about this subject, then we would hold all information necessary to catch a fish on every cast. Perfect knowledge doesn't exist in the fishing world. What we have is general knowledge that allows predictions.

Here's what we know: We know that water temperature is the primary predictor of smallmouth behavior. Water temperature drives smallmouth location throughout the seasons. It drives the time of the spawn and whether the spawn will be successful. Temperature dictates when fish start feeding after the winter doldrums, when they stop feeding after the fall binge, and how much they feed to cope with their raging summer metabolism. Water temperature controls their diurnal movements as they shift between resting and feeding areas. Water temperature prescribes when and what forage becomes abundant and available.

Winter

Not long ago winter was thought to be a time for watching the last of the football season and preparing for college basketball's March Madness. It was a season spent in other pursuits, months to be endured before the warm weather returned to stir the fish into angler cooperation. In some parts of the West where the lakes freeze and even the rivers are mostly frozen, that thinking still exists because it is a reality.

Without mincing words, winter is the worst season for catching smallmouth, but it is not without evidence of redemption. Water levels are low, making it easier to scout ledges, rock humps, drop-offs, undercuts, creek channels, and other fish-holding structure. While scouting, take notes, or even better, take pictures. Dial in coordinates of structure on a GPS unit so each can be located when visual clues are hidden by higher water levels. Winter is a time for learning more about the structure under the water.

In more temperate parts of the West, anglers can adapt fishing techniques to the existing water conditions during winter. Not every day is a good day to be on the water. Stay home when the air temperature drops below 32 degrees, when the wind blows, or when a cold front hits, as the fish don't feed under those conditions. On the other hand, a day or two, or even a few hours of sun may gently nudge up the water temperature and stir a few fish into feeding. On those days when the temperature increases, go fishing in the warmest part of the day. You'll likely be the only person on the water, even in those well-known spots that see plenty of anglers in the prime fishing months.

As in any other season, common sense on the water must prevail. In winter, dress in layers of synthetic fibers for heat retention, with an outer water- and wind-blocking shell suitable for the weather. If fishing from a boat, have an extra set of clothes on the boat in a dry bag; otherwise, leave them in your vehicle. If you get soaked, dry clothing is the key to warding off chill. A marvelous winter fishing product, Crazy Thermoband, a wrist band which warms the blood flowing into the fingers, makes it possible to fish without gloves.

So where do the fish live in winter? In cold winter climes like the high plains of Wyoming and Montana where winter shows up early and stays late, stream smallmouth winter over in the deepest slack water pools and eddies. The key is that slack water allows the fish to hug bottom without expending precious energy holding themselves in place against the current. This slack water fish den isn't necessarily in the deepest areas of the river, as some wintering areas may be only a few feet deep.

Recent studies question that conventional wisdom, concluding that winter habitat and activity levels are unrelated to winter severity and instead vary from river to river within similar climates. In the systems like the Snake River, bass follow convention by going deep and staying there until spring. In others, bass remain active all winter, avoiding the deep holes. Locating the fish on any given water requires time on the water. Unfortunately that knowledge gained is not transferable to other rivers.

Lake smallmouth are more predictable, as they tend to concentrate in mid-depth areas. In glacier-carved Lake Washington, winter bass are found on rock humps 65 feet deep—mid-depth compared to the yellow perch which are down over 100 feet—but still out of normal fly rod reach. Contrast that with Lake Powell where the smallmouth are oriented on rock structure in 20 to 30 feet of water, the same level they seek during the hottest summer months when daytime air temperatures hover near triple digits. Determine the water temperature near those rock structures that hold fish, then you will find smallmouth elsewhere in the lake where that temperature and rock structure coincide.

Water temperature will not be uniform throughout a river or lake. As on land, each body of water has microclimates created by prevailing wind, shade, current velocity, composition of substrate, tributaries, underwater springs, and other factors. The fish concentrate in the microclimates that offer the best combination of food, shelter from current, and security from predators. Sunny south-facing rock walls which continue underwater raise the surrounding water temperature a degree or two—just enough to attract food that in turn attracts smallmouth. Dark patches of weeds or rocks in the streambed or a shallow lake bottom absorb more energy from the sun's rays. Shallower areas with springs or groundwater seeps will hold fish if the inflow is warmer than the surrounding water. Concentrate on those areas because the fish do.

After discovering the holding area, the next puzzle piece is locating fish within the holding area. Smallmouth remain structure-oriented no matter the water temperature. As Utah Division of Wildlife Resources (DWR) Lake Powell Fisheries Program Manager Wayne Gustaveson says, "They have an inherent need to be around rocky structure." To be more precise, look for broken rock and cobble because that is where their primary food lives.

Winter smallmouth are sluggish. The colder the water, the more they avoid current. In their cold-water-induced lethargy, they don't exhibit their aggressive summer ambush feeding behavior. Winter steelheaders will understand the need to land the fly near the head of winter bass, as neither winter steelhead nor smallmouth will move far for dinner. Smallmouth metabolism is slowed by the chilly water, so they eat less frequently. When they do answer the dinner bell, they prefer to be served a large meal.

The observed preference for large prey items in the dead of winter may not be so much a preference as a reflection of what is available. There are no juvenile crayfish, no young-of-the-year forage fish, and no recently hatched dragonfly nymphs. Big flies tied with soft, wavy materials that provide plenty of action when slowly bounced along the bottom are the ticket. Crayfish patterns like D-Dub's Crawdad Candy are excellent, though I would keep them on the small side—3 inches or less. Minnow patterns that imitate the full-sized adult of the prevailing forage fish work best.

Unlike the feeding frenzy in the heat of summer, winter fishing is not a big numbers game. However, it is a big fish time. Most winter-feeding fish will be females stoking the fires in preparation for the spring spawn.

Spring

Unlike reveille's bugle call in boot camp, which instantly transforms recruits from somnolence to hurried activity, spring comes to smallmouth waters in fits and starts. A few days of warm weather stir fish from their winter snooze only to have a cold rain drop them back into winter funk. As the water gradually warms, smallmouth move from their winter haunts into spawning sites. It doesn't happen in a linear fashion on any body of water, nor does it happen in every river or lake at the same time.

In lakes, wind-protected shallow coves on the north shore warm first because they get the most sun. North shore smallmouth move into the shallows several days before their south shore brethren. A river fed by snow melt, like Washington's Yakima, starts to warm and then chills from the flush of newly melted snow. A low-gradient stream like California's Russian River warms faster than a high-gradient river like Oregon's John Day.

What this demonstrates to the smallmouth angler is how important a thermometer, time on the water, and careful note-taking are to angling success. Until the water warms, match the speed of the retrieve to the water temperature. The fish are hungry, but their bodies have yet to get revved up.

Spring is best broken into four periods: early prespawn, mid-prespawn, late prespawn, and spawn period. The distinctions, while somewhat arbitrary, are important because the fish will be at different levels, in both activity and the water column.

Early Prespawn

This is the period of the first primal stirring from winter. When the water temperature tops the mid-40s, male and female fish begin to actively feed after going perhaps all winter without taking food. They rise from winter depths after a period of warm, pleasant weather, and a few head toward the shallows. If a cold front blows in, they retreat down in the water column. Anglers aching to get on the water during this phase need to pay attention to the water temperature. If it shows an upward trend, even a degree or two for a few days, then it's time to fish. When the

Washington's Grande Ronde River receives an influx of smallmouth each spring from the Snake River. They come to spawn in the warmer water, spend the summer, then drift back to overwinter in the Snake.

mercury drops back down on a cold or windy day, spend the next few days tying flies or getting the boat rigged because the fish will have turned off.

Mid-Prespawn

When the water temperature rises, topping 50 degrees, smallies are on the move. The entire mature population points toward the shallows. Males and females energetically feed in preparation of the spawn. Some males will check out potential nesting sites between eating sessions.

As in winter, presentation should match fish activity level. Slow presentation is the ticket to catching fish because the smallies still suffer from winter's cold water and need a higher body temperature to get into full-on chase mode. Weighted flies that hug the bottom work best in areas where there is current. Topwater flies like the Hamster take fish in slack water sections.

In lakes, the fish will be spread across all available cover, such as rock piles, weed lines, large woody debris, and man-made structure. In moving waters, focus on slack water, back eddies, and cobble bottoms. Not all cobble bottoms are created equal. Look for those with a mixture of rock sizes ranging from cobble to car-sized boulders. These will hold amazing numbers of smallmouth of several sizes. Small fish will be pushed to the edges where habitat becomes marginal, while the biggest fish

station themselves in front of and behind the best rock structure. Take advantage of this time because fishing will slow as the water continues to warm.

Late Prespawn

When the water temperature rises above 52 degrees, smallmouth waters transform yet again. Males that are going to spawn get busy picking out and building nests, activity that deflects their attention from feeding. Once the site is selected, the male cleans the nest site of rocks and gravel and sweeps it clean of silt. The shallows are almost barren of females at this stage. The numbers of actively feeding males are reduced, but there are still plenty of feeding males in the shallows.

To find females you must go deeper. They have moved into slightly deeper water, awaiting the courtship that is soon to follow. Look for females in water 3 to 5 feet deeper than where the males are doing domestic chores. That means if the males are staging in water 3 feet deep, the females will be in 6–8 feet of water.

Biologists used to think smallmouth lived their entire lives within a single pool, never traveling more than a few hundred yards. Turns out some of these fish have signed up for frequent flyer miles. River fish travel farther than lake fish, up to 40 miles to find acceptable spawning habitat. The distance traveled

The unsettled spring weather can play havoc with the fish. A cold rain can send them back into deeper water. A warm rain may spur them into spawning.

The manicured shoreline reveals no clues to the submerged boulders that attract spawning smallmouth. The rocks, visible only at low water, were spotted late in the year when the water was down.

is based on each discrete stream environment, apparently unrelated to latitude, climate, or even conditions in the next drainage over.

The Columbia River stretches four hundred miles north to south across Washington and then runs another three hundred miles west forming the border between Oregon and Washington. The Columbia and its major tributary, the Snake, have huge resident populations of smallmouth. Each river also has a large migratory population of fish that leave their winter home in the big river to spawn in the warmer waters of smaller tributaries such as the Grande Ronde, Salmon, Walla Walla, and Yakima.

The WDFW did a long-term research study on the Yakima River, studying how smallmouth and other species interacted with wild and hatchery salmon and steelhead fry and smolt. In the course of the study, biologists tracked water temperature in the Columbia and Yakima Rivers. In March, the Yakima's water temperature averaged 47 degrees while the Columbia checked in at 41 degrees. By June, the Yakima ramped up to 65 degrees while the Columbia lagged at 59 degrees. All that warm water flowing into the Columbia sent a signal to pre-spawn smallmouth staging in the Columbia. Message received. When sampled on March 2 there were 985 fish, 150 mm or longer in a Yakima River section below Horn Rapids Dam. On May 4, the smallmouth population on that same section had exploded to 28,145.

A rainstorm and a rising water level can trigger the fish to bite. A bright baitfish pattern, quickly stripped across a cobble bottom took this fish and several more.

Submerged roadbeds run across many western reservoirs. Fish spawn in the drop-off along the edges of the beds, like this one under Banks Lake.

The downside of fall in the West is that irrigation reservoirs are at their lowest level of the year and can become unfishable.

As long as the water temperature of any given body of water remains above the mid-50-degree mark, smallmouth will stay out of deep water because their primary forage—mostly minnows—is in shallow water. Bass may retreat into deeper water at night only to return to the shallows as the day and water warms. In lakes holding threadfin shad, stripers, and smallmouth, it's not good to be a shad. Stripers herd them into shallow back-bays where smallmouth await in ambush. If the survivors try to break out to open water, the stripers force them back to the smallmouth. The cycle continues until the shad escape or the predators are sated. A two-fly combination of a Miyawaki Beach Popper with a small marabou Clouser about 18 inches below can result in hooking fish on both flies at the same time.

As the water continues to cool with longer nights and less daytime heating, bass go through one more feeding binge at the 50-degree mark, before settling into their winter habitat. To find the fish, think like a smallmouth. In other words, focus primarily on protection from the elements and from predators, with food being a secondary object. In streams, they head for deeper pools and rocky areas, which provide protection from strong current and the opportunity for an occasional bite of food. In flushes of high water, stillwater fish head for similar structure. They want protection from wind and waves and to be near a food source. The depth where they locate depends on the water temperature, as they will avoid the coldest part of the lake.

Smallies can be caught in every season. Just be sure to pay attention to the water temperature. Now let's talk about gear.

CHAPTER NINE

Gear: The Basics and More

When I started fishing smallmouth, I had one fly rod, a fiberglass Fenwick 9-foot, 7-weight. I used it for Atlantic salmon in Hosmer Lake. I carried it into the Wyoming wilderness for alpine trout, packed it across the Washington desert for seep lake rainbows, and even caught a few saltwater fish with it. The old Fenwick still gets occasional use if only as a reminder of how far modern fly-fishing rods and equipment have advanced.

Rod manufacturers have, by and large, switched over to composite fibers like graphite, though some speciality makers still build traditional bass rods out of split cane bamboo.

The major manufacturers have created new rod tapers specially designed for bass fishing, along with special-purpose fly lines. The click and pawl reels of yesteryear have been largely displaced by engineering marvels crafted from aluminum barstock or composites. The medium and large arbor disc drag reels border on being works of art—and are priced as such. It's easy to drop multiple thousands of dollars outfitting a couple of rods with reels, extra spools, and lines for each. It's also easy to pony up a few hundred bucks for gear that will catch just as many fish. Spend whatever your budget allows and makes you happy.

When boat fishing with a partner, we each rig two rods equipped with floating and sinking or sinktip lines. The rods allow us to fish different water depths effectively without having to stop and change lines.

duck hunters and winter steelheaders. Neoprene waders' greatest asset is warmth, but the fabric does not breath, making it much less comfortable than waders made of breathable materials. Layering to fit the weather and water conditions under breathable waders is a better way to go.

When breathable waders were first introduced, they were quite expensive. Equipment manufacturers have continuously improved the product, including fashioning styles made to fit women, and are now more affordable. Waders and hip boots come in stocking foot and boot foot models. Boot foot models are warmer, make dressing faster as you don't have to fiddle with boot laces, and have fewer appendages to snag weeds and other river debris. Stocking foot waders allow for a more custom fit. Buy the wading boot that fits your foot instead of slipping your foot into a generic boot designed to fit several foot sizes. This is especially important if your foot size is not in proportion to the rest of your body.

Float tubes and pontoons designed for use on lakes come with a solid or mesh stripping panel that keeps the line from tangling around the angler's feet or wrapping around an underwater obstruction while it's being retrieved. If the boat doesn't have a stripping panel, they are easy to make with nylon mesh, a grommet tool, and shock cord. A stripping basket worn around the waist is handy for the wading angler. The basket keeps the stripped line out of the weeds and makes long casts easier to execute. Hard-sided boats like sleds and johnboats can be equipped with stripping baskets as well. Bob Day, a San Diego Bay saltwater fishing guide, uses a lightweight, collapsible round fabric bag to contain the retrieved line. There is nothing more frustrating than seeing a big fish cruising, plotting an approach, and making a cast, only to have the fly fall short because the line catches underfoot.

Even with felt-soled boots or sandals, safely wading some rivers can be problematic. Wading staffs provide that third leg of the wading triangle. They come in one-piece or multipiece collapsible models made of wood, metal, fiberglass, and composites. One model even has a grappling hook on one end, which can be embedded in the ground to help pull yourself up a steep riverbank.

Floating western rivers is one of my favorite ways to fish for smallmouth. Most of those rivers have serious whitewater that calls for wearing Coast Guard approved personal floatation devices. Paddlers and rowers prefer models cut to allow free arm movement. Avoid the type that automatically inflates when immersed because it will inflate when you get splashed on the first rapid you run.

Chest packs, backpacks, fanny packs, lanyards, and multipocket vests are some options available to the wading smallmouth

Sandals are my favorite fishing footwear for summer and fall fishing. Look for ones with Vibram soles and toe protection. If wading, felt soles are the best.

Chest waders make coldwater fishing more enjoyable. Some models feature a waterproof front zipper.

fisher for carrying flies and other gear. Chest packs don't work for me because they get in the way of the digital single lens reflex camera I carry, but they work well for some fly fishers. Lanyards filled with gadgets and tippet spools are popular, but hook on streamside brush and get in the way of casting. Backpacks comfortably carry a ton of gear, but they must be removed to extract a fly box when changing flies.

A shoulder sling pack is a good compromise. Fanny packs are great when it's too hot to wear a vest, but don't hold much and can restrict wading if they are not waterproof. The mesh vest is the best compromise with pockets for fly boxes, tippet spools, spare reel spools, food, water, and extra clothing while cooler than the traditional vest. Bass flies are generally bigger than trout flies so bass fly boxes are bigger as well. Check the size of the vest pockets before buying to make sure the pockets are big enough to hold your fly boxes.

Upstream or Downstream

Traditional dry-fly trout fishing, as practiced by dry-fly purists, is always fished facing upstream. Any other way is considered unsporting at best and, more likely, uncouth. To my way of thinking, such a rigid, dogmatic approach to fly fishing steals the fun from the sport. Casting upstream makes sense if that's the best way to present the fly under a given set of conditions. The benefits are many. It's easier to get a natural drift whether fishing topwater or subsurface. The fish are less likely to be disturbed by the wading angler. When fishing weighted flies, less weight is needed because the cast can be made far enough upstream to get the bug down to the feeding zone.

But consider for a moment how steelheaders fish for those big ocean-going rainbow trout. The traditional cast is quartering downstream and across the current for anglers swinging flies. The neo-steelheaders are drifting nymphs and jigs under a bobber, casting upstream only far enough to allow the flies to drop into the feeding zone. Those same tactics should be employed by smallmouth anglers.

Most of the western smallmouth rivers are best fished from boats of some nature, which are extensively covered in the next chapter. Wading is tough for a number of reasons, including restricted access through private property, steep and deep canyons, and the sheer size of the rivers. When drifting, the focus is always downstream, trying to locate and hit the next fish-holding spot before the current sweeps the boat past. Western smallmouth river fishing is an exercise in reading the water, discerning the best structure to fish, and making the first cast count—there often is not a second chance.

CHAPTER TEN
Boating for Bass

Western River Float Trips

There is something about a multiday float trip on a western smallmouth river that calls to me. Partly it's the challenge of whitewater—the Class II, III, and IV rapids with well-earned names like Widowmaker, Snow Hole, Waterspout—that gets my pulse racing. Partly it's the remoteness of the rivers that run beyond the reach of cell phones. Partly it's the unhurried pace of fabulous smallmouth fishing in splendid scenery.

Floating a river in search of smallmouth is my favorite way to fish. Floating allows me to access the river away from boat ramps, bridges, and all the access areas that typically receive the brunt of fishing pressure. Float trips require preparation and planning, whether it's a day trip or a week or more. On land, if you forget a raincoat or water bottle, you can walk back to the car and pick up the missing item. Not so on a float trip. Once the boat leaves the launch, you need to have all necessary gear on board. Rowing back upstream is often not an option and many western rivers flow through canyons that make walking out arduous at best, impossible at worst.

Smallmouth live in many types of western waters from 186-mile long Lake Powell (roughly the same distance as Baltimore to New York City) to step-across creeks like East Fork Gila River. On big waters, some form of floating craft comes close to being a necessity to get the angler where the fish live. When selecting a boat to own, remember every boat is a form of compromise—some are loud and expensive to own and operate; still others are slow with limited range—however, all have features that make them the perfect boat under a particular set of circumstances. A fishing buddy of mine has 23 "perfect" boats, not one of the them is an exact duplicate of another.

Before venturing into a boat dealer, take some time to evaluate your needs, wants, and budget. It makes sense to start with budget first, as that may eliminate all but the least expensive craft. A top-of-the-line, sleek and glittery, tournament-style bass boat will run $50,000 to $70,000. A top-of-the-line float tube barely tops $400. Part of the budget discussion is whether you own the kind of vehicle required to haul the boat and recover it from a launch site. Will the boat require a trailer, fit on a cartop rack, or break down to fit into the trunk? Another part of the budget is the cost of owning and operating the boat. Gas and ordinary maintenance expenses can eat into the discretionary money. Liability and physical damage insurance will take an additional bite. Consider the ease and cost of repairing motors, cracked hulls, and blown tubes.

Single person kick boats come in all sizes. My boat is rated for Class IV whitewater and features a wide frame and long, stable pontoons.

After establishing a realistic budget, next consider storage space. Float tubes and other inflatables can be deflated and rolled, so they need little space. Kayaks and canoes can be hung from garage rafters above a car. Any boat that requires a trailer takes up more space, and local ordinances or home-owner association covenants may require it be stored out of sight. That might mean having to rent off-site storage space, which increases ownership costs and adds the inconvenience factor of having to go get the boat instead of merely hooking up the trailer.

How much time do you have to use a boat? Unless the budget is without constraint, you'll likely want to spend less for a boat that mostly sits on dry land.

What kind of water do you intend to fish? Small lakes and ponds require less boat than huge western reservoirs or rivers. Do you plan to use improved launch sites where you can back the trailer directly into the water? Or will you seek remote locations requiring long carries through brush, or winches and cables to launch and recover a boat up a steep slope?

Are you a person who never fishes alone, or someone who always fishes alone? Are you a minimalist who revels in rough-ing it, or a person who demands creature comforts like padded seats and room for an ice chest, or a live well? Whatever your style, make a list of features separated into three categories: must have, would be nice, and deal killers.

After massaging all these factors, then its time to talk with other anglers—members of a local fly club, a person you run into at a boat launch, or someone who has a boat outfitted like your dream boat. More than likely your dream boat will evolve as a result of these conversations. That's a good thing, because if you had rushed to the local boat shop and plunked down your credit card, you could easily be stuck with someone else's dream.

One last question needs to be answered before buying. How much time and energy are you willing to spend to learn how to efficiently, effectively, and safely operate whatever boat you want to buy? Don't buy a drift boat, raft, or cataraft with the intention of running rivers if you are not willing to learn how to drive the boat and come back alive. If outboard motors baffle

When floating, frequently consult the river map. After a few hours on the river, all the curves start to look alike, making it easy to miss the intended campsite.

This boat has everything you need for a two-person, week-long float trip on a desert river.

you—to the extent that knowing how to hook up a fuel line is the outer limit of your skill set—then don't buy a boat with a motor.

Once the basic questions have been pondered, then it's time to buy. New, name-brand boats come with a warranty. Used boats may or may not have a transferrable warranty. Buying a boat is a lot like buying a car. Buy new and you have a dealer and manufacturer to rely on if there's a warranty issue. Buy used, and save some money, but it's buyer beware.

Here's a brief description of the most common types of floating craft.

Float Tubes

Float tubes have dramatically improved from the truck inner-tube wrapped in a nylon shell to the lightweight, bladderless, V-hulled tubes of today. Float tubes are perfect for ponds and near-shore areas of lakes. They can be launched wherever you can get to the water. Chest waders, fins, and a personal floatation device complete the package. Since you sit low to the water, a longer than normal fly rod works best. It's hard to sight fish from a tube, but the benefit is you can sneak close to the fishing spots. Float tubes are the least expensive watercraft option.

The donut model float tube has largely been replaced by the U-boat or V-hull designs which are easier to get into, especially when wearing fins. All work well in warm weather. GENE TRUMP

Loading a raft to maximize safety and utility is part art and part science. Here the camp table doubles as a casting platform on the John Day.

Tube Boats

Pontoon-type boats come in many sizes and styles, from one-person lake boats to three-person guide boats complete with rigid seats and casting platforms. Pontoons can be further broken into three subcategories: kick boats, pontoons, and catarafts. All share the same basic design: two parallel inflatable tubes joined by a rigid metal frame, with one or more rigid seats attached. How they differ is in size and construction of the tubes, in whether the frame includes a standing platform, the type of anchoring system, and in the propulsion system.

Kick boats typically have tubes 8 feet long or less and are powered by oars or fins. Lightweight, they can be carried and launched wherever you can get to the water. They work well for lakes and for sluggish rivers lacking whitewater. Care must be exercised when anchoring in moving water, as the force of the water pulling against the tubes may cause them to dive underwater and flip the boat. Once off the water, the tubes can be deflated, the frame disassembled, and everything packed away in the trunk of a car.

Pontoon boats have bigger and longer tubes, wider frames, may have standing platforms, and accommodate one to three people. They carry enough gear for extended river trips and have an anchoring system that can be used in moving water. They can be hauled to the launch site, then assembled. Most owners carry them fully assembled on a small flatbed trailer.

Catarafts are bigger yet with tubes as large as 28 inches in diameter and up to 18 feet long. The frames are stronger, heavier, and wider than pontoon boats. They have enough cargo space to haul all the gear used for extended river trips for groups of three or more and are powered by oars or a small outboard motor. Their size and lack of maneuverability when compared to kick boats, pontoons, and rafts makes them better suited as point-to-point transport instead of on-the-go fishing platforms. They can be broken down into component parts and hauled in a pickup. More often they are hauled on a flatbed trailer.

My favorite day-trip boat is a kick boat rated for Class IV rapids. It has long but small diameter tubes with low water and wind resistance, is light enough to be maneuvered with fins while I fish either still or moving water, and can be inflated in minutes. It fits in my pickup bed with the deflated tubes attached to the frame.

Rafts

Inflatable rafts ranging in length from 13 to 16 feet and, fitted with rigid rowing frames, are perfect for two or three people on extended river trips. Rafts can carry all the gear necessary for night after night on the river. They are maneuverable and safe in the hands of an experienced and competent boat driver. More importantly, they are terrific fishing platforms with one person on the oars guiding the boat into fish-holding spots, the other casting from the front of the boat. The trip is even more enjoyable if

Kick boats and pontoons are equipped with oars for maneuvering through rapids and traveling long distances. Fins allow a subtle approach to nab big fish like this one.

Pontoons with standing platforms provide a higher sight window. A sunhat and polarized glasses help in spotting fish.

Note how most of the gear is loaded behind the rower. It counterbalances the weight of the front passenger and increases maneuverability.

both boaters are competent on the oars so it's easy to switch places regardless of what the river throws at the boat. Be aware that it's not all fun and games. Western rivers are known for gusty upriver winds that can make rowing downstream an exceptionally aerobic workout.

Inflatables come in two varieties. Self-bailing boats have an inflatable floor that forces water entering the boat to drain to the edges and out the holes along the sides. They are heavier and cost more than traditional rafts. Solid floor rafts, also known as bucket boats, require a bailing bucket to remove any water. Self-bailers actually serve to keep the occupants dryer and safer than the bucket boats. When a bucket boat fills with water, the boat driver now has to pilot a water-logged, heavy craft through the remainder of the rapid until the water is removed and the craft lightened.

Kayaks

Kayaks are another option for day-tripping or extended trips when supported by a gear boat. Kayaks, either the fiberglass traditional cockpit or the molded plastic sit-on-top variety, are fast, easy-to-maneuver, and they allow the angler to get close to the fish without spooking them. They are light and easy to toss in a pickup bed or atop a car rack. Basic models are inexpensive. As bells and whistles like anchor systems, rod holders, and other fishing accessories are added, the price climbs. One style comes with a pedal-powered propulsion system. Kayaks, like canoes, have a slim profile that allows access through narrow, tule-choked passages where other boats cannot go.

Anyone operating a cockpit model must know basic safety maneuvers like the Eskimo roll and how to extricate oneself when the boat is upside down. Storage space is limited so if you're the kind who likes to carry a ton of gear, kayaks won't work. You'll always have wet hands from water dripping off the double-bladed paddle. There is almost no dry area on a sit-on-top boat, limiting the use of expensive nonwaterproof cameras and cell phones. Sitting so low on the water makes sight fishing a challenge. Less susceptible to wind because of the low profile, they lose steerage as soon as the paddle is put down. The wind and current quickly whisk you away from where you intended to fish. Manufacturers have attempted to deal with the propulsion issue by adding pedal-powered fins or building a hole in the middle of boat so it can also be finned like a float tube.

At least one company is touting standup paddle boats as fishing craft. They are quick and easy to paddle, but they are a real challenge to fish from in the wind and limit the amount of gear carried.

These paddle-powered boats easily traveled upstream on the Flathead River. Pedal-powered models are becoming more popular as they can be maneuvered while the occupant fishes.

Canoes

We don't see many canoes on western rivers. Canoes are lightweight, easily carried on a cartop rack, launched and retrieved nearly everywhere, and hold up to three people in the longer models. They are constructed of aluminum, fiberglass, wood, or plastic, with plastic being the best overall choice for durability, ease of maintenance, and stealth. Casting is done from a sitting or kneeling position that strains my back just thinking about it. If the canoe is fitted with an outrigger, it's possible to stand up to cast, but the outrigger makes the canoe unsuitable for whitewater. They work best on lakes and rivers without whitewater. I've seen more flipped canoes on western rivers than any other watercraft.

Drift Boats

The drift boat, patterned after the McKenzie River boats designed by Tom Kaarhus and made famous by Woodie Hindman, feature a wide, flat bottom, high flared sides, narrow flat bow, and pointed or squared-off stern. This aesthetically pleasing, extremely stable fishing platform is a favorite of northwest fly fishers. The shallow-draft boat features a continuous rocker that allows it to spin on its center for easy maneuvering. First constructed of marine-grade plywood, most are now either aluminum or fiberglass, 16 to 18 feet long. Built to carry three people on day trips or two on extended river trips, in the hands of an excellent boat driver, they handle whitewater quite well and keep the occupants the driest and warmest of all human-powered boats. These high-sided boats get buffeted by those same upstream winds as other high-profile boats. Some manufacturers have responded by building low profile drift boats that offer less wind resistance but suffer a corresponding loss of ability to handle whitewater. My brother favors fishing from his drift boat because he can stay dry, stand up, move around, and anchor when necessary. The boats with a squared-off stern will accept a long-shaft outboard or electric motor. Basic hull weight of a fiberglass boat is roughly 250 pounds; aluminum runs three or four times as much. The size and weight requires a trailer. Most owners restrict themselves to designated launch sites. The adventuresome have been known to winch their boat down rock cliffs to access water not easily reached.

Johnboats

Johnboats, flat-bottom, low-side, square-end boats, get some use in the West. Built in sizes from barely big enough for one adult to more than 20 feet long, they are riveted aluminum, with one or more bench seats. In the smaller sizes they weigh about 100 pounds so they can be tossed in a pickup bed or on top of a car, then hand-carried to the water. Bigger sizes call for a trailer. Their low sides make them resistant to our western winds but susceptible to taking on water if piloted through rapids. They have plenty of floor space and make excellent fly-fishing craft on smaller lakes and slow-moving rivers. Some owners outfit their johnboats with an array of electronics like the bass tournament boats. The whitewater found on most western smallmouth rivers and the size of western lakes and reservoirs generally limit the use and popularity of johnboats.

Jet Boats

Big-water rivers like the Columbia and Snake see plenty of jet boats. Developed first in New Zealand, they are big, powerful, aluminum boats that rely on a waterjet that draws water through a series of impellers and stators in ever-increasing velocity. The high velocity water exits the pump through a moveable nozzle. The jetstream both steers and propels the boat. Lacking a propeller, jet boats can run up and down rivers in only inches of water. However, once the power is turned off, they turn into rudderless drifting barges. For that reason, and since the boats are too big to be rowed, they are most often used for moving from point to point where the occupants jump ship, then fish from shore or wade the shallows. Even under power they are not useable fly-fishing platforms.

A concern with jet boats, even on a river as large as the Snake, is that their sheer size, bulk, and speed create substantial wakes that swamp smaller boats, batter shorelines, and stir up sediment that chokes spawning redds. In the minds of many who float the Lower Salmon and Snake Rivers in human-powered craft, jet boats substantially detract from the experience.

V-Hulls

V-hulled boats, especially those extra-wide models up to 14 feet long that can be rowed, make good lake and slow-moving-river fly-fishing boats. My brother and I have explored many a lake and river in a 12-foot aluminum lake boat. We maneuvere it close to shore so the caster can toss flies into the bank structure. When anchored, it is stable enough for both of us to stand up and fish. The pointed front end is too cramped and unstable to fish from so we stow the anchor and gear there. If budget and personal tastes allow, a small outboard or electric motor can be added.

V-hulled boats are heavier than johnboats of the same size. They can be trailered, carried on cartop racks, or lashed into the bed of a pickup. A 14-footer is a challenge to wrestle into the water, but anything shorter can be hand-launched wherever two people can get it to the water.

Glitter Boats

Bass boats like the ones used by bass tournament pros are excellent flatwater fishing platforms, if you can get past the sticker shock and cost of operation. The broad beam, flat deck, and center console design have limited obstacles or obstructions to catch the fly line. The low sides make landing fish a breeze. Their glitzy paint, noise when under power, and conspicuous-consumption image might raise eyebrows among the fly-fishing

The V-hull can be modified to accommodate a stable fishing platform in the narrow front end. BEN ROMANS

Well-appointed boats come equipped with a rod holder. Aftermarket rod holders are available to fit any boat. If negotiating whitewater, make sure the rod is securely fastened in the holder.

community, but that could just be jealousy turning green. The best fly-fishing power boats share common characteristics—a center console, plenty of flat deck space, enclosed storage for gear, and a shallow draft.

Boat Accessories

The single most useful accessory for any fishing craft is a rod holder. Even when fishing from a float tube, I always have two rods rigged and ready for different fishing conditions. A strap-on rod holder can be easily added to a float tube to protect the second rod and keep it out of the way while fishing the first rod.

Newer models of drift boats are equipped with rod holders that run along the gunwale. Some raft rowing frames also have built-in rod holders. Boats lacking them are easy to retrofit in one of two ways. A length of flexible plastic tubing or 2" PVC can be attached to the gunwale with worm clamps and small screws. The reel hangs out the end, so if more than one rod is stored, the angler can run two tubes and insert one rod from either end. In the second approach, the foam-filled brackets attach to the gunwales. It's easier to get rods in and out of the brackets; the tubes provide more protection.

The second most useful accessory, and some would argue *the* most useful, is a second anchor to keep the boat from swing-ing in the current or wind. The second anchor is important when fishing deep in a lake, as it's next to impossible to maintain contact with the fly or get a good drift with a boat swinging and yawing in the wind. Of course, a second anchor necessarily implies having a first anchor. Small fishing boats rarely need fancy fluke-type anchors—mushroom anchors or lead triangles work under most flatwater fishing conditions. River anchors, especially on rivers with ledge rock or boulder bottoms, should be lead triangles or lengths of large-link chain, bundled and secured with a carabineer. These type are least likely to get hung up on the bottom. To avoid hangups, fluke anchors should only be used on rivers with mud, sand, or grass bottoms.

Always use the anchor when the boat is beached so you don't have to chase your boat downriver after a gently bobbing current unties the line wrapped around a bush. Wind gusts blast across the water without warning, so always wrap the anchor line around a tree or large rock. On rivers like the Columbia, which are subject to daily water release fluctuations from irrigation and power generating dams, you must exercise special care in anchoring. When beaching your boat for lunch or wade fishing, instead of dropping anchor in the water, land stern-first and pull the tail end and the anchor onto shore. The safest way to anchor is to establish a routine and follow it each time.

If other boat traffic allows, you can anchor a hard-sided boat or raft in fairly fast current. Pontoons should only anchor in soft current, and operators should make sure the bow is facing

When beaching your boat, pull the anchor onto shore. Wrap the anchor around a nearby tree or large rock, or bury it in the sand.

upstream directly into the current before anchoring. Otherwise, the pontoons may catch and be driven under by the current, flipping the boat. Let the oars trail in the water to keep the boat aligned with the current.

Folks often knot the end of their anchor rope to keep the line from slipping out of the pulley system. Bad choice. Eliminate the knot; if the anchor gets caught and heavy current starts to pull the boat under, you can slip the line and save your boat. Better to lose the anchor than lose your boat.

Fish Finders and Other Gear

These gadgets are essential for locating deep underwater structure, bait concentrations, and suspended smallmouth bass in stillwaters. Lake Washington is estimated to have 18,000 catchable-sized smallmouth spread across 18,000 surface acres. Blind casting is a near-futile exercise because most of the lake is barren of bass. Mounted on the front of the boat, a fish locator that looks down and out into casting range reveals whether fish are nearby and helps an angler avoid fishing where there are no fish. Small units fit pontoon boats and kayaks.

Waterproof gear bags, also referred to as dry bags, are used for holding the gear you don't want to get wet. On extended float trips, my tent, sleeping bag, sleeping pad, camp shoes, and personal gear go in one dry bag that gets strapped down to avoid being washed overboard in whitewater. A smaller dry bag holds my clothes for protection against weather changes. It includes fleece gloves, a nylon windshirt, balaclava, rain pants, and raincoat in addition to several light layers of clothes. If the weather turns nasty, I can stay on the water and catch fish rather than running for the beach.

A plastic ice chest, when not used to chill food or liquids, does double duty as a dry box. Make sure it's strapped down so it doesn't bounce out when running a rapid.

If you are on the water at night, make sure the boat is equipped with the necessary running lights, a headlamp for each occupant, and extra batteries.

Clear the Decks

This old naval expression directing sailors to stow gear and prepare for battle is apropos for fly fishing. All boats are festooned with objects that catch, snag, crimp, or snarl fly line when it is stripped off the reel. Loose floor boards, exposed screw heads, and metal braces that are not flush with the side of the boat drive me batty. Strap buckles, flapping straps, and open zippers on gear bags do the same. Anything that *can* catch a fly line *will* at some point, usually when the big fish of the day is in sight.

I recently fished with a friend in his boat, which had an annoying feature. The front seat had a retaining strap which snapped onto the seat back when the seat was folded down. When the seat was in use, the strap hung down about 8 inches

When not filled with ice, the ice chest can be used to store extra clothes, lunch, or extra fishing gear.

below the seat. I didn't have a stripping basket, so my fly line tangled on the strap with every cast. I quickly traded comfort for casting distance. I closed the seat and snapped the strap down. Sitting on the deck was a small price to pay for unhindered casting. Removable shock cord would be a better solution than the seat strap. The cord would hold the seat down when trailering the boat and could be removed before launching and stowed in the vehicle.

Before leaving home, inspect the boat for those line-catching objects, then tighten, tape, or otherwise cover them. Duct tape works well as a temporary cover; use silicone caulk for a more permanent fix. Don't use water-soluble caulk for obvious reasons. When on the water, keep zippers closed, buckles tight, tuck strap ends under the strap, and store gear bags where they are most likely to be out of the way. A nylon mesh bag can cover the motor and fuel lines when not being used. Stow all removable running lights, antennas, and other items that can get in the way of casting.

GPS

Several of the western smallmouth rivers like the Lower Salmon, Grande Ronde, and John Day are managed by the Bureau of Land Management. That agency produces a user guide and river map for each river it manages. These spiral-bound maps, printed on waterproof paper, detail boat launches, camping sites, rapids and other navigation hazards, as well as items of geographical and archeological interest. Each morning when I'm on the river, I'll review the map pages that cover that day's float, slip the map under a cam strap where it can be easily retrieved during the day to periodically refresh my recollection, then head down river.

But like all printed river maps, it's out of date by the time it hits the press. The always changing river adds to and subtracts from gravel bars, islands, and other landmarks with each high water event. And that's where a good GPS unit can make a difference. If you are doing a 70-mile float in five days, it helps to be able to pinpoint your position each day so you can break the float into manageable sections and finish the trip on time without having to slog through 20 miles of rowing against an upstream wind on the last day.

Drag Anchor

A drag anchor is a length of large-link chain attached to a line that is attached to the boat. It is used to slide along the bottom of slow-moving streams while holding the boat in the current, allowing the angler to cast without operating the oars. It is an effective method of boat control that allows a solo angler to fish likely looking spots while on the move without needing to control the boat with oars.

Here's why it should not be used. Dragging that chain along the bottom stirs up sediment that increases the turbidity of the water. If the chain runs over spawning nests or redds, it damages the site. It can easily shred weed beds that harbor insects and provide cover for young-of-the-year fish. It scrapes and scours the bottom in a manner not all that different than a scallop or oyster dredge. The river bottom is the beginning of the food chain, a chain that feeds every invertebrate or vertebrate that lives in the water or depends on anything that lives in the water. One person using a drag anchor on a river one time is not likely to irreparably damage that food chain. The risk of damage increases exponentially with each additional person who runs a drag chain down the same reach. It is a selfish way to fish without any regard for the environmental damage caused. It's also dangerous when used in fast current or broken bedrock as the chain may get wedged and pull the boat under.

When float-fishing without a partner, use a float tube or kick boat easily controlled by fins. The low profile and quiet approach—no chain dragging and clunking along the bottom—allows you to get closer to the fish without alerting them. Getting closer means a shorter, more accurate cast. Less line on the water makes for a greater chance of detecting the strike and hooking the fish.

Drift Casting

Like hitting a great drive in golf, there something quite satisfying about stripping handfuls of line, loading the rod and double hauling the longest possible cast to a fish on the other side of the river. But it's too tiring to do all day long. Most float-trip casts are short. The target is a chute, run, and foam pocket you get one chance to hit before the boat sweeps past and the next target of opportunity appears. Short, precise casts that put the fly in the best possible position to attract attention catch more fish than any other. The boat driver and caster work together—the driver maneuvering the boat within 50 feet of the target and the caster hitting the spot the first time.

Casting Safety

Two fly fishers casting out of a small boat with 9-foot-long rods can be a disaster complete with frayed nerves, tangled lines, and broken rod tips. Or it can be a pleasant experience filled with conversation, companionship, and two fish on at the same time. What determines the result is following a few simple guidelines, which become more important when using sinking lines and multiple weighted flies. A 250-grain Sink-Tip, looped to 15 feet of T-14 and followed by two weighted flies, makes for a potentially dangerous package in the hands of a caster who fails to follow the guidelines. Any lapse in concentration while casting can easily result in driving a hook into the caster or worse, the fishing partner. To minimize that risk, both casters should cast parallel to each other, either in the same direction or on the opposite side of the boat. They should never cast over or across each other.

Most fly fishers are right-handed. When shooting toward the shore, the person in the front of the boat will face the bank or slightly downstream and cast so the line passes over the bow, the fly headed toward the bank. The caster in the stern, if casting in

The Lower Umpqua Fly Casters hold a "tube-a-rama" outing on the river. A personal flotation device would complete the picture.

the same direction as the bow caster, will have the line pass over the middle of the boat, between both anglers. Because of the increased risk of injury caused by the line and sharp, pointy things passing between the anglers, the more skillful caster should be placed in the stern. When there are three in the boat and two are casting in the same direction, it is critical to have the best caster in the stern to minimize the risk to the person rowing the boat. Lefties, make the proper adjustments.

If the casters have never fished together—so each is unaware of the other's skill level and casting tendencies, it makes sense to communicate one's intention before beginning the cast by saying "casting." The cast should be completed before the other angler begins to make a cast. Anytime the rod tip is elevated, it's a good practice to alert the other angler by saying "tip up."

Boating Safety

There are no surprises in the American Canoe Association study of kayak and canoe fatalities. The top five deadly mistakes are:

1. Failure to wear personal floatation devices
2. The water or weather was too cold
3. The victims were inexperienced
4. Alcohol or drugs were involved
5. The victims were nonswimmers

My father was a Red Cross swimming instructor who taught all his children to swim before we could read. We also lived on a river for years growing up, spending most summer afternoons in the water. No smallmouth is worth drowning for. Before venturing out on the water, learn to swim. This increases survival chances if the boat dumps. Check with the local Y, park district, or American Red Cross for when and where swimming lessons are offered in your community.

Know that alcohol or drugs have no place on the water. They impair judgment and reflexes, and they contribute to dehydration on hot days and hypothermia on cold ones. Additionally, you can get cited for operating a boat under the influence. Save the alcohol for the beach when you are done for the day—it will taste better when you are safely ashore.

Inexperience can be mitigated with a dose of common sense, coupled with planning and organization. When you get a new craft, curb your impulse to immediately launch on a new river. Instead, take it to a flatwater site and practice rowing to determine how it responds with different oar strokes. Notice how fatiguing a front stroke is compared to a back stroke. Practice the pivot stroke and cross stroke so you can execute them on moving water without thinking or hesitation. My fishing buddy's pontoon reacts slower and draws more water than my kick boat. That means I have learned to pick a different line through rapids and set up that line sooner when driving his boat.

Once you know how your boat handles, get river-running training by a professional. Think back to before you got your first driver's license. Before you could take the license exam, you had to take Driver's Education, which included classroom work and several hours behind the wheel where you were trained by a professional. Getting trained in river running by a professional—learning how to read rivers, how to use your boat, and how to perform basic rescue techniques simply makes sense.

Now to the issue of cold. Free-flowing western rivers are mostly snowmelt, so early season runoff brings bone-chilling, muscle-cramping temperatures. Do not count on being able to swim in frigid waters. Even in spring and early summer, though air temperatures may hit 90 degrees, the water can easily be 50 degrees or less. Idaho's Clearwater River stays cool throughout the summer due to cold water released from the bottom of Dworshak Dam, despite daytime air temperatures exceeding 110 degrees.

Getting dumped into the cold water induces what is known as cold shock response. When your body gets dumped into cold water, that immersion triggers an automatic gasp reflex. If your head goes under or a wave splashes your face, water can be sucked into your lungs during the gasp. And things only get worse. Wearing a personal floatation device (PFD) is the best way to keep your head above water. Properly fitted floats are designed to do just that. If you can beat the first phase of cold shock response, then you can focus on executing the maneuvers necessary to get out of the water.

Fly fishers are wedded to waders that do a good job of protecting against wind and cold so long as they don't fill with water. If you fish on the edges of the season when water and air temperatures get downright cold, think seriously about trading your waders for a dry suit, like those worn by kayakers. They have zippers in all the right places and keep you dry and warm.

Remedial Rowing

Rowing a boat is really pretty simple. To move forward, dip the oars and push forward. Repeat. The forward, or push stroke, is the weakest rowing stroke, as it uses only the small arm muscles. To move back, dip the oars and pull back. Repeat. The pull, or backward stroke, is the strongest as it involves leg, upper body, back, and arm muscles. To pivot the boat, dip one oar and pull back. To spin the boat, dip both then pull back on one while pushing forward on the other.

A key to safely operating a boat is to understand the effect of those simple strokes. For example, the pivot stroke will turn the boat, but also moves the craft laterally. The cross (spin) stroke turns the boat without repositioning it relative to the bank. The push stroke accelerates the downstream momentum

Fair-skinned fishers need to pay close attention to sun protection. Buff, hat, gloves, long sleeves, and long pants effectively cover all the skin. A quick dunk in the water prevents overheating.

while the pull stroke slows the boat, allowing more time to fish likely looking water and avoid obstacles. To learn these strokes and how they affect your boat, find flatwater and practice, practice, practice.

If you're like me, your day job puts you at a desk pushing computer keys, not a task designed to prepare your hands for the rigors of rowing. Wearing bike or weight-lifting gloves will protect your hands from oar-induced blisters. Frequent switches between fishers and rowers on two-person floats also calms friction hotspots, but make those position changes only when beached or in calm, shallow water.

Basic Avoidance Maneuver

In order to avoid "obstacles," a word that encompasses more than fixed objects, the rower needs to recognize and understand them. OFPA, the name for the basic avoidance maneuver, is easy to remember: Observe, Face the danger, Pull, and Align.

1. Observe. While you are multitasking—positioning the boat, dodging trees and awkward casts by your boat partner, spotting fish, and eating a snack—make sure you look downstream to observe upcoming obstacles.

2. Face the danger. Once an obstacle is observed, point the bow (downstream end of boat) toward the obstruction, do a couple of quick pivot strokes to create an escape angle which puts the boat about 45 degrees across current from the obstacle.

3. Pull. Use the back stroke to overcome the downstream momentum. The first few strokes control the speed, the next few strokes ferry the boat away from the obstacle. Learning how many strokes are necessary is much like learning to steer a car; most beginners row a zigzag course until they learn how their boat reacts to each current.

4. Align. Use the cross stroke to straighten the boat so the bow is downstream and you are running parallel with the bank again.

If avoiding the obstacle takes you away from the preferred fishing line or puts you too close to the bank, point the bow at the bank and repeat steps three and four until you have achieved the correct casting distance.

On rivers, match the rate of observation, information processing, and action to the current: the more obstacles and the faster the current, the faster you need to OFPA in order to set up for the next obstruction.

Steep canyon walls means the rafters are committed for long stretches of river before the next take-out. Experienced boaters always carry emergency and repair equipment.

A sunshade can be fashioned using a tarp, lengths of line, a few tent stakes, and a lightweight aluminum pole.

Gear for overnight river trips is listed in the Float Trip Appendix. The clothing list should be adjusted to fit the season of the float—just know that even in the heat of summer, getting soaked in a thunderstorm and chilled by a brisk wind are possibilities. I rarely use the foul weather clothing listed in the appendix, but I never leave home without it.

Float Trip Logistics

Long before launching a boat, you need to plan and prepare for the adventure. In other words, you need to determine the logistics of the trip. Start with a basic checklist of items, then address these specifics to your planned adventure:

- Type of boat
- Water conditions
- Skill level of each boat driver
- Camping facilities available along the route
- Miles to be traveled each day
- River hazards
- Optimal floating time
- Mandatory gear for the specific water
- Required permits
- Best fishing time period

Several western smallmouth rivers, like the Lower Salmon and John Day, are managed by the BLM under a permit system. When planning a trip to any western river, first determine the management authority, then carefully read their river rules. For example, the Lower Snake requires a permit, a self-contained toilet, a fire pan (all ash and charcoal must be carried out), and group size is limited. The John Day limits the number of launches from May 20 through July 10 on some portions of the river. Half the permits for the restricted period are released March 1, the second half on May 1.

Once you've selected the river, the next choice is what reach of the river are you going to float. Make sure the planned daily mileage is not too long to be comfortably fished in the available daylight. Running a river at night is asking for trouble. Current velocity, your style of fishing (run-and-gun, or probe every spot), time to wade, and the number of fish hooked are only a few of the variables affecting the distance traveled in a day. I've spent all day on the water barely covering 2 miles, landed the boat at dusk, and walked back upstream to get my truck. I've also covered 15 miles and had to use a flashlight to spot the cut in the shoreline brush where I'd left the truck. Missing the spot would have added another 5 miles to the float in full dark and the same number of miles hiking back to the truck. On wilderness rivers, 5 to 8 miles per day is a good rule of thumb. Rivers with developed access generally have boat launches separated by a normal day's float.

When selecting a camp, consider what time of day it will get sun and shade. Early morning sun makes it easier to get everyone up and ready to get on the river.

Part of the planning process is familiarizing yourself with water flows for the selected stretch so when you hit the river it's in shape to fish. When the John Day River is running 25,000 cfs, it's possible to run Clarno to Cottonwood—a distance of 70 miles—in a day, but fishing, from boat or bank, is out of the question. At 6,500 cfs, the river allows plenty of fishing time while still covering 15 miles in a day. To cover that same distance at 400 cfs, plan on run-and-gun fishing while rowing. Below that level, expect to drag even the lightest boat through some reaches.

The USGS National Water Information System (www.water data.usgs.gov/nwis) offers real-time and historical water flows on most every river of importance in the West. The most useful searches are by state or drainage. Once the real-time flow is known, that can be compared with the flow recommendations on the BLM websites based on the type of boat you plan to use. For example, on the John Day, the BLM Boating General Information webpage suggests 800 cfs is the minimum flow for a drift boat or 500 cfs for an inflatable raft.

The various editions of the *DeLorme Atlas & Gazetteer* are good general resources that show primary and secondary roads in great detail. Benchmark Maps also publishes a *Road and Recreation Atlas* for each of the 11 western states. I have both for several states, and between the two, I can find my way to even the most remote boat launches and water access sites. Google Earth is another excellent resource for tracing river

routes and potential camping spots. Bear in mind that the satellite photos may be a few years old, and river courses, hazards, and channels change with each high water event. What you see on your computer monitor may differ from what you actually experience on the river.

Local fly shops in the area you intend to float are a good source of information. Many of them keep tabs on water levels, navigation hazards, and current fishing conditions. Phone conversations are nice, but face to face works better, particularly if you first spend some money in their shop as part of the exchange. Local paddling clubs found through the magic of the Internet are another source of water and perhaps fishing advice.

The gathering of all this knowledge is intended to allow you to plan a trip that matches your goals, your boat's performance capabilities, and your skill level. You want to end each day and the trip as healthy as when you started. Kick boats work just fine on lakes and reservoirs, but are unsuitable, even hazardous, on Class II and above whitewater rivers. My kick boat is rated for Class IV rapids, but I've seen some Class IV rapids that would eat my boat. If faced with a hazard beyond your skill or the boat's capabilities, lining the boat through the sticky spot or portaging downstream are both time-honored and safe ways of dealing with those situations.

What follows are some basic terms any prospective rafter needs to understand.

Class

River sections have a class designation and are rated according to the American Whitewater Affiliation International Scale of River Difficulty. Individual rapids also carry a class designation using the same scale. Class I is the easiest to boat, having only a few riffles and small waves. At the complete other end of the spectrum is Class VI, bordering on the extreme of navigability, nearly impossible and very dangerous. Class II has easy rapids with waves up to 3 feet. Class III has high, irregular waves and narrow passages that may require complex maneuvering. Class IV features long, difficult rapids with constricted passages requiring sequential, precise maneuvering in turbulent water. Class V is more difficult than Class IV but not quite as dangerous as Class VI.

Western rivers that offer multiday trips all run through remote country. Contrary to the notion that smallmouth only live in placid streams, these smallmouth rivers are all rated Class II and above—partly a function of the rapids themselves and partly because of their remote locations where help, in the event of a mishap, may be days away. Many of the rivers have poor cell phone reception. Even satellite phone signals, which travel in a straight line, may not escape the deep canyons, save when the satellite is directly overhead. It's important to have all the appropriate gear and requisite water skills to insure that the trip really is an adventure to remember for all the wonderful companionship and outstanding fishing, rather than for unpleasant mishaps created by lack of preparation.

The difficulty or ease of running a rapid varies with the amount of water flowing through the hazard. Some become more difficult in lower flows, others more difficult at higher flows. If any boat operator in the group has doubts about how to safely navigate a rapid, take a few moments to stop and scout the run. Talk about it. The more experienced boat operators should describe their read of the water, point out what to avoid, explain the best line through the rapid, and discuss what to do if a boat gets in trouble so that others get the benefit of their experience.

Buy and wear either a Type I or III personal floatation device and make sure it is properly adjusted. Do not assume you can don your float "as needed." I've been knocked out of a boat by a sweeper in an otherwise benign reach of the river. Most casual boaters leave the straps too loose, trading perceived comfort for safety and effectiveness. Once the float is on and the straps tightened, have your boating companion yank upward on the lapels. This simulates pulling you out of the water into the boat. If the vest shifts, the straps are too loose. An improperly adjusted float won't keep your head out of the water and may even hamper your ability to swim to safety. Attach a pealess whistle to each personal floatation device.

Lower Clarno rapids on Oregon's John Day has reversals and holes in high water that demand full attention and competent boat driving. At low water, it turns into a rock garden.

Take the time to beach the boat and scout the rapid. Flipping a boat and losing all your gear and perhaps more would be a tragedy.

Western rivers are susceptible to strong upstream winds that have blown unsecured gear out of boats. Make sure anything left in the boat is securely fastened to prevent its loss.

Some states, like Oregon, require floats be worn at all times by those under a certain age. Enforcement officers are on the river to make sure the rule is followed. If the wearer is mature enough to know when and how to use one, add a PFD-mounted river knife.

Flow

The rate at which water runs past a measuring gauge is expressed in terms of cfs, or cubic feet per second. The actual rate may vary above or below the gauge depending on additional water from tributaries or water diverted into irrigation canals. As you gain experience on a river, the flow numbers begin make sense and allow you to anticipate river hazards.

Gradient

Expressed as the number of feet per mile the river drops over its course, gradient of most smallmouth streams is less than that of trout rivers. The John Day drops an average of 11 feet per mile. By comparison, the upper part of Oregon's McKenzie River cascades an average of 60 feet per mile, while the same river where the valley widens near Springfield only drops 7 feet per mile. Once the river runs into the Willamette, smallmouth start showing up in the catches.

Hazards

Strainers are obstructions, usually trees or logjams, resting in the water with part of the obstruction underwater. They are easy to see but must be avoided, as the current pulls people and boats under the tree and strains them through the branches. If you end up in the water, never try to swim under a strainer. Water flowing at 3 miles per hour exerts 64 pounds of pressure per square inch against a solid object, making extrication challenging. Try to swim over it or climb on top.

Sweepers are trees overhanging the water, sporting branches that sweep passing boats clean of occupants and gear.

Stoppers are waves where the crest curls back upstream on itself, flipping boats or filling them with water.

Holes are river features created by water flowing over and around an obstacle at a near-vertical gradient, causing the current to circulate back up to the obstacle. Boats can get flipped or trapped in holes.

Low-head dams are a seductive hazard found wherever rivers are diverted for irrigation. Their smooth, steep drop gives the appearance of an amusement park water slide. In reality, they create the ultimate hole with little chance of escape. Portage around them. If you doubt the danger, do an Internet search on "the drowning machine."

Horn Rapids Dam on the Yakima River, a 12-foot concrete low-head dam located a quarter-mile below Horn Rapids Park, is an shining example of how an innocuous-looking man-made structure can be a killer. Nothing more than a high ledge, the water pouring over the dam creates a reverse hydraulic, trapping whatever floats over it. The force of the water falling over the dam excavates the stream bottom into deep holding water. In the interest of angler safety, the area is wisely closed to fishing for 400 feet below the dam. Despite the danger, every few years someone tries to run the dam in a power boat. All have failed. Some have died.

Right and Left

River right and river left are always determined from the perspective of an observer looking downstream.

The All Important V

Most river obstacles that can harm a boat—rootwads, barely submerged trees, sharp rocks, and more—leave a disturbance on the water surface in the form of a V with the pointy end directed upstream. Put the boat into position to avoid the pointy end, as well as the ripples curling upstream and the surrounding edges, which may indicate tree branches or other obstructions.

Conversely, when viewing a rapid, if the pointy end of the V, also known as the tongue, faces downstream, following the tongue provides the safest path. On long stretches of white water, like the John Day's Upper and Lower Clarno Rapids, which are filled with obstructions, you need to make successive maneuvers to take advantage of successive downstream Vs. If there are multiple Vs pointing downstream in any given rapid, the one with the longest legs is the best route.

River Bends

As the northwestern rivers drift through deep canyons cut into lava from the Columbia River Basalt Group, they wend around oxbows, those U-shaped sharp bends in the river. Those bends present a different challenge. Understanding physics makes reading water easier. The current at the outside edge of the turning arc travels faster than the inside edge. The faster current is usually over deeper water but tends to drive boats into the bank. The slow current on the inside edge may be too shallow to navigate. Your task is to split the difference by taking a line that avoids the hazards at each edge. Look for the current seam that allows safe passage.

River Braids

As flows drop and midchannel gravel bars appear, the river may separate into one or more braids, some of which may not have enough water for safe passage. All other elements being equal, the braid on the downhill side of the river will have the most water. It has the water you see plus water percolating through the gravel bar into the braid.

Lava deposits of the Columbia River Basalt Group shape and channel the desert rivers of Washington, Oregon, and Idaho.

Point to Point Floating

Point to point day trips usually involve two or more anglers, two vehicles, and one hard-sided boat or two inflatables. One vehicle is left at the take-out, the other loaded with gear and driven to the launch site. At the end of the float, the anglers load up the boat and gear and retrieve the upstream car. I've managed several solo trips where I dropped my boat at the launch, drove to the take-out, then rode my bicycle back to the launch. You can reverse the car and bicycle ride, but I've found that after a full day of fishing, I'm not really in the mood for a bicycle ride in the dark.

Multiday trips often involve a commercial shuttle service. An extra car key is dropped off with the shuttle operator before you head to the launch site. The shuttle operator picks up the vehicle from the launch site and drops it at the take-out, timed for the day you arrive at the take-out. The best shuttle operators move your vehicle from the launch site and store it at a secure location until the delivery date to minimize the risk of the smashed window syndrome.

Still another floating variation is a possibility. If the boat has an outboard or electric motor, run it first upstream, then float back down to the launch. I've even done this on rivers with modest flows, rowing a kick boat or drift boat upstream to get to a great run not otherwise accessible, and fished my way back to the launch.

If the trip involves more than one boat, consider yet another option. Fishing styles differ, rowing styles differ, and boat driving skills differ. My tendency is to thoroughly fish the good water and push quickly through the less favorable water. Other boat drivers are deliberate in setting up their boat for running a rapid, while the more experienced and skillful drivers prefer making on-the-spot decisions. How this all plays out is that boats with different driver-types may get separated—out of hearing, sight, and signal. Those differences make it important to discuss a plan before getting on the water each day. The plan should include a clear understanding of the intended camping or take-out site for the day, as well as the no-later-than time for all boats to be at the appointed spot. It's no fun to be on a river with no effective means of communicating with the other boats when it's time to be at the camping spot but you are not clear on the location or think you may have floated past the site while focused on fishing.

The plan should include a clear understanding of which rapids will be scouted and from which side of the river. If the boats are beached on both sides of the river, it's difficult to discuss the hazard, determine the best line to avoid the hazard, and gain the collective wisdom of all hands shouted over the roar of the rapid. As part of scouting, the group should determine which boat, generally the one with the most skilled driver, will go first. The other boats then follow the line, gaining experience in reading the water.

Look for campsites where the boat can be safely tied up. The best ones have a flat, wind-protected spot to set up the kitchen and nearby flat tent sites.

Note how all the boats are properly secured. Anchor lines are set, the boats are rafted together, and they're tethered to large rocks.

If you intend to release your fish, crush the barb before tying on the fly and carry forceps to remove any deeply hooked fly.

The release or retain decision should include, among other things, an understanding of the level of fishing pressure on the water, capacity of the water to support fish, the time of year (prespawn, postspawn), the relative size and overall number of fish in the water, and the smallmouth life cycle. In other words, fly fishers should approach the release or kill decision with as much effort at educating themselves as they put into learning how to catch the fish in the first place. Stewardship and conservation of the resource should not automatically result in catch-and-release of every smallmouth on every water.

Not all fish are suited for all waters. As the fisheries biologists learned over time and mostly by error, brook trout are not well suited for living in alpine lakes. They reproduce in waters where rainbows and cutthroat cannot, and quickly populate the water in greater numbers than the food supply in the water can adequately support. The brookies stunt and develop long, snakey bodies that are mostly head and mouth. In short, they lose their sporting appeal.

Smallmouth may have that same capacity. Fisheries science demonstrates that smallmouth sometimes dominate and outcompete other species. Before smallmouth were introduced into the Yakima River, northern pikeminnow were the apex predator. Once the smallmouth established themselves, they replaced the northern pikeminnow. In fact, in all the years that

In some western rivers, the numbers of fish outstrip the available food supply, leading to huge numbers of small bass. Those hungry fish can decimate a food source, altering the web of life in that water.

I've fished the reach of the Yakima where smallmouth reign, I've never caught a northern pikeminnow. According to Washington fish biologists, smallmouth dominate largemouth and increase their numbers more effectively despite their relative equal fecundity.

For years in my writing and my speaking engagements, I took the position that every large female smallmouth was sacred, to be returned to the water with great haste and care. I no longer believe that to be good stewardship when practiced in all waters. It depends on a number of factors present in the lake or river.

Some smallmouth waters have a huge biomass of fish. There is one western river, the John Day, where it takes no special skill to hook 50 smallmouth from a single riffle, 200 bass in a day. The numbers of fish in the water are simply staggering. Yet the numbers of desirable-sized fish are relatively few. Most are 8 to 11 inches with only a few multipound fish. That's because the food supply of this fertile river is consumed by an excessive number of mouths. Every fish gets some food, but few fish get enough food to grow to quality size. There's the rub. Do we want a fishing experience based on quantity—where what matters is the number of fish hooked? Or do we want the experience of quality? Do we want a day on the water with fewer fish to the net, but with a greater likelihood that one or more of them will be a trophy?

Oregon adopted a set of retention regulations on the John Day River some years ago intended to create a quality fishing experience on a select portion of the river. Retention is allowed throughout the river, with no minimum size. However, a slot limit is imposed in the most heavily used section in an effort to minimize the number of large fish killed. On the middle reach of the river, all smallmouth between 12 and 16 inches must be released, and only one fish longer than 16 inches may be retained each day. The slot limit makes sense, at least in theory. I'm not sure that science supports the entire regulation. My sense of the matter, based on more than half a century of fly fishing, is that science and angler behavior—fly fishers in particular—don't mesh. Science doesn't take into consideration how well fly fishers have embraced Lee Wulff, nor does science account for those anglers who fail to read or follow the regulations.

The management issue goes back to a combination of the catch-and-release mindset and the tendency of anglers to retain the big fish. I freely acknowledge being part of the catch-and-release problem. Until recently I had not intentionally killed a smallmouth bass since 1972. To cease being part of the problem required a significant change in my thinking, but I now believe retention is necessary on waters that are overpopulated with small fish in order to achieve a quality instead of quantity fishing experience. On waters with a high density of smaller bass, anglers should retain some fish. The finite food supply then benefits a fewer number of fish resulting in more bigger fish. It may also require fishery managers to increase daily bag limits on selected waters.

Of course, not all smallmouth waters have a high density of bass. When fishing places like Duck Valley Reservoir, producer of the Nevada state record smallmouth, which have a low den-

Ever-expanding smallmouth populations can result in exciting, fast-paced fishing. Aggressive management regulations like slot limits and increased bag limits may be necessary to preserve the quality of the fishery. GENE TRUMP

sity of fish, it makes sense to employ the catch-and-release ethic. In order to make that determination, anglers need to educate themselves about each water they fish. Conservation and stewardship is not a "one size fits all" proposition.

Here's an analogy: You are an educated consumer about to buy a house for your family that includes school-aged children. Before finalizing the purchase, during the review period, it's time for due diligence. It's important to learn about the quality of the local schools your children will attend. You get on the Internet to check how the school district and the individual schools where your children might attend are rated. You want to live in a safe neighborhood, so you drive the area around the prospective house, looking for cars up on blocks, sketchy characters, and other such issues. You might even park your car, walk around the neighborhood, and ring doorbells of prospective neighbors to inquire about any neighborhood issues. You check out the local shopping to see how far it is to the nearest grocery store, shopping mall, coffee shop, and gas station. You might even check the level of police activity, review flood plain maps, determine the nearby zoning, and check with the planning department to inquire about any new roads or planned commercial development. What you won't do is buy the first house for sale that you see.

I'm not suggesting that the decision to keep a fish is as important as buying a house for your family. I am suggesting that it's important to actively participate in conservation and stewardship of our fishing resources. It is not someone else's job. It is not solely the state fish and game department's job. It is not solely the task of national organizations like the International Fly Fishing Federation, Trout Unlimited, and Izaak Walton League. Nor is it solely the job of local fly-fishing clubs. It is the task of everyone who uses the resource.

Salmonid versus Smallmouth: A Northwest Conundrum

Smallmouth were first introduced into a private lake in Washington's San Juan Islands in 1923. The following year some 5,000 fish originally slated for Seattle's Lake Washington were planted in the Yakima River, near the town of Prosser. Within two years, a 6-pound Yakima River fish took second place in a *Field & Stream* fishing contest. A mere 40 miles of river and a single low-head dam separated those smallmouth from the Columbia River. A few miles south of the Yakima confluence, the Snake and Columbia Rivers join. All three rivers run through courses cut into the lava of the Columbia River Basalt. In other words, all three rivers are excellent smallmouth habitat. Those 5,000 bass successfully spawned in the Yakima. Their progeny ran downstream and found the Columbia equally hospitable. Soon the smallmouth spread into the Snake and elsewhere. A world-class fishery was born, but all was not well in those rivers.

Those in favor of smallmouth bass populating rivers where salmon, steelhead, and trout swim clash head-on with those who champion salmonids. The die-hard salmonid crowd slurs the smallmouth, calling it an invasive species and the ruination of the great salmon runs of the past. In truth the negative impacts of overfishing in the ocean, dams with no fish ladders, logging and road-building practices that choke spawning streams, and

Climate change results in warmer water temperatures in what has been anadromous salmonid spawning and rearing habitat. The warmer water has drawn smallmouth into that territory, leading to more bass-salmonid interactions.

Northwest bass fly fishers rarely face competition on the water. There never are more than an handful of fly fishers on this 28-mile long prime smallmouth lake.

Smallmouth have been introduced into western desert reservoirs. In the proper setting, they help maintain a balanced fishery.

urban sprawl that lays waste to travel corridors, spawning grounds, and rearing habitat are what have caused declining salmon populations. It's much easier to blame a fish than to look in the mirror and lay blame where much of it lies. The more rational merely refer to smallmouth as a nonnative species and recognize that smallmouth are here to stay. Salmon and steelhead have the law on their side with protections in both state and federal statutes; smallmouth have the benefit of that old saw, "possession is nine-tenths of the law," as they live in the rivers year-round while the salmonids merely pass through. Rather than a rule of law, smallmouth's possession of a river is a rule of force. Smallmouth chow down on salmon fry and some smolts. Rarely, if ever, is the reverse true.

The salmon-smallmouth issue has an interesting twist: the fly-fishing and tournament smallmouth anglers predominantly practice catch-and-release. The salmon anglers who damn the smallmouth for eating salmon fry and smolts are a consumptive crowd who kill every legal-sized fish they bring to the boat.

Federal and state legislators are in the fish management business. For example, the Washington legislature imposed the following mandate on the Fish and Wildlife Department:

The department shall conserve the wildlife and food fish, game fish, and shellfish resources in a manner that does not impair the resource. In a manner consistent with this goal, the department shall seek to maintain the economic well-being and stability of the fishing industry in the state. The department shall promote orderly fisheries and shall enhance and improve recreational and commercial fishing in this state.

In an effort to cater to all constituent groups while pleasing none, the legislature created multiple competing interests in those few words. Food fish are different than gamefish, so conserving one may come at the expense of the other. Conservation of resources may clash with economic well-being and stability of the fishing industry. Recreational and commercial fishing interests are clearly at odds when it comes to salmon. Enhancing one interest necessarily restricts the other, as evidenced by the new Columbia River Management plan that realigns catch quotas to allocate more fish to recreational anglers. A recent state appellate court case, much to the dismay of the commercial fishers, interpreted the phrase "fishing industry" to include both sport and commercial fishing interests.

Salmon is the cultural king of northwest fish. The Native American tribes were salmon-based societies and that culture continues today. A substantial commercial salmon fishing industry targets different salmon species depending on relative abundance and market price. Add to the mix recreational salmon fishers who hit the water when the fish return from the ocean.

Washington classifies salmon as a food fish. Smallmouth are a gamefish. By mandate, the WDFW manages salmon, at

Baitfish patterns like the Clouser Minnow are excellent imitations of salmon smolts. Smaller patterns best imitate the fall chinook fry. Both will catch fish for weeks after the naturals have migrated downstream. JAY NICHOLS

the expense of gamefish. That's what the law implies and that clearly reflects the culture of the northwest where salmon is king. Northwest steelhead, biologically nothing more than rainbow trout that runs from freshwater to spend years pigging out in the ocean before returning to freshwater to spawn, is the regent in waiting. Fishing writers from Zane Grey forward lionized steelhead as the acme of freshwater gamefish to such a degree that the fish has attracted aficionados who attribute almost mythical qualities to it. In Washington, the steelhead is a gamefish and it too, by federal statute, is managed over the top of smallmouth.

Before anyone's hackles get raised over the management hierarchy that elevates a food fish over a gamefish and selects one gamefish at the expense of another, know that the hierarchy is supported by science. Dietary studies demonstrate that smallmouth, particularly those of a certain size, eat fish. To experienced smallmouth fishers, that doesn't come as a surprise, as many of the best smallmouth flies imitate forage fish. But that was not the thinking last century.

Ben Hur Lampman, author of *Coming of the Pond Fishes*, wrote, the bass "would prove himself, if given the opportunity, the best friend of our salmon and trout." David Starr Jordan, a noted ichthyologist of that era and first president of Stanford, asserted the smallmouth would limit their diets to minnows, suckers, and chubs. The state and tribal fisheries biologists in Oregon, Washington, and Idaho who are trying to retain, establish, or expand anadromous salmonid populations,

many of which are Endangered Species Act–listed populations, wish those earlier words were true. They are not and may never have been true.

The WDFW did a decade-long study of species interaction on the Yakima River prior to adding more hatchery salmon and steelhead to the river. The river has spring, summer, and fall chinook and steelhead runs that spawn in the upper river basin. After a successful spawn, the fall chinook fry, spring chinook, and steelhead smolts head downriver and must escape the hungry maws of northern pikeminnows, channel catfish, and smallmouth bass. The scope of predation depends on a number of factors, including water temperature, velocity, and turbidity; however, one fact is clear. When fall chinook fry meet concentrations of bass, the bass wreak mayhem on the fry. Interestingly, naturally spawned fry suffer the most, as they are smaller than hatchery fry and available in the river for a longer period of time. Other studies show that the more days subyearling chinook and smallies occupy the same river space, the more chinook fall prey to the bass.

On rivers controlled by dams or those which receive hatchery supplementation, fish managers have tricks they can use to minimize predation. Since studies show that size is the biggest variable in whether smallmouth eat natural or hatchery fry, hatcheries could hold their fry longer to allow them to attain greater size. Holding fry longer in the hatchery has its own set of concerns. And on dam-controlled rivers, the water managers could increase the volume of water releases timed to flush fry out of the river faster, making them vulnerable for a shorter period of time. As might be expected, problems abound with this practice as well.

Logic would indicate that the greatest consumers of salmon fry would be the largest smallmouth, if only because the large fish have a greater total calorie consumption demand. Yet logic fails here. The greatest offenders are the 8- to 12-inch small-mouth. And, as mentioned, the consumption all runs one way. According to WDFW Warmwater Fish Program Manager Bruce Bolding, he knows of no studies showing that salmonids prey on or have any impact on smallmouth.

Responding to the legislative marching orders that pit species one against the other, WDFW has tweaked the Yakima River smallmouth bass retention regulations several times over the past few years. The most recent change intended to combat the growing relative abundance of smallmouth, completely removed all size and retention limits. The WDFW is also trying to reach out to the fly-fishing community in an effort to get more fly fishers hooked on smallmouth. Both actions are an effort to encourage anglers to harvest smallmouth from that river.

Similar circumstances occur in other western states. Oregon's North Umpqua River is a destination steelhead stream that draws fly fishers from around the world to fish its storied waters. Any river sporting a section named "The Holy Water" attracts

Culling a few bass of this size would help restore the balance between the fish and the food that feeds them all. GENE TRUMP

Thoughtful conservation insures the continued pleasures of fishing for generations to come. We all owe intelligent stewardship to the sport we love.

Western smallmouth country is gorgeous country.

plenty of attention and defenders who strive mightily to protect that fish run. Summer steelhead that run the gauntlet of natural and manmade hazards to spawn in the upper reaches produce offspring, which must navigate the mainstem Umpqua's plentitude of smallmouth bass to reach the open ocean.

Smallmouth are not native to the river and, unlike John Day River bass, were not intentionally introduced. One story has the 1964 flood swamping a fish hatchery and releasing thousands of smallmouth into the river. Another story holds that the fish escaped from a flooded private pond. Whatever the real story, the bass have made their home throughout the river, to the delight of smallmouth anglers and the dismay of salmonid fishers. In 2013 Oregon's Department of Fish and Wildlife bumped the smallmouth retention limit up to 15 fish per day and removed all size restrictions in an effort to dent the bass population.

Oregon introduced smallmouth into the John Day River above Tumwater Falls in 1971 after carefully conducting studies to determine the potential impact smallmouth would have on out-migrating salmon and steelhead smolts. The Oregon Department of Fish and Wildlife determined that the lower river was mainly a migration corridor for anadromous fish and the only resident fish population was northern pikeminnow. The studies showed that the smolts headed downstream during periods of spring runoff with cold water temperatures before the

smallmouth began actively feeding. Stomach sampling done after the smallmouth were introduced confirmed little smallmouth impact.

The natural order of our world is evolutionary change. Much of the change is apparent only when viewed in geologic time of thousands or even millions of years. Climate change is more rapid as the effects are measurable within a few years or decades at the most. 2012 was the hottest year on record in the United States. If those record temperatures are repeated over the course of years into the future, coldwater fish will suffer. Their niche will be filled by warmwater fish like smallmouth. Natural disasters like the Wallow Fire in Arizona altered the relationship of trout and smallmouth in the Black River. The sediment washed into the river by snowmelt and rain killed the trout and smallmouth expanded to fill that gap.

Researchers from the University of Washington School of Aquatic and Fishery Sciences and School of Environmental and Forestry Sciences have documented an increase in water temperature on the John Day and predict a drastic reduction of habitat for salmon, rainbow trout, and bull trout of up to 100 percent by the end of this century. The uptick in water temperature has caused smallmouth to expand their range into the forks of the John Day and encroach on critical habitats for endangered spring chinook. Habitat changes are not the only threats to salmon. Researchers have demonstrated that juvenile salmon don't recognize smallmouth as predators, lacking a history of predator-prey relationship. The implications of climate change will manifest themselves in the fishing regulations of the future as fisheries managers weigh enhancement, restoration, and conservation options.

Managing a river that flows through more than one state presents additional challenges. It becomes infinitely more difficult when nonnative species cross the border from a neighboring state and pressure homegrown native fish. That describes Washington's Spokane River where smallmouth swim into Washington from Idaho. The bass have established themselves in what was native redband trout country. Some local anglers would like to extirpate the smallmouth, but even if possible at any given point in time, more would swim downstream from Idaho to fill the void. Changing the regulations from catch-and-release to adding a retention limit for the section of the river with the highest concentration of smallmouth is not a solution either. The Washington Department of Health advisory recommends no fish from the Spokane River be consumed due to lead and PCBs—contaminants flowing into the river from Idaho silver mines.

Some fishing regulations are designed to maintain diversity of species or to balance competing species. Utah's Division of Wildlife Resources has removed the bag limit on smallmouth in several waters in an effort to protect trout. Yet even the highly competitive smallmouth gains protection when it swims with an even more aggressive predator. In the Utah portion of Lake Powell, anglers are encouraged to kill every striper caught in an effort to keep their numbers down and allow the smallmouth and largemouth a chance.

Some fishing regulations are designed to combat illegal introduction of unwanted fish species. New in 2013, Utah required anglers to immediately kill any smallmouth taken in the Green River. Washington has a similar regulation for northern pike on the Pend Oreille River.

All this talk about the impacts of smallmouth might seem to be antibass or prosalmon and prosteelhead. Nothing could be further from the truth. The northwest conundrum of salmonids and smallmouth is geographically isolated. Western states that don't have salmonid-smallmouth interactions don't face those complex management issues. However, every western state does have fish species interaction issues that can be solved only by unbiased scientific research interpreted and rationally applied by the agency legally empowered to manage the resource.

In most places in the West, smallmouth are adapting quite nicely on their own. Dr. Henshall was correct when he pointed out that a smallmouth "has the faculty of asserting himself and making himself completely at home wherever placed."

But we must promote diversity of species and provoke thoughtful discussion among and between the angling public and among and between those who manage or attempt to manage the fish. If the result of the education, diversity, and discussion is better-reasoned conservation and stewardship decisions, then we—the angling public—all win.

Boat and Accessories

Boat (raft, cataraft, canoe, drift boat, or pontoon)
Rowing frame and straps for lashing frame
   to boat
Oars or paddles
Extra oar or paddle
Oar locks and two extra oar locks
Throw bag
Air pump
Dry bags
Bailing bucket
Straps, hoopie, carabiners for lashing gear to boat
Personal flotation device for each person
Rowing gloves
Maps in waterproof case
GPS
Signaling devices
Safety and rescue equipment (slings, carabiners,
   prussiks)
Bow and stern lines
Extra rope for lining boat through rapids
River permit
Invasive species permit

Repair Kit

Frame repair tools: vise grip, channel lock pliers,
   screwdriver, wrench
Leatherman-type tool
Bailing wire
Pipe clamps
Extra washers, nuts, bolts, and screws for frame
Duct tape
Patching material appropriate to boat type
Heavy thread and awl

Waterproof First Aid Kit

First aid book
Sawyer Venom Extractor Pump Kit
Triangular bandages
Gauze rolls—2" wide
Benadryl or cortisone cream
Neosporin or other antibacterial ointment
Antidiarrhea medicine
Moleskin for blisters
Assorted size Band-Aids
Sterile pads
Butterfly strips
Safety pins
Adhesive tape
Elastic bandage
Ibuprofen
Antacid tablets
Tweezers
Personal medications
Feminine hygiene products (double as absorbent bandages)
Prescription medications
Eyeglass repair kit
Outdoor blanket or space blanket

Lightweight sungloves protect against the harsh sun typically experienced in smallmouth country. The fingerless design affords the necessity dexterity to tie knots in the leader or change flies.

Clothing

Wide-brimmed sunhat
Bandana
Raincoat
Rain pants
Quick-drying shorts
Quick-drying sports bra or swimsuit top
Poly T-shirt
Poly underwear
Long-sleeved shirt
Fleece pants
Fleece vest
Poly long underwear
Fleece jacket
Synthetic neck gaiter
Wool or fleece stocking cap
Camp shoes
Water or wading sandals

Camping Gear

Sleeping bag
Sleeping pad
Tent with poles, stakes, and rain fly
Ground cloth
Head lamp with spare bulb and batteries
Personal toiletry items
Pocketknife
Sunscreen
Bug dope (insect repellent)
Water bottle
Lip balm
Polarized sunglasses with safety strap
Camera
Binoculars
Pelican case for nonwaterproof camera
Towel and hand towel
Camp chair

Polarized sunglasses make spotting fish possible in glaring desert sun. They also provide protection against errant casts. Use a tether to keep from losing them. WAYNE GUSTAVESON

Group Equipment

Food
Waterproof plastic food containers
Ice chest
Water in plastic containers (1 gallon per person per day)
Water purifier filter
Toilet paper
Portable toilet system
Plastic garbage bags
Plastic wash basin
Plastic rinse basin
Biodegradable dish soap
Bleach
Stove and fuel
Cooking equipment
Eating utensils
Dishes
Portable table

ACKNOWLEDGMENTS

This book would not exist without many people it gives me great pleasure to acknowledge. I owe my first debt to my mother and father, and grandparents Sukey and Ty, who took me fishing and taught me to love the tug on the line (though I initially spent more time chasing frogs and crawdads). They made being outdoors fun, as did my sister, Nancy Alderson, and my brother, Michael T. Williams; it's still a pleasure to hang with them in the out-of-doors after all these years. And many thanks to every person I've ever fished with—I've learned something from each of them. Three fishing buddies in particular require special mention: Steve Bohnemeyer, Sue Morrison, and Peter Maunsell, the best companions on the water.

For the technical aspects of this book, I relied on the assistance and expertise of fisheries biologists from all of the 11 western states. Without fail, they willingly shared their knowledge and their time while staring budget cuts and job pressures in the face. Their dedication and enthusiasm demonstrates the true meaning of "public servant." Among them, three individuals stand out: Paul Hoffarth, District 4 Fish Program Biologist, Washington Department of Fish & Wildlife; Bruce Bolding, Warmwater Fish Program Manager, Washington Department of Fish & Wildlife; and Wayne Gustaveson, Project Leader, Lake Powell Fisheries, Utah Division of Wildlife Resources.

Finally, I thank my first and best editor, my wife, Q Lindsey Barrett. Everything I write is better for her touch. Plus, she and my daughters, Courtny and Megan, willingly support my fly-fishing obsession. My girls rock.

David Paul Williams has been fishing since before he was old enough for kindergarten. He's caught numerous species in all types of water, but smallmouth bass top his list as the most fun to catch. As a freelance writer and speaker, he loves sharing his knowledge about fishing and his enthusiasm for the printed word. He can be found online at www.thewriterealtor.com and contacted at thefishingwriter@gmail.com.

INDEX

accessories: boat, 169–171; fishing, 156–157
Afternoon Delight, 139
anatomy, 51–53, 84
anchors, 169–170, 171
Aurora Reservoir, CO, 15

backing, 153
banks: steep, 63, 77; undercut, 69–71
Banks Lake, WA, 77
Barr, John, 132
bass species, other, 6–7, 45
Belle Fourche River, WY, 41
bends and curves, 48, 63, 65, 179
Bennett, Michael, 124, 125
Bennett's: Baitfish Perch, 124; Baitfish Smolt, 125
Black River, AZ, 9–10, 190
Black Tadpole, 89
Black Teeny Egg Sucking Leech, 123
Blitzen Hopper, 88–89, 127
Bloom's M.R.S. Bugger, 117
Blue Winged Olive, 108
boats: accessories, 169–171; selecting, 161–163;
    types of, 164, 166–167, 169
Bohnemeyer, Steve, 123
Book of the Black Bass (Henshall), 1, 3, 6–7, 9
Boo Radley, 83, 89, 136
bottom composition, 73, 74
Box Canyon Reservoir, WA, 38–39
breaks and chutes, 68
Brooks, Joe, 9
Brown Lead Head, 129
Brownlee Reservoir, OR, 30
bulges, 63
Burkem, Monte, 4

Cachuma Lake, CA, 15
camping gear, 194
canoes, 167
Carey, Col., 135
Carey Special, 87, 135
Carrie Stevens streamers, 107

casting: drift casting, 171; mimic movement with, 91–92;
    retrieves, 101–103; safety, 171–172; tips/techniques,
    91–92, 95–97; topwater flies, 108, 109, 114; two flies,
    99–100; upstream, 100, 159
Casual Dress, 86, 87, 117, 123
catarafts, 164
catch and release, 146, 183–185
Chernobyl Ant with Body Armor, 122
Chickabou Crayfish, 129
Chuck and Duck, 117
chutes and breaks, 68
C.J. Strike Reservoir, ID, 16
Clearwater River, ID, 17
Clinton, De Witt, 3
clothing, 141–142, 157–159, 173–174, 177, 179, 182, 194
Clouser, Bob, 9, 112
Clouser Deep Minnow, 93
Columbia River, WA, 4, 6, 36–38, 51, 56, 72, 73, 78–79,
    82–83, 145–146, 186
conditioned fish, 56, 103
The Confidence Fly, 105
crayfish, 51, 82–83, 85–86, 92, 107, 108, 110–112, 149
Crayfish Leech, 129
Culley, Aaron, 122
current, understanding, 73–75, 76
curves and bends, 48, 63, 65, 179

Dale Hollow Reservoir, 4, 56
Day, Bob, 158
D-Dub's: BananaRama, 105, 110, 134; Banana series, 34, 107;
    Bleeding Minnow, 44, 130; Chartreuse Caboose, 86, 97,
    105, 106, 107, 137; Crawdad Candy, 86, 134, 142; Fighting
    Craw, 85, 130; Fry, 131; Maribou Minnow (Brown and
    Olive), 34, 84, 136; Orange Banana, 108; Prickly Sculpin,
    82–83, 84, 133; Rabbit Bugger, 6, 86, 112, 131
deadfalls, 72
depth of habitat, 73
diet: autumn, 149–150; casting to mimic, 91–92; feeding
    style, 56; feeding times, 81–82; the fisherman's, 98–99; life
    cycle, 51, 83; preferences, 3, 82–83; senses role in, 53–56,
    92; targets of opportunity, 89. *See also specific foods*

docks, 77
Dominic Singh's Spicy Stinger, 121
drift boats, 167
drop-offs, fishing, 77
drowning, 182
dry bags, 170
Dumb-G-Bug #1, #2, #3, 128
Dworshak Reservoir, ID, 17, 49, 56

East Fork Gila River, NM, 26, 28
eddies and seams, 68–69
Eichman, Jimmie, 117
Elkhead Reservoir, CA, 16
At-Em Bomb, 126

feeder creeks, fishing, 72
Fighting Craw, 85
Flaming Gorge, UT, 31
Flathead River, MT, 19–20, 45
flats, fishing, 71, 76–77
flies: barbs and hooks, 107; color, 107–109; durability, 106;
    and lines, matching, 103; materials for, 84–85, 105–106,
    139; movement, 106; shape, 107, 108; the silver bullet,
    105; size, 107, 108–109, 110, 113, 149; sound, 107–108;
    texture, 109–110; weedguards, 106; weighting, 112.
    See also specific patterns
float trips, 161, 175–176, 180–182, 193–195
float tubes, 158, 163
fly patterns, about, 85–86, 100–101, 107–108,
    111–113, 149
Fontenelle Reservoir, WY, 39, 40
footwear, 157

Galloup, Kelly, 1–2
glitter boats, 167, 169
gloves, 173–174
Golden Triangle, 4, 62
Gordon, Hal, 122
Grandaddy Ty, 43
Grande Ronde River, WA, 58, 143
grasses habitats, 71–72
gravel bars, 71
Green River, UT, 191
Greyrocks Reservoir, WY, 41
Gustaveson, Wayne, 58, 142

habitat, learning about, 62–63. *See also specific*
    habitat types
Hamster, 97, 108, 109, 133, 143
Hara Kiri, 118
Hare's Ear, 86
Hayes, David L., 4
hearing, lateral line and ears, 54
Henry Hagg Lake, OR, 30
Henry's Fork, ID, 9
Henshall, James A., 1, 2, 3, 6–7, 9, 191
Hexagenia Quigley Cripple, 88

Hex Nymph, 88, 123
Higgins, Jim, 118
Hindman, Woodie, 167
Hi-Vis Foam Beetle, 89
Hobby Lobby #1, 130
Hoffman, Henry, 129
Horsethief Reservoir, WA, 36
Hughes, Dave, 123
Humboldt River, NV, 22–23
humps, fishing, 77
hybrid water, fishing, 78–79

Ice House Reservoir, CA, 12, 15
insects, 86–89, 108, 113
It Works, 118

jetboats, 167
Joe's Smallmouth Sculpin, 115
johnboats, 167
John Day River, OR, 28, 29–30, 58, 62–63, 67, 71, 72,
    73, 86, 86–87, 142, 146, 175, 179, 185, 190
Jordan, David Starr, 188
Jordanelle Reservoir, UT, 31

Karrhus, Tom, 167
kayaks, 166
Kermit, 132
Keyhole Reservoir, WY, 39, 41
Kings River, CA, 12
knots, 156
Kreh, Lefty, 93
Kristof, Joe, 115

Lacepede, Bernard, 52–53
Lake Havasu, AZ, 11–12, 149
Lake Powell, UT, 32–33, 49, 58, 76, 79, 83, 142, 146,
    149, 191
Lake Washington, WA, 58, 76, 142, 170
leaders, 154–156
ledges, fishing, 69–71
leeches, 89, 113
Lewis, Gary, 138
lines, 103, 153–154
Little Brook Trout bucktail streamers, 9
Little Brown Trout bucktail streamers, 9
Little Rainbow Trout bucktail streamers, 9
Luke, John, 116
Luke's: Bass Tube, 116; Flipping Fly, 116

Marabou Clouser, 150
Marabou Damsel, 88
Matalone, Sam, 118, 119, 120, 121
McKenzie River, OR, 43, 179
Meat Whistle, 132
Mega Craw, 124
Miyawaki Beach Popper, 150
Morris, Skip, 122

Muddler Minnow, 114
Murdich Minnow, 107
Mystic Mouse, 125

Navajo Lake, NM, 24
nesting, 49–51, 73, 77, 143, 146, 171
Nevada, 21–23
night fishing, 99, 170
Night Rider, 137
North Umpqua River, OR, 189–190
Noxon Reservoir, MT, 18–19

O'Keefe, Brian, 117
Olson, Eric, 117
oxygen, dissolved, 72–73

packs, chest/back/shoulder/fanny, 158–159
paddle boats, 166
Pale Evening Dun, 108
Pat's Stone, 86, 88
Pend Oreille River, WY, 39, 97, 191
personal floatation devices, 158, 173, 177, 179
Petersen, Devin, 121
Pineview Reservoir, UT, 31
points, fishing, 77
pontoons, 158
pools and rapids, 66–67
Potholes Reservoir, WA, 34, 36
Prickly Sculpin, 83, 84
Purple Bunny, 126

Quick Baitfish Imitation, 120
Quick Shad Pattern, 120
Quincy Reservoir, CA, 15

rafting terms, 177, 179
rafts, 164, 166
rapids and pools, 66–67
Red Ass Ratt, 103, 125
Redeye Crawbooger, 122
Red-Eyed Clouser, 127
reefs, offshore, 78
repair kit, 193
retrieves, 101–103
riffles and runs, 65
Rio Grande River, NM, 23–24
riprap habitat, 72, 76, 78
riverbed habitat, 77
roadbed habitat, 77, 145
Rock Creek Cove, WA, 38
rock piles, fishing, 77
rods and reels, 152–153
Roosevelt Lake, AZ, 10–11
Rosborough, Polly, 117, 123
rowing, 173–175
Rufus Woods, WA, 49
runs and riffles, 65

Russian River, CA, 12, 13, 142
Rustin, Matt, 10
Rye Patch Reservoir, NV, 21–22, 76

safety, 158, 170–173, 173, 177, 179, 193
salmonid-smallmouth issue, 186–191
sculpin, 83–84, 91–92
seams and eddies, 68–69
senses, 53–58, 103
shad, 83–84, 91, 149–150
Shad Fry, 135
Shad Imitation/Shad Imitation #2, 119
shadow, 49, 61
Sheep Creek Reservoir, NV, 23
sight, 53–54, 58
Silver Fox, 117
Singh, Dominic, 121
sinkers, 157
Skues, G. E. M., 7
Slaymaker, Samuel, 9
Small Black Fly, 121
smallmouth bass: in fiction, 9; geographic distribution,
    3–4, 45; life cycle, 49–51; migration, 75; record weights,
    4, 10, 52, 56, 75, 186; senses, 53–58, 103; tactics,
    1–3, 84
smell, 55–56
SMP, 11, 115, 122
Snake River, ID, 17–18, 73, 142, 145, 175, 186
South Fork Reservoir, NV, 22
Sow Belly, 4
spawning, 51, 58, 77, 79, 113, 142–146
Spokane River, WA, 191
springs, fishing, 77
Stalcup Adult Damsel, 88
stewardship, 183–191
Stewart, Joel, 116
stream armor habitat, 72
streamcraft, 93–95
stripping basket, 158
strip strike, 103
structure, understanding, 47, 49, 59–61, 61, 62, 76,
    78–79, 142
sunglasses, 157
sunken woody debris, 78

tadpoles and frogs, 89, 113
taste, 56
Teeny, Jim, 123
Tongue River Reservoir, MT, 20–21
topwater flies, 11, 107, 108, 114
touch, sense of, 56
tributaries, 72
trout fishing, 7–8, 43, 113–114, 159
Trueblood, Ted, 9
Trump, Gene, 11, 115
tube boats, 164
two flies, 99–100

Umpqua Clouser #1, #2, #3, 138
Umpqua River, OR, 27, 28–29, 73
Ute Reservoir, NM, 24, 26, 149

Verde River, AZ, 10
vests, 159
V-hulls, 167, 168
Violet Gurgler, 109

waders, 157–158, 182
wading staffs, 158
waters, learning the, 97–99
water temperature, effect of, 58, 72, 82, 141–150
weather, effects of, 58
weed bed habitat, 71–72

western silvery minnow, 83–84, 91
Whitman Craw, 121
Williams, David Paul, 129, 130, 131, 132, 133, 134, 135, 136, 137
Williams, Michael T., 1, 126, 127, 128
Wood, Bob, 118
Woolly Bug, 116
Woolly Buggers, 89, 100–101, 107, 113, 114
Wulff, Lee, 182, 183, 185
Wyatt's Wonder, 126

Yakima River, WA, 6, 34, 35, 72, 86, 142, 145–146, 179, 186, 188–189
Yampa River, CA, 15–16
Yellowstone River, MT, 21